THE MYTH OF
INEVITABLE
PROGRESS

THE MYTH OF INEVITABLE PROGRESS

FRANCO FERRAROTTI

Contributions in Political Science, Number 115
Global Perspectives in History and Politics

To Wolf

from Franco

Greenwood Press
Westport, Connecticut • London, England

Library of Congress Cataloging in Publication Data
Ferrarotti, Franco.
    The myth of inevitable progress.

    (Contributions in political science, ISSN 0147-1066 ;
no. 115. Global perspectives in history and politics)
    Bibliography: p.
    Includes index.
    1. Progress. 2. Industrialization—Social aspects.
I. Title. II. Series: Contributions in political
science ; no. 115. III. Series: Contributions in
political science. Global perspectives in history and
politics.
HM101.F39   1984   303.4′4   84-589
ISBN 0-313-24329-8 (lib. bdg.)

Library of Congress Catalog Card Number: 84-589
ISBN: 0-313-24329-8
ISSN: 0147-1066

First published in 1985

Greenwood Press
A division of Congressional Information Service, Inc.
88 Post Road West
Westport, Connecticut 06881

Printed in the United States of America

10 9 8 7 6 5 4 3 2 1

Contents

Preface

This book is in the first place a caveat against technocracy in its refined present-day form. Old-fashioned technocracy is obsolete because it is clearly self-defeating. Its claim to solve all political and social problems in terms of purely technical know-how is so directly and blatantly presumptuous that there is hardly any need to explode it. I have dealt with it extensively and systematically in some of my previous books, notably in *Sindacato, Industria, Società* (*Unions, Industry, and Society*), *An Alternative Sociology*, and *Max Weber and the Destiny of Reason*. Today technocracy appears to be more insidious since it presents itself as a rational systematic theory that pretends to be both self-evident and self-justified, and therefore not in need of either a historical dimension or a democratic legitimation. No wonder that a radical version of structural functionalism seems to be reemerging. Naturally, most sociologists and political scientists who couch their structural-functionalist bent in systems theory terminology and are technocratically inclined would resent being labeled as technocrats or, to use Albert Salomon's formula, willing servants of the "tyranny of progress."

It is nonetheless true that among sociologists and political scientists today a rather "weak" notion of legitimation is widespread, to the extent that, on one hand, they diligently bring out the psychological-behavioral aspects, and, on the other hand, stress the formal characteristics or at least those able to be completely translated into formally codified institutions. To that extent the concept and the very term of "society" become absorbed into the more structured and "manageable" one, as it were, of state organization. However, one needs hardly comment that thereby legitimacy runs the risk of being confused with legality and that the living essence of the problem is being lost. The fact is that the basis and the main source of legitimacy lie in what we are used to terming the "underlying population." It is here, not elsewhere, that the leaders of society and the power they dispose of, find or may hope to find their legitimation.

The publication of this book, which at least in part reflects an earlier stage of my intellectual work, would not have taken place without the friendly insistence of George Schwab and of Dr. James T. Sabin. Arthur J. Vidich and Stanford M. Lyman, and Daria Martin have offered, during my recent stay at the New School for Social Research, useful comments on some key points. The care of Mildred Vasan, at Greenwood Press, has also been helpful.

THE MYTH OF
INEVITABLE
PROGRESS

1

The Enlightenment Idea of Progress

PROGRESS AS A RATIONAL INQUIRY

The crisis of civilization has now been under discussion for well over fifty years, occasionally with gloating insistence. In the eighteenth and nineteenth centuries progress was discussed with that same insistence, albeit with the vehemence of controversy and a greater seriousness. Considered continuous and irreversible, it became conceptualized a priori as the self-motivating supreme force of order, on God's authority. In the lamentations of today's doom-portending literature there is a substantially rhetorical attitude resembling the choral incantations of the professional advocates of progress. It would be unfair and, from a cognitive point of view, deceptive, to renounce the distinction as a matter of principle, since there is a radical difference between seventeenth-century rationalism and the need for rationality as valued by Enlightenment thinkers, which cannot be ignored. Furthermore, the eighteenth-century lay religion of progress became the pure and simple nineteenth-century mythology of expansion, as the tears shed by Ortega y Gasset on popular rebellion were qualitatively different from those shed today on mass culture. It is still the same movement, towards critical analysis of nature and history, but has lost faith in its final flowering—impregnated with inevitable happiness for the human race.[1]

It is certainly easy today, on the basis of the experience and information afforded by two centuries of history, to scoff at the abstract character of the abundant illusions about the "magnificent and progressive lot" of human nature, the infinite perfectability, still praised as late as Carducci. It is necessary, however, to consider the polemical interpretations: the fundamental significance of the Enlightenment—and above all the French Enlightenment—as far as it elaborates and affirms the concept of progress rather than a providential design, has long been misrepresented by historiographical schematism deriving from Idealism. This schematism only underlines the characteristically unhistoric aspects of abstract rationality and the weight of purely negative critical instances. That which escapes Idealism, or, more precisely, that which Idealism is inherently incapable of understanding, is in point of fact the fundamental characteristic of the Enlightenment, which demands an explicit empirical price for each truth acquired; it faces, with neither logical protection nor religion, not only the problems of natural science, as the new seventeenth-century science wished to, but also those of history. Sacred designs and cyclical theories are removed from historical study, leaving it completely open and consigned to man as his daily toil and essential task. Turgot affirms: "The people that has first acquired a greater knowledge has quickly become superior to its own neighbours: every step forward facilitates further progress. In this way the development of one nation accelerates day by day while others remain in their state of mediocrity, determined by particular circumstances, and still others continue to live in a barbaric state.''[2]

The concept of progress, rather than the concept of history as the history of human civilization, as the movement of civilization, past, present, and future in a desirable direction,[3] has its classic formulation in Voltaire's "Essai sur les moeurs et l'esprit des nations," and its most eloquent propagandist in Condorcet. This constitutes the Enlightenment's cardinal idea and clarifies the character of man's optimistic taking possession of himself and his faculties, the Kantian awareness of coming of age. "The Enlightenment is nothing but the Kantian feeling that man had reached his majority, and a distinct consciousness of his truly sovereign dignity. He was not already made divine: a man-god would have nothing to do, as the architect of the universe now has nothing to do, having already done too much. Total freedom would annihilate him. His place is half-way between all and nothing, a situation which seemed tragic to Pascal but which now seemed an obvious departure point for concrete and effective thought.''[4]

In Kant's 1784 text, referred to here, the sense of human dignity conceived as the fruit of the scientific application of intelligence to the solution of the problems of reality, whether natural or socio-historical, emerges with clarity: "The Enlightenment is the exit of man from a state of minority that he must impute to himself. Minority is the incapacity to value his own intellect without the aid of others. This minority is imputable to him, if the cause of it does not depend upon a deficient intellect but on his lack of decision, and lack of courage to use his own intellect without the aid of others. Have the courage to avail yourself of your intelligence! This is the motto of the Enlightenment.''

It is in fact true that each day has sufficient problems of its own, but it is also true, in the words of Turgot, that "every step forward facilitates further progress.'' The use of critical intelligence had already been proclaimed by Cartesian researches, but according to Descartes such important areas of analysis as politics and religious belief had, on principle, to be considered subsidiary to rational criticism. The Enlightenment limited the power which Descartes attributed to reason, connecting it to the binding lessons of experience, though at the same time not accepting limits or exceptions regarding the scope of rational inquiry. Voltaire, with his habitually jesting tone, pointed out with extraordinary analytical acumen the consequences of Descartes' system: "It is worth noting that Descartes' self-styled principles of physics are far enough from inducing the mind to recognize its creator. . . . I declare that the Cartesian system made Spinoza's system possible; I declare also that I have met many people led by Cartesianism to recognizing no other god but the immensity of things, and that, on the other hand, I have never met a follower of Newton who was not a theist in the correct sense of the term.''[5]

AGAINST TRADITIONAL WISDOM

During the Enlightenment, rational inquiry included every system of knowledge or belief without exception, whether natural, ethical, political, or religious. For the Enlightenment no truth is privileged or can escape the onus of proof; no truth is absolute or can claim exemption from verification. Each truth is therefore confirmed or corrected, if need be modified in its essential terms, or simply left to fall away as no longer true. In this sense the basic attitude of the Enlightenment is rigorously empirical. From this derives, on the other hand, its revolutionary meaning, its intransigent, belligerent anti-traditionalism, which, isolating its abstract polemical aspect, has been mistakenly confused with anti-historicism. The classic expression of this Enlightenment anti-traditionalism is found in Bayle:

It is a pure and simple illusion to pretend that a conviction passed on from century to century, from generation to generation, cannot be completely false. A cursory examination of the reasons why certain opinions establish themselves and are handed down from father to son will show that nothing is less reasonable than such a pretence. Undoubtedly one needs to recognize that it is easy to persuade people of certain false opinions which dovetail with their childhood prejudices or passions of the heart—such opinions, for example, as the supposed rules of forebodings. One requires nothing more, because these opinions become eternal, since, with the exception of an occasional philosopher, nobody bothers to establish whether what everybody says is true. Everyone considers that an opinion has already been examined several times, and that the Ancients have already taken precautions against error, and goes on in his turn to teach to posterity, as if he were dealing with an indubitable fact.[6]

Tradition as the principal, if not the only, source of truth, is therefore challenged. It is not a question of anti-historicism. Indeed, it is precisely with the Enlightenment's vigorous application of radical criticism to every belief and part of knowledge that the demise of the "great traditions," as the cultural anthropologists call them,[7] occurred, and that a historicist attitude giving precedence to man was founded, freed of metaphysical designs or pre-established harmony. It is, besides, a question of a particular historicism, still bearing the influence of Lockean empiricism, from which, among other things, the Enlightenment draws a necessary scepticism which justifies the orientation of reasoned distrusts towards traditional truth. Voltaire honestly recognized the Enlightenment's debt to empiricism:

After many thinkers had romanticised the soul, there came a sage who modestly made history. Locke explained human reason to man as a good anatomist illustrates the energy of the human body. He always resorts to the light of physics; sometimes he dares to speak affirmatively, at other times he goes so far as to doubt; and instead of defining everything we do not know, he proceeds to examine by degrees the things we want to know. . . .Locke, having destroyed innate ideas and given up the folly of believing that one always thinks, ascertained that all our ideas derive from the senses, examined simple and complex ideas, and traced the human spirit in all its activities, showing the imperfection of human language and which word abuses we make at each moment.[8]

The following are the defining characteristics of the mental climate of the epoch preceding and preparing for the great "crisis" of the twentieth century: anti-historicism, the critical use of reason, on a substantial and linguistic level as an instrument of domination over nature and history; fundamental optimism, "human, too human," which corresponds to the relative decline of a sense of mystery; the widespread conviction that the concept of progress and, later, in the nineteenth century, the inevitability of development, constitute intrinsic and necessary laws of human society which it would be useless to question too severely. Lamettrie, with the usual blunt brutality which marks his style, sums this up well: "Let us not lose ourselves in the infinite: we are intended to have but a minimal idea of it; it is absolutely impossible for us to arrive at the origin of things. For the other part, for our calm, it is all the same whether matter is eternal or has been created, whether or not there is a god. How foolish to torment ourselves over something it is impossible to know, and that, on the other hand, would not make us happier were we to know it."[9]

A REVOLUTIONARY IDEA

We seem to be dealing with a minimalist attitude, sceptical as far as final causes and the absolute are concerned, an attitude pervaded by fundamental common sense. But it is an apparent minimalism whose real revolutionary influence finds verification of extraordinary precision in French history. It is in France, in fact, more than England, Germany, or the United States, that the *ancien régime* presents itself closed and impermeable, from a reaction which admits only one form of contact with new ideas and the classes which carry them into history, that is, frontal assault. England already had her "glorious" revolution in 1688, the United States with Jefferson's "declaration" were becoming God's country, in which fact and value tend to coincide, and Germany had known the Reformation two centuries earlier.

The situation in France is different and is demonstrated by the powerful summarizing term *"l'ancien régime."* According to Méthivier the *ancien régime* is made up of the following components: (1) a political regime, understood as a monarchy of divine origin tending towards personal and authoritarian absolutism. It develops on a body of medieval structure, in which, however, there is a new national force—the bourgeoisie, which is capitalistic, individualistic, utilitarian, and secular; (2) a society whose structure has three aspects: (a) It is "coutumière," or habitual. Medieval practices and customs are considered law, born of an ancient social contract between the three orders which regulates the relations between individuals and communities in the same country. These were the basis of the private law of every province and fief. As Dumoulin, the great sixteenth-century jurist, tells us: "Our customs are our true common law." (b) It is besides a "corporative" and "hiérarchisée" society.[10] The individual is considered only as a member of a social group. The social groups cannot be considered castes, being only partly open and accessible. This society is dominated by an ascending force which individual citizens create in order to improve themselves in the material oral and legal geriarchy of these collectives. They are indifferently called "corps," "communautés," "compagnies," "états," etc.; each one has its own laws, regulations, liberty, franchise, and privileges. These innumerable organized and active bodies form the authentic dorsal spine of the *ancien régime*. (c) Finally, this society is catholic. The Catholic religion is the state religion. From birth to death it is the citizen's guide and counsellor. The clergy control the birth, marriage, and death registers and are responsible for children's education from primary to higher levels. Most human activities take place under the auspices of the church, which organizes every body or community in co-fraternities which take a patron saint. Relations between Church and State are governed by the 1516 concordat, which grants spiritual and doctrinal authority to Rome and temporal, disciplinary power to the king. This division is always a matter for controversy.

As a sociological phenomenon, the *ancien régime* developed slowly to emerge with its specific characteristics during the sixteenth-century. In the next century it put itself, with its organization and influence, at the disposition of the monarchic state, which had reached the apogee. The monarchy availed itself increasingly of all the best things that the *ancien régime* had created. In fact, monarchic institutions had arrived, roughly speaking, at their ultimate form under Louis XIV; his grandson, Louis XVI, governed with the same ministers and counsellors.

If, however, Louis XIV knew how to take the monarchic system to a position of authority never again attained, he did not manage to give it a coherent and logical form. After his reign one could say that "despotism is everywhere and the despot nowhere." National unity makes further progress in the eighteenth century, thanks to the development of communications and economic relations and the diffusion of classical culture. Towns and provinces maintain their privileges; the North retains its customs while the South follows Roman law. The multiplicity of weights and measures, of tolls and internal customs-posts, impede the economic unification of the country. Confusion and disorder remain the characteristic traits of administrative organization; legal, financial, military, and religious areas superimpose upon one another. France, in Mirabeau's words, is only an "agrégat inconstitué de peuples désunis." The *ancien régime* is therefore caught in a state of acute fragmentation by the Revolution, and forced onto the defensive. The monarchy is always of "divine right." The King of France is believed to be the representative of God on earth, enjoying absolute power for this reason. However, this absolute regime lacks the will to govern. Louis XVI had ceded his absolute power to the hands of the aristocracy. In spite of numerous, if not hypertrophic, administrative personnel, the attempts of Machault, Maupeou, and Turgot at structural reform came to a halt in the face of obstinate resistance from the Parliament and the provincial states, the foundations of aristocratic power. This type of administrative organization never improves, while, since the sixteenth century, the sudden enrichment of holders of capital, the rising of early industries, and a new distribution of wealth prepare a new distribution of power.

France of the *ancien régime* is therefore a heterogeneous and complex society, characterized by a great variety of occasionally feudal arrangements, different from one region to the next with some more modern, though not necessarily free of feudal concessions as a result. But the ensuing events damage some traditional social groups while favoring others. According to Méthivier, "la gentilhommerie rurale," a large number of needful families obliged to serve the king, must be counted among the former; the monarch helps them by lavishing pensions on the old officers, "priorates" or ecclesiastical prebends for their younger sons, and sending their first-born to the military academy of Saint-Cyr. These families live on their land with the income derived from it. The middle and lower bourgeoisie "de métiers" has been damaged above all by the uncertainty which has hit the luxury trades in their hands. The "paysannerie," finally, seems to be hit by the lowering of grain and wine prices and the increase of taxation and service costs. Unemployment follows for the working classes.

The explosion of popular anger is thus explained, and the fears of 1700–13, precursors of 1789, that pushed crowds of the poor and vagabonds towards stocks of grain, against the "gabeleurs" and "maltôtiers.'' On this matter the writings of Fenelon, Vauban, and Boisguilbert eloquently underline the results of the official inquests of 1687 and 1698, the ''doléances'' of the bishops and curates.

On the other hand the haute bourgeoisie and high court nobility were favored. The former was composed of ''gens d'affaires,'' bankers, financiers, ''fermiers généraux,'' arms suppliers, treasurers and tax collectors (Samuel Bernard, Crozat, Legendre), armorers, and monopoly concession holders. The latter, the high nobility, ''Noblesse de Cour,'' and ''Noblesse de Robe,'' knew how to turn events to their advantage; the nobility of the court profiting from their proximity to the king, and his graces; those ''de robe'' enriching themselves from their own lands. But the nobility, like the clergy, does not present a social unity; it proposes to share power with the king, offering resistance to reform in exchange. In its opposition to royal absolutism it demands liberty, but its intentions turn towards the past; it is animated by an impossible dream of restoration. The bourgeoisie, on the contrary, turns towards the future; by attaining wealth, economic strength, culture, and knowledge it hopes to gain participation in political power. For this reason the bourgeoisie no longer limits itself to claiming political rights and freedom; it begins to demand the abolition of aristocratic feudal privileges and the equality of rights. Clinging to its privileges, throughout the eighteenth century the aristocracy rendered the solution of the problem impossible and forced the economic crisis, whether agricultural, industrial, or commercial, to the breaking point.

It is not possible to scratch the closed impenetrability of dominating oligarchic groups without attacking at base the tradition which constitutes the foundation of legitimacy, and at the same time attacking the pressures coming from the fourth state, which first blocked and then frustrated the peaceful revolution attempted by Turgot. A peaceful revolution, but above all judicial. It will be necessary to liquidate feudal privileges, but the equality of all citizens with respect to positive laws will not mean the pure and simple universal extension of political rights, because only the landowners are citizens in the correct sense. Condorcet clarifies: ''In civil countries it is the territory which constitutes the state; it is therefore property which makes citizens.''[11] With a Louis XVI on the throne and a fourth state which is rapidly acquiring a consciousness of itself and does not seem prepared to act merely as a stool for the bourgeoisie or the deserters from the rising aristocracy, Turgot's enlightened and paternalistic reform could not but fail.

Apart from the resistance of oligarchic groups, Turgot's own ambivalence is clearly reflected in his plan: he was not insensitive towards the popular classes (in Condorcet's phrase, "this unhappy species who suffer in silence"), but was basically a conservative and bureaucrat; he was a fervent promoter of free and secular compulsory education, while at the same time respectful of religious traditions which recall the tone and climate of the Prussian Enlightenment. Turgot's plan is therefore stricken by internal contradictions. In administrative action as in theoretical justification this results in an incompatibility with the principle of Enlightenment as it has been defined by Kant:

A government based on the principle of goodwill towards the people, that is an 'imperium paternale' in which the subjects, as minors unable to distinguish between the useful and the harmful, are forced to behave passively—to wait for the state to judge in which way they must be happy and only expect what generosity the state decides upon,—this government is the worst imaginable despotism (a regimentation which takes all freedom from the subjects, who therefore have no rights). A paternal government is of no use; a patriotic government (imperium non paternale, sed patrioticum) is the only conceivable form for law abiding men, even in relation to the benevolence of princes.

The failure of Turgot's plan is instructive in more ways. In the first place it is a significant measure of the French socio-economic structure's rigidity, which, unlike its English equivalent, does not allow more or less phantom-manipulated mediations and dilutions. But this is not all. It indicates several points of extreme weakness, both conceptual and practical, in the ideology of progress. In particular, Turgot's resignation means the fall of the illusion that one can discreetly utilize the fourth state without recognizing the right to make first person history and assume complete economic and political freedom—including the freedom to make mistakes. In other words, progress cannot maintain the exclusive possession of an enlightened elite, which may be benevolent but is intrinsically authoritarian. In his stance as an efficient official, Turgot represents the arrival of the technocrat for whom social dimensions of the problems of development, with their typical indeterminancy and irreducibility to rational plans, remain substantially extraneous. He sees the social dimensions as of secondary importance, not imposing an organic restructuring of the plan in which they are fundamental components. For Enlightenment thinkers the perspective is individualistic in the most restricted sense, that is, spotlike, and legal-abstract.

Even when one speaks of the people, one does not mean all the citizens in their diversity and specificity, but only the landowners, who are further subdivided according to strict discriminating criteria in proportion to the extent of their property; alternatively, one means the "people" in Rousseau's sense as an abbreviated expression for the "volonté générale," which is not the "volonté de tous" as understood by the professional organizations (such as unions and cultural or social organizations) existing between individuals and the state, but the abstractly conceived will of an individual citizen. The man whom Locke discusses is Abbot Parini's "young gentleman." Schumpeter observes that the sociological type or social matrix of Turgot recalls the English "country gentlemen" and landed gentry, together with the Prussian Junkertum.

THE INDIVIDUALISTIC PERSPECTIVE

It should be remembered that even the third great Enlightenment revolution, the American Revolution, owed much to a group of intellectual "humanists," who were mostly of patrician origin and fond of classical literature and country life. There is no "people" in the sense of a combination of working classes and peasants, that is, as a combination of the lower classes, properly understood. It is the individual and his freedom that count. It is necessary to free him from the legacy of the past, from social conventions, and from the shackles of tradition and custom. The genius of Marx lies in his having intuited the presence of a new, unrecognized, human condition, that of the proletariat; but even the Marxian perspective is spotlike and legal. From the atomistic individual one suddenly passes, without mediation, to the working class understood as a "general class," a mythical vehicle which saves humanity in saving itself. From this comes Marxian schematism as far as it concerns class war, which lacks sociological substance—being concerned with merely abstract individuals instead of the fight of groups and families; this schematism is fixed forever in the plan of a dialectic which is still naturalistic, dogmatic, and therefore deceptive. Also from the mythical "general class" derives the singular incomprehension of the short-lived organizations in defense of workers, such as unions, from which—quite correctly from the Marxist point of view—Lenin will theorize the function of "transmission belts," and whose lack of autonomy in reality opens the door to bureaucratic regression and to the commisarial conception of the revolutionary process. Then, again from the same myth, derives the instrumental impossibility of foreseeing the weight and function of a new middle class in an industrially developed society, and thereby a mechanical and restricted interpretation of the phenomenon of fascism which is incapable of taking account of history as it unfolds and, furthermore, content to apply the same univocal, pseudo-scientific formula to qualitatively different historical situations.

Outside the polemic which divided the Encyclopedists, Jacobines, Saint-Simonites, and socialists, the peremptory affirmation with which Rousseau opens "The Social Contract" is indubitably the meeting point: "Man is born free, but is enslaved everywhere." Today their faith in the individual and his destiny, and their optimism, have a pathetic ring. Later, even for Comte, working towards the construction of a ferociously socio-centric system, the scientific liberation from the past constitutes an unrenounceable principle. This liberation comes, explicitly or implicitly, in the name of individual judgment against the principle of authority. This is at the same time the instrument and prize gained by the rational individual, who by means of the critical use of reason fulfills himself and takes possession of the world; he conquers it against the mysterious, irrational reasons of tradition and custom.

The individual appears, in the first place, as a self-sufficient reality, a complete product of nature, indefinitely perfectible per se: "Man is the product of nature. . . . The frequently made distinction between physical man and moral man is widely abused,; moral man is nothing but this physical being considered from a certain viewpoint, that is, in relation to some of his ways of acting owing to his particular make-up."[12] If man is nothing but a product of nature, he must return to nature. This return to nature will have in Rousseau its eloquent apostle, with details which only seem to contrast superficially with the general Enlightenment orientation. Rousseau's return to nature is not intended as the idealization of the simple life, like the romantic cliché of primitive communities. The return to nature is only a stepping-stone to the reform of society and the rediscovery of a new, ahistorical and thus immutable, legitimate basis for social order, in comparison with which the existing order will soon reveal its oppressive and corrupting characteristics: "It is easy to establish that the first origins of the differences which distinguish men must be sought in the successive changes of human constitutions; in fact, as is commonly recognized, men are naturally equal as all animals were before various physical causes introduced in them the differences that we recognize."[13]

The return to nature proclaimed by Rousseau must not therefore be interpreted as a possible return to the "saturnia aetas," even though it does not lack phrases and tones of nostalgia for the "bon sauvage," but as the formulation of a comparison which morally justifies reforming intervention with respect to present society. For Rousseau also, therefore, the return to nature means in the first place a fight against social conventions and, with respect to these, the liberation of the individual, who is "naturally good." This is a point of fundamental coincidence which Rousseau, notwithstanding his noted hostility for the Encyclopedists, binds to the various theories and general orientation of the Enlightenment: faith in the individual, in his natural resourcefulness and his autonomous capacity for equilibrium.[14]

NOTES

1. For the distinction between seventeenth-century rationalism and the Enlightenment, see the fundamental work by E. Cassirer, *Die Philosophie der Aufklärung*, Tübingen, 1932 (Eng. trans., *The Philosophy of the Enlightenment*, Boston, 1951). The idea of progress in its origin and successive development has found a diligent historian in J. B. Bury, *The Idea of Progress*, London, 1932. There is an abundant literature about the transition from the idea of progress to simple evolution; among others, see the less known, VV.AA., *Evolution in Modern Thought*, New York, n.d., especially p. 264, C. Bougle, "Darwinism and Sociology."

2. Cfr. Turgot, *Plan de deux discours sur l'histoire universelle*, Schelle, ed. Paris, 1823, I, p. 303 (Eng. trans., Ronald Meek, *Turgot on Progress, Sociology and Economics*, London, 1973, pp. 61–118).

3. This is the definition offered by Bury of the concept of progress when he writes, "This concept means that civilization has moved, is moving, and will move, in a desirable direction" (cfr. Bury, *The Idea of Progress*, p. 2).

4. Cfr. A. Cento, *Condorcet e l'idea di progresso*, Florence, 1956, p. 71.

5. Cfr. F.M.A. de Voltaire, *Eléments de la philosophie de Newton*, in Oeuvres, XXII, p. 404 (Eng. trans., T. Smollett, et al., *Works*, Vol. 5, p. 26, London, 1762). The relationship between Descartes and the Enlightenment writers has been variously investigated; interesting, among others, the study about *Diderot and Descartes* by A. Vartanian (Princeton, 1953), centering the attention on "scientific naturalism."

6. Cfr. P. Bayle, *Pensées diverses sur la comète*, Paris, 1820 ed., p. 100.

7. Cfr., for example, R. Redfield, *Peasant Society and Culture*, Chicago, 1956, especially ch. 3, "The Social Organization of Tradition," pp. 67–104.

8. Cfr. F.M.A. de Voltaire, *Lettres philosophiques*, XIII (Eng. trans., *Philosophical Letters*, Indianapolis, 1961).

9. The thinking of Lamettrie can be found in an eloquent synthesis in *L'homme-machine* (Eng. trans. *Man à Machine*, Chicago, 1912), which remains the exemplary text of mechanistic philosophy.

10. Cfr. Martin Oliver, *L'organization corporative de la France d'ancien régime*, Paris, 1938.

11. Cfr. S. Concorcet, *Oeuvres*, IX, p. 12.

12. Cfr. P. H. d'Holbach, *Système de la nature*, Diderot, ed., Paris, 1822, p. 49.

13. Cfr. J. J. Rousseau, *Discours sur l'origine de l'inégalité parmi les hommes*, Paris, 1754, preface (Eng. trans., *A Discourse Upon the Origin and Foundation of the Inequality Among Mankind*, New York, 1971).

14. For a different opinion, cfr. A. Santucci, *Le origini della sociologia*, Milan, 1962, p. 57: "This explains his hostility against the Encyclopedists. Rousseau noted that it is quite possible that material progress has been prompted by intellectual progress, but has contributed to the separation of man from his simplicity. Man that lived in small groups and in communities preserving traditional customs has been lost in recent civilizations, which are the victims of luxury, restless ambition and sterile scepticism. This is the point, and the difference: social *bonheur* depends first of all on customs, and customs on education of the heart rather than on education of intelligence."

2

The Crisis of the Individual

BELIEF IN THE INDIVIDUAL

Belief in the individual defines the modern world. It has been justly observed that the individual is prized for himself; his creative gifts are considered his fundamental essence; the free development of the human personality is exalted as an ideal by Renaissance artists, the Elizabethans, Locke, Voltaire, and Rousseau. This vision of a man who freely extends himself, happy in the fulfillment of his quality, is shared by individuals with absolutely different ideas, such as a Jefferson and an Edmund Burke. It is the figuration that Hegel had of the heroes of Napoleon's time and that Karl Marx, as much as it may surprise those who have not read him, had of the artisans and workers he admired.[1] That man, whether modern or ancient, advances on the shoulders of previous generations, is a facile paradox that has become commonplace. Modern man means essentially ''secular'' man, that is, in his attitude towards himself, his dealings with others, and his decisions and actions. To be modern is to renounce the tutelage of an intermediate authority and the protection of the powerful; it is to accept the deepest meaning of a rigorous separation between that which is private and that which is public.

Individualism is the connecting thread that is found everywhere in the complex weft of the epoch stretching from Leonardo to the first decade of the twentieth century. It has found its monument in Herbert Spencer's sociology, but Spencer's individualistic extremism was only the exaggeration of a widely diffused belief, and that is to say that, at least as regards the economic aspect of social life, there exists a self-regulating automatic mechanism which operates in such a way that the pursuit of the personal interests and objectives of the individual results in the greatest possible satisfaction of everybody's needs. The Enlightenment revolutions are typically individualistic revolutions. The most radical, the French Revolution, with the vote for the end of feudal rights in the National Assembly on the 4 August 1789, made France a country of small landowners, closed in their exasperated and anarchic individualism, who lacked the English type of landowner's counterbalance. With regard to industry, the Revolution acted as a powerful stimulus towards freedom and individual initiative, bringing about the abolition of various medieval corporations and restrictions of medieval origin.

The idea of progress, which is the cardinal idea of the modern world, develops within a perspective of individualism. Strictly related to the new conception of science, it changes the idea of the world. "For medieval man," Romano Guardini observes, "science exclusively represented the search for truth through the study of authoritative sources. . . . But from the second half of the fourteenth century and particularly in the fifteenth century a change occurred. The desire for knowledge goes directly to the reality of things. Man wants to see with his own eyes and examine with his own intelligence, reaching a judgment based upon criticism, independent of previous models."[2] On the level of social organization the primary groups and intermediate associative groups, in which we recognize today an importance as the instruments of mediation between the individual and history and between the individual and the state, have been urgently liquidated in the name of individual freedom, the emptiness of this freedom only being recognized later. The progress of the individual creates the principal concern. This progress is considered directly proportional to the degree of his emancipation from social conventions. It is a secure, single-minded progress, but requires as a preliminary condition that the individual be conceived in a desert, that on his way there are neither rules nor obstacles; he is free to fulfill himself, to give reign to his destiny.

History does not close its cycle in this way, of course. History has no cycles; history, like progress, is necessarily an open, constantly moving, irreversible, single-minded process. The rebellion of the Enlightenment is a positive rebellion, an explosion of optimism. When the individual finally succeeds in freeing himself from social morals and current prejudices, which limit initiative and brake impulsiveness, spontaneity, and creativity, he finds himself in a happy state of reconciliation with nature, at peace with his profound being, in equilibrium and secure. It is a common theme in nineteenth-century theater; Ibsen is one example among many. The important thing for the individual is to be authentic, that is, to be himself, putting aside and suspending as a sort of universal methodical doubt all ties of family, friendship, and work, which give sense to everyday life. The individual, thus stripped by Enlightenment rationalism of every familial link, and detached from his own socio-cultural matrix, is ready to fulfill his historical mission. This consists in substituting rationality for wisdom, communicating freshly and fully with nature, and guaranteeing the general progress of civil society, towards which end an "invisible hand" inexorably guides individual progress.

THE INDIVIDUAL AS AN AUTONOMOUS AND SELF-SUFFICIENT REALITY

According to Vernon L. Parrington, a classic example of such a child of nature is presented by Mark Twain when he describes the picaresque adventures of Huckleberry Finn. He is a happy rebel against the tyranny of family ties, against artificial social conventions, and generally against the strict morals of the village; he is sure of himself, of his own individuality, and of his inexhaustible self-sufficiency. In his apparent amorality, or even immorality, the story of Huck is pervaded by a feeling of profound moral passion and a refusal that is primarily ethical, even if it is colored by a simple, picturesque antipathy for the adulterated, calculated mores of respectable, urban society. This refusal finds its last outlet in his flight from everyday routine to help Jim evade slavery, against the rules of conventional morality, and to put himself at the service of a new god, a natural god, the great Mississippi River: "a whole mile broad, and awful still and grand."[3]

It is not by chance that the Enlightenment revolt against tradition and formalism profoundly incised American cultural and social life, finding an immediate, ideal, and practical response. The United States is in fact a nation without prehistory, born with a written constitution as rigid as any product of reason compared with the fluidity of habit. The United States is the "country of God," or, literally, the "country of miracles." For the Pilgrims and founding fathers in flight from Europe, from its injustices codified by custom and positive law, from its vertical inflexibility, the American world offered itself as the ideal land for the great experiment, for the miracle of renovating spiritual life and civil society "ab imis." The "open frontier" and the absence of a feudal past are here a point of departure, rather than the lacerating and suffering outlet of a long tension. It is a gift from the gods, a point that is the original right of "civis Americanus," a point that is at the same time a factual reality and a value judgment, an aim to achieve. It is at the base of the American constitution as a myth for the lower classes of Europe. From this derives the optimistic and burning individualism, the "rugged individualism" of the pioneers. It is an individualism which does not deny sociability, but does not know the social values of tradition. It led Jefferson to be stupified and scandalized by Burke's volte-face, which involved his favoring the American Revolution, which was permeated by a concrete, pragmatic spirit, while violently opposing the French Revolution, which he judged to be dominated by theoretical dogma and thus subject to the logic of totalitarian terror.[4]

THE MYSTICISM OF SCIENCE

An American scholar, in clearly Burkean tones, has, with considerable finesse, revealed the influence of a progressive-individualist perspective on the ambitions of the social sciences and their presupposed methodologies, up to the present day:

What was scientific psychology if not the study of the mental forces and states of the natural individual, who was always assumed to be autonomous and stable? The political and economic sciences were interested in legal and economic atoms—abstract human beings—and in impersonal reports supplied by the market or a particular general legislation. The rationalists converted all social and cultural differences into differences of intensity and quantity, of individual passions and aspirations. Individual stability was in function of his unalterable instincts and sovereign reason: the stability of society was guaranteed by laws of historical development. The two elements—scientific universality and moral emancipation from the past—became nearly indistinguishable in the philosophy and social science of the time. That Bentham boasted of being able to make laws for the whole of India from the recesses of his own study hardly constitutes an indication of personal eccentricity. The boast rose from a belief, whether in reason or in the uneradicable uniformity and stability of individuals, everywhere.[5]

The fight for emancipation from tradition therefore prepares a new despotism, that of anti-traditionalism, the tyranny of progress as a necessary law of historical development. Here we touch the second limitation of the Enlightenment: the individual perspective in a legal atomistic sense suggests an idea of progress which pays for its presumed universal validity by lacking organic historical roots, with the extreme fragility of its own guarantee and with its own tools of practical realization. Nobody can deny the importance and positive contribution of the challenge to tradition, but it is clear that the equation of tradition and error is simplistic and utterly unsustainable. Such an equation is the result of undue, that is mechanical, rigorous application of the analytico-scientific method to the socio-historical sphere. This is the root of technocratic illusions and of the confusion between technical progress and moral progress, and from this derives the conversion of scientific need into scientism and naive sociology. In a word, the quantification of the qualitative on one side, and, on the other, the trespass of the scope of scientific analysis into the romantic and doctrinal conception of historical development as a progressive realization of a providential design, from Augustine to Hegel. Alternatively, the trespass, as in Saint-Simon and Comte, into the mystical need for a complete regeneration of humanity by the scientification of political judgment and the absolute rationalization of social structures and functions.

As I have elsewhere observed, what characterizes the post-Enlightenment systematic sociologists and their methodological planning is precisely this confusion between scientific rigor and the need for total regeneration, which acquires the tone and meaning of a religious experience. Science makes progress possible; indefinite, complete, and historically determinable progress. Evolution is already commenced by humanity, as it is documented in the passage from nomadic tribes to the city-state, and thus to nations. With science it must conclude in the supreme vision of an organic, brotherly humanity, removed from all particulars pertaining to tradition and custom. This tendency reaches its apex and complete formulation in Comte's work, where science and mysticism coincide and progress is transformed by philosophical conviction into a religious message.[6] Comte is, in this sense, an exemplary case. He exhaustively illustrates the conception of historical development and the evolution of the idea of progress as a single-minded, necessary development from one social type to another immediately superior, by rationally intelligible stages which are scientifically predictable in their essential characteristics. This is in precise antithesis to the other conception of historical development, the pessimistic and cyclical conception, which we can call Spenglerian. According to this conception, far from being destined to perpetual peace, industrial societies, by concentrating human masses in cities, disintegrating territorial and blood-related communities, and at the same time rousing ambition and power lust, cannot avoid serious conflicts of extraordinary dimensions.

PROGRESS AS A PROBLEMATIC HUMAN ENTERPRISE

We are indebted to J. B. Bury for the most complete study of the idea of progress, its origins and development from classical antiquity to the evolutionary theory of Herbert Spencer and to Comte's law of three stages. He says that the idea of progress is a theory which implies a synthesis of the past and a prophecy of the future, that it is based on an interpretation of history in which society slowly but ineluctably progresses is a desirable direction, and that this process will continue indefinitely. It also implies that everybody will enjoy a condition of general happiness which will justify the whole of the process of civilization, since otherwise the direction would not be desirable. For Bury there is yet another implication: the process must be the necessary outcome of man's physical and moral nature, otherwise there would be no guarantee of his continuity and of his escape from the problems of the world. The idea of progress would then fall back on the idea of Providence. But this is not the case, as Hegel saw perspicaciously, with the affirmation of the inevitability of progress, in itself inconceivable because, if progress is really conceived as a necessary process, history is reduced to taking account of graduations of inevitability. In this case, history is simply what it is and, for better or worse, cannot be interpreted otherwise. That is to say that progress is transformed into pure and simple development, and Croce, not forgetting Hegel's lesson, frees himself from both optimistic and pessimistic interpretations to observe: "What is the reality of the spirit and of history? A continuum developed and linked by events, which are the works of man; works, and not emotions, feelings, tastes or pains; works which will be philosophical concepts, scientific formulae, poetic creations, practical actions, generous and religious actions."[7]

In other words, progress is restored to human initiative; no law of development can really guarantee it. Comte's law is little more than a utopian dream, deduced with no great rigor from insufficient introspective notations and from a brief examination of European history, unduly presented as the history of all humanity. The First World War marked the end of the dream, the brusque interruption of a *belle époque*, which like all *belles époques*, was believed to be eternal. In fact, the 1914 war closes the nineteenth-century, the century of positivism, the romanticism of science and belief in progress. Nietzsche died in August 1900, but his prophecies were still a simple curiosity, the eccentricities of a mad professor. The superman phenomenon was little more than a limited aesthetic fashion; Nietzsche's intuitions had not shown all of their tragic character. It is a fact that the nineteenth-century outlived itself; the avant-garde movements of the first years of the twentieth-century, Marinetti's Futurism and the artistico-literary rebellion, are possible because they flowered on the solid basis of a bourgeois society which knows, or believes itself to know, what it is and where it is going. The first manifestation of the crisis coincides with the outbreak of the first global conflict, when the equilibrium of nineteenth-century Europe disappears in fragments. Now, in everybody's view, the resigned, genuine desperation of modern man begins; his perplexity, his bewilderment at the great transformation. He vaguely feels himself entering a new era, treading on fresh ground, beginning a journey on which all the old reference points are of no value. Progress is not inevitable. History does not possess autonomous organizational powers. Progress and civilization are not automatic, but are only human enterprises which are exposed to setbacks, have no guarantee against regression, corruption, and failure, and are dominated by uncertainty and fear.

NOTES

1. This view has been forcefully and persuasively presented in *The Western Intellectual Tradition* by J. Bronowski and B. Mazlish, New York, Harper, 1960.

2. Cfr. R. Guardini, *Das Ende der Neuzeit*, Basel, Hess Verlag, 1950, p. 35; (Eng. trans., *The End of the Modern World: A Search for Orientation*, New York, Sheed and Ward, 1956).

3. Cfr. L. Trilling's contrary view in *The Liberal Imagination*, New York, Doubleday, 1957, p. 104. Trilling argues that Huck finds his real father in Jim as Stephen Dedalus does in Leopold Bloom, that the boy and the Negro slave form a family between them, a primitive community.

4. I have noticed elsewhere the curious coincidence between Marx and Jef-

ferson's judgment of Edmund Burke concerning the French Revolution; cfr. my book, *La sociologia come partecipazione*, Turin, Taylor, 1961, p. 70.

5. This criticism of abstracted utilitarianism has been voiced especially by R. A. Nisbet in his study, *The Quest for Community*, New York, Oxford University Press, 1953, which I have translated into Italian under the title *La comunità e lo stato*, Milan, Comunitā, 1957.

6. For a comprehensive comment in this connection, may I refer the reader to my essay, *Una teologia per atei*, Bari, 1983, published in English by Associated Faculty Press, 1985.

7. Cfr. B. Croce, "Progresso come stato d'animo e concetto filosofico," *Quaderni della critica*, July 1948.

3

The Problem of Technology

MACHINE AND MAN

Technology poses us a problem which has displayed, and still displays, portentous symptoms. We have been accustomed to a cultural tradition which sets up an opposition between humanism and technology, between man and machine. Such an opposition cannot be discounted, yet is not acceptable as it stands. In particular, one must not be led astray by its rhetoric. Humanism is not an armchair.

It is an interesting fact that anti-machine feeling has been propagated most eloquently by men with no professional mechanical expertise. The machine retains in their eyes all the fascination of a mysterious and frightening reality. But at the same time it is born with the shameful mark of what Thorstein Veblen called "manual contamination, the sign of useful, 'servile' work."[1] This leads to the emotional and passionate defining nature of anti-machine feeling: the "heroic" shout of Carlyle, Ruskin's sarcasm, Bernanos' romantic and eschatological sense of the catastrophical, the *reductio ad absurdum* of Georg Juenger and his present-day imitators, who are legion. The feeling against machines cannot be reduced to a real doctrine; it is more a state of mind, a psychological reaction more or less intellectually mediated, that a writer coherently expresses in conceptual terms. In the humanist intellectual it reveals an aesthetic vocation threatened by the machine, and prepares its own theoretical justification. Emmanuel Mournier has justly observed: "Anti-machine feeling is less a doctrine than an effective and passionate current."[2] Its verbal violence, its refusal on principle of research limited to the machine and its real short-term effects on human beings, and the predicatory fervor which sustains it, all declare its limits.

ANTI-MACHINE FEELING AS A PROTEST

Within the diffuse and complex attitude which we cursorily indicate with the term "anti-machine feeling," one can distinguish three different human situations. In the first place, there is the anti-machine feeling of pre-technological or paleo-technological human groups. The difficulties which rural-born workers encounter on beginning to work in a factory are well known. Georges Friedmann has written interestingly of this question.[3] The wide research conducted in technically underdeveloped countries documents the socio-psychological lacerations from which social groups suffer in the stage of transition from the peasant world to a highly mechanized industrial society. It is not only a question of certain difficulties of psycho-motorial adaptation, as is attested by tests in use with the great majority of company managements. Workers of peasant origin, for example, suffer relatively more from noise, from heat conditions, and from the rhythm of certain machines than workers of urban-industrial origin, and are consequently more exposed to industrial accidents. Resistance to machines is, in this case, manifest in naive forms, such as absenteeism, small self-inflicted accidents, noncollaboration, and minimal production. It is substantially a question of protest against technical innovation which tends to defend the worker's physical integrity and his socio-psychological habits.[4]

In the second place, the anti-machine feeling which consists of pure and simple physical destruction of machines should be considered. This type of feeling takes its name from the English worker Ludd, who, failing to win a dispute with the workers of a shoe factory, vent his anger on the factory's machines. The first group of Luddites appeared in Nottingham in 1811, and a deep vein of anti-machine feeling has generally distinguished the early phases of the modern worker movements. But one should not believe in simple reactions which spring spontaneously from the psycho-physiological incapacity for adaptation. Luddism is brutal and violent, but derives from groups of workers already within an industrial tradition. Besides, these workers know from direct experience that their immediate enemy is the machine, because the machine produces more quickly, within stricter margins of tolerance, and with a more constant production rhythm. Their machine-breaking fury needs no ideological or doctrinal justifications. It explodes with the violent and natural readiness of legitimate defense. The machine condemns the worker to unemployment and poverty. Furthermore the machine lowers an impersonal and mechanical diaphragm between employee and employer. It marks the end of direct human contact and the "family spirit" at work. The impersonal and anonymous discipline of "work rules" substitute paternalism, which although authoritarian is human. The old-fashioned employer, who chose the best workers from the most lively boys of his parish, is succeeded by the university-educated engineer.[5]

ANTI-MACHINE FEELING AS A BOURGEOIS MYTH

Anti-machine feeling properly understood, that is, as a conscious, embryonic, reflective position which is not part of the worker's world, consists of a bourgeois myth, full of deep nostalgia for an idealized pre-technological, peasant civilization, with its intact green fields and clean air.[6] Writers, poets, artists, and men who live on an agrarian income in rapid decline or are strictly integrated in a pre-technological way of life see a mortal threat in the advance of large-scale mechanization and the manipulating and standardizing practices which accompany it. They realize that their values are in peril and that their culture is becoming irrelevant.

When small industries, developed in the old *régime* as a sort of complementary activity to large-scale landowning, grow and enlarge their field of operations (a possibility due to new discoveries which allow a qualitative and quantitative rise in production),[7] until they give way to the first accumulation of capital and make large-scale mechanization technically possible and economically convenient, the consequences for social institutions and values, or way of life and "culture," are immediate and profound. Culture, as "otium" contrasting with "negotium," that is, solitary culture, essentially narcissistic contemplation and self-cultivation, as a terminal point of a formative process which excludes work and its technology as servile, this culture is in crisis. But here the third type of anti-machine feeling, which we are delineating, divides into two subcategories which we can indicate respectively as the mystique of craftsmanship and the refusal of the modern world.

It is not only a question of Queen Elizabeth in the sixteenth-century limiting the expansion of the iron industry in order to save the rich English forests. The mystique of craftsmanship reproaches the machine for technological disoccupation of the hands. It surrounds with suspicion, if not with a sacrilegious aura, everything that is "adulterated," impersonal machine products, which have not known the "unique" craftsman's touch; products of a violation of natural laws. The machine makes mass production possible, but such production is not commensurate with the real, "natural" needs of human beings. Its advantages are apparent: soon after its creation by man, the machine becomes his tyrannical master. The mystics of craftsmanship are not anti-technology on principle; they accept technical progress with reservations. They recognize the advantages of technical progress but fear that the price to pay is too high. They intend to "control" technical progress and mechanization because they feel the internal contradictions. Far from waiting to push them to extremes in order to destroy them, they run to cover on the level of politics and customs; they propose decentralization, they preach against the mania for the colossal and size in all its aspects. Their most coherent representative is Proudhon.

MARX AND PROUDHON

The polemic between Marx and Proudhon is exemplary in this respect. Compared with Marx, who, believing in the secular dogma of dialectic, expected the solution of the social questions from the frontal clash between two classes, Proudhon seems to be completely aware of the extreme variety of the Marxian "general class" or proletariat, which he prefers to call the "people." He does not believe in an automatic dialectical leap, which seems to him more destructive than positive in the long run. He never tires of affirming the "plurality of irreducible and antagonistic elements" which essentially characterize both the physical and the moral world, a plurality which is in precise antithesis to Hegelian-Marxist monolithic monism.

It is above all in the *Philosophie de la misère* that Proudhon's preoccupations find expression inasmuch as they concern gigantism in industry and technology, which transforms itself from a tool to an aim. "It is from this essential contradiction in our ideas, realizing itself in work and operating with enormous power in society, that a contrary sense is given to each case, conferring on society the aspect of a reversed tapestry or an animal with its head hung low. Through the division of work man must raise himself little by little to science and liberty; in reality, through the division of work and the use of machines, one is brutalised and enslaved."[8]

The remedy suggested by Proudhon to the antimony of capitalist society, for its own pure linearity, consists of an "idealist" target which is too easy for Marx's sarcastic rigor.[9] For Proudhon it is a question of finding a "general equation" for all the economic contradictions of society, an equation which, as a Platonic archetype, will be the "nec plus ultra" of human development and will at the same time point towards the solution of all problems. Proudhon already foresees this equation:

We must arrive at a law of "change," a theory of "mutuality," a guarantee system which resolves the old forms of our civil and commercial societies and satisfies all the conditions of efficacy, progress and justice which criticism suggests: we must arrive at a society which is not merely conventional but real; which transforms fragmented divisions into a scientific tool; which abolished slavery by machines and prevents the crisis of their apparition; which benefits from competition and gains security for everybody from monopoly; which, by the power of its principle, puts capital and the state to work instead of requesting credit from capital and protection from the state, etc., ... a society, in one word, which being at the same time organization and transition, escapes the temporal, guarantees everything, and enforces no obligation.[10]

The mystique of craftsmanship, which we may consider admirably summarized in this eloquent passage from Proudhon, finds its fulfillment in the feeling against machines when it is elaborated into a reflective myth, or as a conscious refusal of the modern world.

Marx, using a paradigm, examines Proudhon's considerations with regard to the division of work and machines.

1. Good side of the division of work	"Considered in its essence, the division of work is the way in which equality of conditions and intelligences realizes itself." (Proudhon)
	"The division of work has become for us an instrument of poverty." (Proudhon)

VARIANT

2. Bad side of the division of work	"Dividing work according to its inherent governing principle, which is the principal condition of its fecundity, it reaches the negation of its aims and destroys itself." (Proudhon)
3. Problem to resolve	"Find a way of reassembling which cancels the inconveniences of the division whilst conserving its useful effects." (Proudhon)

In the first place Marx reproaches Proudhon for having made an "eternal law" or abstract category of the division of work. History, Marx observes, does not proceed by categories. It needed a secular evolution in Germany to actuate the large-scale division of work which determined the separation of town and country. Besides, depending in which of many epochs it took place, the division of work assumed particular features which "would be difficult to deduce from the one word 'divide,' or from the idea or category." Proudhon had noticd how economists dwelt at greater length on the advantageous consequences of the division of work than on the negative consequences. According to Proudhon, only Say had recognized that what produces good from the division of work is also the source of what is bad. Marx replies that, even before Say, the problem had been proposed by Adam Smith, who based it on a work of Lemontay, and that even before Smith and Lemontay the problem had been presented by Ferguson. For Marx, Proudhon has limited himself to establishing a parallel between the printing worker of his time and the medieval worker, and between the literary figure of his time and of the Middle Ages. The prisoner of an explanatory plan, he sees the logical cause of the decrease in wages in the division of work, as well as the source of individual deprivation. Marx presses home: "The division of work reduces the worker to a degrading function; this degrading function corresponds with a depraved soul; the depraved soul corresponds with an ever-increasing reduction in wages." And to show that this wage reduction suits a depraved soul, M. Proudhon says, to salve his conscience that the "universal conscience" wants it that way. Is M. Proudhon's soul counted in the "universal conscience"?

Then Marx goes on to analyze the part regarding machines, which Proudhon defines as "logical antitheses of the division of work." According to Marx, Proudhon, departing from his premises, arbitrarily transforms the machine into a factory: "After having conceived the modern factory in order to show the origins of poverty in the division of work, M. Proudhon supposes the division of work itself to have generated poverty; then he considers the factory, and represents it as the dialectical negation of this poverty." Marx considers the Proudhonesque dialectical proceeding defective at every point and criticizes the fact that Proudhon has deviated from his original categorical definition of the division of work, assuming that "the handmill supposes a different division of work to a steam-mill." Proudhon wanted to begin with the division of work in order to be able later to arrive at the machine as a specific production tool. But "machines are not an economic category in the same way that bulls drawing a plough cannot be. Machines are only a productive force. The modern factory which depends on the application of machines is an economic category," as Marx observes. There is more: the division of work, which according to Proudhon predates machines, only really exists in the modern world and does not date from the birth of the world. Marx deeply criticizes Proudhon's thesis that the factory is born from the division of work and the wage-earner. With this in mind he examines a series of facts which contribute simultaneously to the development of manufacturing industry, in order to demonstrate that the division of work presupposes the gathering of workers in a factory.

Marx writes, "There is no evidence, neither in the sixteenth nor in the seventeenth century, that the various branches of a single trade have been used separately to the point at which it was sufficient to gather them in one place to make a complete factory. But, with men and tools together, the division of work which existed in the corporations necessarily reproduced or resembled the inside of a factory." Proudhon therefore saw things precisely in reverse. One can say the same of his definition of the machine as a synthesis capable of re-establishing the unity of previously fragmented work. Marx adopts the definition of a machine given by Rabbage in the "Treatise of Political Economy": "When in the division of work each particular operation has been reduced to the use of a simple tool, the conjunction of all these tools, powered by one engine, constitutes a machine." The concentration of work-tools would therefore be, according to Proudhon, the negation of the division of work, in reality, the precise reverse is true: "While the concentration of tools is developed, the division is equally developed, and vice versa. This is why each mechanical invention is followed by a greater division of work, and each increase in the division of work brings, for its part, new mechanical inventions.''

In fact, according to the lesson of English history, one can see that the most significant progress in the field of the division of work began precisely with the coming of the machine. The first weavers and spinners were mostly peasants, and it was the invention of machines which separated manufacturing industry from agriculture: "The weavers and the spinners, recently united in one family, were separated by the machine." It was in virtue of the application of machines that the division of work assumed such great proportions that industry, once detached from the soil, came to depend exclusively on the world market and international exchanges.

Proudhon speaks at great length of a "providential" or "philanthropic" aim of invention and the application of machines. Marx replies that such a philanthropic aim is pure illusion. The machines declared this themselves when it was seen that the English market had developed so much that there was no longer sufficient manual labor. For the rest, factual conditions make any discussion of "providential aims" sinisterly ironic: "Children were kept at work with the whip; they became objects of trade, and contracts were made with orphanages.... The worker saw so little of the rehabilitation or "restoration" that Proudhon had predicted from the use of machines that in the eighteenth century he resisted the dawning empire of automatons for some time. The division of work within society grew with the introduction of machines, which simplified the factory worker's job. Capital has been re-gathered, and the individual has been seriously divided. Proudhon leans on the authority of Adam Smith, but one must remember that Smith wrote of a time when the automatic factory was in its infancy.

In his *Philosophy of Manufacturing*, written when industry had already evolved considerably, Ure documents how in a system which breaks down a process in order to reduce it to its principal constituent parts, submitting all the parts to the operation of an automatic machine, these same parts can be entrusted to an unskilled worker after a cursory training period. Moreover, it is possible to transfer the worker from one machine to another as circumstances dictate. Marx, remembering the famous example of the pin factory, concludes: "Such mutations are in open opposition to the old system of work division, which gives one worker the job of making the pin head, and another the point." Proudhon is correct when he notes the difference between a country farrier and Geuzot's worker, to the advantage of the former. But at this point, introducing the division of work, Proudhon—according to Marx— "proposes that the worker makes only the 12th part of a pin, then proposes that he makes all 12 parts. In that way the worker would arrive at the science of, and understanding of, the pin." Proudhon has not sufficiently proved his notion of "synthetic work." Moreover, throughout his work Proudhon stresses the difference between the contemporary world and the Middle Ages, but in such a way has not managed to go beyond the petit bourgeois ideal. And to realize this ideal, he conceives no improvement above returning to the worker, or at most the medieval master-craftsman. Affirming that to feel oneself genuinely a man it is enough to have produced one masterwork in a lifetime, he does nothing but turn backward. Marx asks: "Is this not, in form and substance, the masterwork required by the medieval guild?" On Marx's diagnosis the principal fault of Proudhon lies in this desire to return to the Middle Ages, this desire to *wallow in superficial contradictions without seeing in them any positive aspect for the formation of future society*. In fact, Marx declares that *"an oppressed class is a vital condition of all societies based upon antagonism between classes."* The redemption of the oppressed classes necessarily implies the creation of a new society.

The mystique of craftsmanship sees a danger in the machine as far as the technological perfection of the machine is in proportion to its success in reducing manual labor, while perfection of craftsmanship means the perfection of manual workmanship.[11] For anti-machine feeling as a refusal of the modern world, the machine puts the concepts of "culture" and civil order in crisis. The modern world, as a rational and secular world, is totally rejected here as a pure and simple absurdity; that is, the modern world as an earthly world, freed from the dogmatic dominion of gods and their caprices, and at least basically exempt from mental habits which are not founded upon rational criteria drawn from scientific research and causal principles. The principle of rationality behind the machine and its operations is correctly seen as the outrider of the secular principle which is fundamental to the modern world. The machine breaks routine and upsets the mental and social rules of tradition. It is an essential part of the "human, too human" modern world; the world which has really "restricted man's opinions and religious faith to the private sphere" and "does not tolerate pressures on the individual's autonomy. . .firstly in the sense that it does not put pressure to inculcate opinions and religious belief if the individual chooses, freely and critically, not to accept them."[12]

This type of anti-machine feeling, the most organic and coherent, registers with undoubted efficacy the split created in society by the first "industrial revolution,"[13] that is, by large-scale mechanization introduced into factories by the division of work, and by the systematic, scientific, and standardizing fragmentation of production flow. But it does not escape heavy overtones of medieval and decadent nostalgia, which unites the need for dogmatic unity such as brings us to a classical obscurantism to the needs of an unforced and socially irresponsible culture—cut off from the problems of everyday life. Novalis already noticed the damage done by science to the "sense of the invisible" and, loudly invoking the "New Jerusalem," declared: "It is impossible that earthly powers find equilibrium; only a third element, which is both earthly and heavenly, can complete this task. Christianity must revive, reactivate itself and make a new visible church."[14]

Technology is seen as the great disintegrating force, which pulls men away from the country to concentrate them in "senseless industrial cities,"[15] taking old insufficiencies to a critical point (for example the fire of London or of Chicago); it allows the use of cheap and unskilled labor (women and children) and takes from the ex-craftsman worker the control not only of his own tools but even of his time and movements.[16] Technology "alienates" him from the product of his work and subjects him to the tyranny of "causalism."[17] It announces the "Decline of the West" and the "Crisis of Western Civilization."[18] Keyserling summarizes for everybody: "Which man embodies the spirit of the modern masses? It is the driver; he is the prototype of the mass era, no less than the priest, knight and gentleman have been for other eras. The driver is the technological primitive. The aptitude is very similar to the forest-dweller's sense of direction; technology is its own evidence; it awakens feelings of freedom and power in the man who is its master, with a force proportionate to his primitiveness."[19] In this way, technology, dispensing power to the primitive, prepares and makes inevitable the lowering of noble values and vulgarizes "culture."[20] The decadent tendency of such an attitude is admirably expressed by Heidegger. Technology has its own truth, but it is a banal truth; "It is the eternal return of the identical."[21]

NOTES

1. Thorstein Veblen attributes important social effects and merits to the "machine discipline," but does not fail to show how the machine eventually produces mental habits and social attitudes which contrast with traditional beliefs and institutionalized behavior. The leisure class, which incarnates such beliefs and traditional attitudes, finds itself, in the technical atmosphere which defines the modern world, to be isolated and no more or less superfluous than an anachronistic residual which no longer corresponds to any precisely determinable function. For informed comment on Veblen, see Joseph Dorfman, *Thorstein Veblen and His America*, New York, 1934; J. A Hobson, *Veblen*, London, 1936; R. L. Duffus, *The Innocents at Cedro*, New York, 1944; P. T. Homan, *Contemporary Economic Thought*, New York, 1928; Lewis Mumford, "Thorstein Veblen," *The New Republic*, 5 August, 1931; A. G. Gruchy, *Modern Economic Thought: The American Contribution*, New York, 1947; D. Riesman, *Th. Veblen: An Interpretation*, New York, 1956.

2. Cfr. Emmanuel Mounier, "La machine en accusation," in VV.AA., *Industrialisation et technocratie*, Paris, 1947, p. 7.

3. A straight poetical tone occasionally characterizes Friedmann's considerations concerning the contrast between the natural and technical worlds. In reality it is well to remember that such a view of things is no longer tenable. At the present time it is more correct to speak of a variously articulated town-country continuum. Cfr. G. Friedmann, *Où va le travail humain?*, especially the first part, "A Worker and Two Worlds," *Le travail en miettes* (Eng. trans., *The Anatomy of Work*, New York, 1962), and the early work, which established his reputation as an industrial sociologist in the grand European sense, *Problèmes humains du machinisme industriel* (Eng. trans., *Industrial Society: The Emergence of the Human Problems of Automation*, Glencoe, Ill., 1955).

4. Resistance to technical change has often been exaggerated, especially regarding workers of industrial origin who tend on the contrary to look upon industrial work as a means of evading their social isolation and thus as an unpleasant but effective instrument of upward mobility and social promotion. More research on this aspect is needed.

5. Cfr., for an impressive example, A. Olivetti, *Appunti per la storia di una fabbrica*, now collected in *Società, Stato, Comunità*, Milan, 1956.

6. Perhaps in England, the cradle of "industrial revolution," one can gather the most eloquent deprecations. The coming industrial mechanization was seen as a cosmic punishment. William Blake, Dickens, and Wordsworth speak of it as an imminent catastrophe, while Carlyle, Butler, and Ruskin try to justify it historically and morally; but of this, later in this volume, in Chapter 8.

7. For example, notwithstanding the high technical level reached by the

textile industry towards the middle of the eighteenth century, the decisive pulse came from the chance to use a new energy source, Watt's invention of a rotary steam engine. Cfr. among others, C. Barbagallo, *Le origini della grande industria contemporanea*, Florence, 1951, p. 66; to be consulted also, the studies of economic history with a social perspective by Carlo Cipolla.

8. Cfr. P. J. Proudhon, *Système des contradictions économiques ou Philosophie de la misère*, Paris, 1846 (Eng. trans., *System of Economic Contradictions: or, The Philosophy of Misery*, Boston, 1888).

9. Cfr. K. Marx, *Misère de la philosophie*, Paris, 1847 (Eng. trans., *The Poverty of Philosophy*, New York, 1971).

10. Cfr. Proudhon, *Système des contradictions économiques*, pp. 410–41.

11. Cfr. Thorstein Veblen, *The Instinct of Workmanship and the State of the Industrial Arts*, New York, 1914; 1946 ed., p. 307.

12. Cfr. F. Lombardi, *Nascita del mondo moderno*, Roma, 1953, p. 294.

13. The common catastrophic notion of the "industrial revolution" has been carefully criticized in F. A. Haye, ed., *Capitalism and the Historians*, Chicago, 1954; it contains papers by T. S. Ashton, L. M. Hacker, W. H. Hutt, and B. de Jouvenel.

14. The thinking of Novalis (Friedrich von Hardenberg) on this subject is perspicuously expounded in his tract, *Christianity or Europe*; see the critical edition of *Die Christenheit oder Europa* in Friedrich Hardenberg (pseud. Novalis), *Werke und Briefe*, München, Winkler, 1957.

15. The phrase is used by Lewis Mumford in *The Culture of Cities*, New York, 1938.

16. The Marxian concept of alienation has recently been rediscovered and quite romanticized, but the two essential meanings given by Marx (*Entässerung*, or "exteriorization," and *Entfremdung*, or "extraneation") do not correspond exactly to present-day use, which has psychoanalytical, existential, and phenomenological overtones foreign to Marx. See, for an interpretation of Marxist thought based on the key of "alienation," Jean-Yves Calvez, *La pensée de K. Marx*, Paris, 1956; see also D. Bell, "The Rediscovery of Alienation," *The Journal of Philosophy*, 5, 24, 1959.

17. It is the title of the English translation of Chapter 9 of Friedrich Georg Jünger's book, *Die Perfektion der Technik*, Munich, 1939 (Eng. trans., *The Failure of Technology: Perfection Without Purpose*, Hinsdale, Ill., 1945).

18. A melodramatic Spenglerian tone pervades F. Burzio, *Il demiurgo e la crisi occidentale*, Milan, 1943, pp. 165–66: "Although nationalism and bolshevism are adversaries on many points, they communicate in the common ideal of comfort, and the technical organization upon which it depends, . . . Caught between the symmetrical vices of Russia and America, what will the probable future of Western Europe be?"

19. This view is especially elaborated upon by Hermann Alexander von

Keyserling in *Predictions of a New World* and in other writings; see the orig. edition in *Die Gesammelte Werke*, Darmstadt, Holle Verlag, 1956.

20. Cfr. on this matter, C. Antoni, "Riflessioni e congetture," *Criterio*, May–June 1958; E. Zolla and N. Chiaromonte, "Massa e valori di cultura," *Tempo presente*, August 1958; noting the insuperable limits and the decanting nature of anti-machine feeling, Chiaromonte writes: "If I grant Zolla his due for a passionate and perspicacious attention to those specific and broadly significant facts that are the phenomena of mass, I must say that I do not share the point of view from which he then rises to judge the phenomena and then, not without pride, contrasts them with the world of 'pure' cultural values."

21. Cfr. Martin Heidegger, *Vorträge und Aufsätze*, Pfullingen, Munich, 1954, especially the first lecture, which is dedicated to the "question of technology."

4

Technology and Social Development

TECHNOLOGY AS A CUMULATIVE PROCESS

The greatest weakness of anti-machine feeling as a refusal of the modern world and mass culture is that, while it condemns technology and deplores mass phenomena in the name of cultural values as such, it does not realize that such values are themselves in crisis and are created because of mechanization and mass society. The problem which anti-machine feeling declares is real, but its attitude of self-satisfied exorcism is contradictory and substantially elusive.

The validity of the opposition between man and machine is limited; it does not go beyond a purely logical, intellectual level. Taken to its extreme consequences, it becomes a pure and simple "fictio mentis," if not a convenient alibi. In its specific terms we can only judge it on the basis of empirical researches into those human situations we want to analyze. A generic discussion of that opposition is a meaningless discussion. In fact, in the reality of historical experience, we always find human groups to be moved by specific intentions, within a given environment, and provided with certain tools. In other words, we always find an ideal tension, a conscious bearing, assisted by a certain technology; that is to say, by a certain manipulatory skill, transforming and utilizing material and usually natural resources, too.[1]

In this sense a proposal formulated by Marx a hundred years ago in the thirteenth chapter of Book I of *Das Kapital* is still substantially valid: it is necessary to write a critical history of technology. Marx observes, "Darwin has created interest in the history of natural technology, that is, on the formation of vegetal and animal organs as instruments of production of the lives of plants and animals. Does the history of the formation of the productive organs of social man, the material base of every particular social organization, not merit equal attention?'' Marx's proposal still seems valid to us, but it is a surprising fact that it has not been coherently developed by Marxism. It is in fact true that Marx is a careful observer and, for his time, informed about industrial machinery. The care which he delineates the technical evolution of productive organization and the introduction of new machines in the twelfth and thirteenth chapters of *Das Kapital* is clear testimony of this. But compared with the reality of the technical process and its essential characteristic, Marx's theoretico-conceptual apparatus soon reveals its limits. This is even more the case with Marxists, who are open to philosophical exigencies and the dialectical plan's impatience, but less sensitive to the necessity of describing the facts about industrial machines and establishing the short-term effects of their limited concreteness on groups of workers. It is not only a question of the basic ambiguity of Marxism, to which Hans Kelsen has recently returned. In Kelsen's view there is a strange ambiguity in the meaning of the relation between reality and ideology which makes the basis of Marx's theory of knowledge extremely problematic.[2] Evidently it is not only a question of the epistemological problem. The ambiguity does not restrict itself to the methodological plan; it seems to me to damage the content of Marxist thought in a profound way. In *Zur Kritik der politischen Oekonomie*, Marx first proposes the ''mode of production'' as the base of the ''general character of the social, political and spiritual process of life,'' but then, with the same turn of phrase, shows the determinant factors of the ''consciousness'' of cohabitants in their ''social being'' (''gesellschaftliches Sein''). It seems to me that the limits and ambiguities of Marxism when confronted by the reality of the technical process spring from this double conception of the determinant factor. Marx writes: ''Generallly speaking the Asian, feudal and modern bourgeois modes of production can be defined as the progressive epochs of the economic shape of society. Bourgeois production relations are the last antagonistic form of the process of social production, etc.... The prehistory of human society therefore closes with this social formation.'' Shortly before he had observed in quasi-deterministic economic terms: ''A social formation never dies before the productive forces it is capable of containing have developed, etc.''

These classic observations of socialist literature could justify an interpretation of Marxism as technological determinism. John H. Hallowell, for example, writes, "History is intelligible for Marx because it is the history of technology; tools are man-made, and what is man-made is intelligible."[3] But such an interpretation, based on a restricted conception of the determinant factor in which it is equated with the only "mode of production" in a technical sense, ignores the other wider and more sociologically informed Marxian conception, in which the determinant factor is identified with the whole "social being." Marx undoubtedly assigns an important role to technological development, as is evident even in his sharp polemic with Proudhon in which he makes summary justice of Proudhon's peasant, anarchist anti-machine rancor. But one can declare that Marx never speaks, except in retort, of a priority of recognizing any particular component of the real social process. He insists upon the intimate interdependence, historically, of social organizations in their various aspects (legal, ideological, political, institutional, etc.) and the tools that are widely used in the production of economic goods, which indicate the prevalent mode and stage of development of such production. Marx never made this interdependence explicit and articulate on the level of the theoretical reasons for his own research. I have elsewhere noted how we can distinguish four structural and superstructural, but constantly interacting levels in the essential core of Marx's thought: (1) the stage of expansion of productive forces; (2) the prevalent mode of production and exchange; (3) the social structure, or "civil society" as he calls it in the *Deutsche Ideologie*; and (4) the specific conditions of a political and cultural nature.

These four levels are certainly inter-relating and inter-reacting, that is, present together and active in a given historical situation, and they condition each other although they are not all on the same level. They are at a different depth to global social structure and have a different capacity for affecting real, that is historical, development. Without such diversification we should have absolute stasis rather than movement. It seems that Marx assigns the role of independent variables (in a relative sense) to point (1), that is, to productive forces, and therefore it appears that Hallowell's interpretation is correct and that the violent criticism of Proudhon's peasant anti-machine position is justified. But for Marx and Engels and for all other orthodox Marxists, it is not technology which governs a given society but the "social structure," or class structure. The notion of "classes" and "class structure" is the determinant notion of Marxism. If the technological factor were the determinant and really crucial factor for historical development, as it would

seem from a certain interpretation of Marx, the first relevant consequence would necessarily be the abandonment of the dialectical plan,
because technological development is not analyzable or more simply,
commensurable to that plan. *Its character is cumulative and evolutionary, not dialectical.* Its analysis depends on a sociological-experimental
verification, not on a historical-dialectical approach.

TECHNOLOGY AND RATIONALIZATION

There are, therefore, good reasons[4] to show how Marx's proposal
for a critical history of technology has not been followed up even in
the world of orthodox Marxist thought. The only technological theory
of historical development, coherently worked out at a safe distance from
the furor of technocrats and from the mysticism of the Hegelian dialectical triad, we owe to the American sociologist Thorstein Veblen and
his subtle analyses of the cultural importance of machines, whether
regarding "the nature of peace" or "Imperial Germany." It is not by
chance that Veblen consciously refuses any pre-established design or
any variant of historical finalism. With most critics, he does not confine
himself to revealing the mortal contradiction of Marxism in Marx's final
hypothetical synthesis—in which dialectic negates itself and the class
war results in a classless society—but observes that such a synthesis
does not belong to, nor can for any reason enter, Darwinism or He-
gelism, neither right nor left. He declares that it is a good quality,
English, utilitarian concept and belongs to Marx for the simple reason
that it is borrowed from the profit system. In fact, he says, it is a piece
of hedonism which derives rather from Bentham than Hegel.

It is not necessary to establish here the origins of such a concept. It
is enough to elucidate that, for the American sociologist, Marx is too
professional, too inclined to "reject life," and thereby finished by falling
victim to logical abstractions without basis in reality, as far as no prearranged goal is discernible in the evolutionary process. Veblen affirms
more dogmatically that it is a question of an essentially mechanical
scheme of "blindly cumulative causation."

It has been observed that the limits of Marxism cannot be simplis-
tically ascribed to the Marxist point of view, which is basically "moral"
and "historical" rather than scientific; nor can they be ascribed to the
dialectical plan, which "needs the negative, or evil, to produce the
positive or good."[5] But it is certain that the adoption of a concept of

social process as purely cumulative allows Veblen an extraordinary freedom of analysis and classification, which makes the danger of writing "thesis history" very remote. In particular, such a concept of the historical process as pure "process," that is, as "flux," confers a perfect commensurability on Veblen's analysis with regard to the technical process and its purely cumulative evolution. While philosophical preoccupations predominate in Marx, Veblen delineates a plan of development, resolving itself in a broad cultural-anthropological typology, in which we see the Western human community pass through four principal stages, characterized by four different technologies: (1) the barbaric economy of a predatory nature, from which today's institutions have evolved (e.g., property, war, the spirit of prowess, wealthy classes); (2) the peaceful economy of the neolithic age; (3) the pre-industrial revolution artisan economy; and (4) the age of machine process, or of large-scale mechanization.

MECHANIZATION AND "NOBLE VALUES"

The striking thing in Veblen's wide, and occasionally discontinuous, analysis is the demonstration, in my judgment conclusive, of the romantic nature and logical inconsistency which mines the contrast between technology and humanism at its base, the contrast between "cultural civilization" and "machine civilization." For Veblen, anti-machine feeling really serves to obscure the pseudo rights of perfunctory ownership, sheltering them from the criteria of rational judgment, protecting them with a "magical" and "mythical" halo, which is the consequence of an "animist," pre-mechanical habit of mind. Veblen sees animistic mental habits, pre-rational behavior, and atavistic customs founded on a code of "honor" and a spirit of prowess literally "swept away" by the new discipline of mechanical processes, based upon a causal connection. He writes that the machine process pervades modern life and dominates it in a mechanical sense. One sees its dominion in the imposition of precise, mechanical measures and adaptations and in the reduction of all ways of life, of all aims, acts, necessities, conveniences, and pleasures to a standardized unity.[6]

In other words, the machine process, becoming the predominant mode of production of consumer goods, "rationalizes" the real social process; that is, it affects not only technical production methods, in the sense of organizing production life at company level, but also the larger society outside industry and its culture, symbols, and values, which define it and create a "social order" within it. The "systems of meaning" and ideas which are the hinges of the social order change after the arrival of large-scale mechanization. They are in crisis, and the groups and social classes which mentally and practically speaking live within their ambit are also in crisis. The technical process constitutes for such groups and social classes a fracture and historical "challenge" at the same time, to which they are not prepared to respond. "The machine process compels the worker to a more or less strained attention to impersonal phenomena and to sequences and correlations whose validity neither depends upon human predilection nor is created by habit or custom. The machine sweeps away anthropomorphic mental habits. It necessitates the adaptation of the worker to his work rather than the adaption of work to the worker."[7]

Large-scale mechanization therefore has, according to Veblen, a destructive potency which, in his view, does not seem to be directly against the "noble values" of humanist tradition but against the ethic of natural law, in which he sees only the fragile defense screen of the status quo. The destructive potency is also usually against pretentious conceptual plots of a metaphysical nature, which, like scholastic Marxism, tend to include all reality, or all possible experience, in their plans and discount the results of research before having effectively conducted it.

What we need to clarify here is that, for both Marx and Veblen, technology is not demoniacal, but on the contrary is simply the tool of production; that is to say, the instrument of man's "metabolism with nature," to use Marx's happy phrase.[8] In other words, technology is the instrument of human work, and human work is the distinguishing characteristic between men and other members of the animal kingdom.[9]

THE SCIENTISTIC MISUNDERSTANDING

It is curious that Veblen, the theorizer of the "instinct of workmanship," which in more than one place coincides with the Marxian concept of production as the self-creation of men, who becomes "animal rationale" besides "animal laborans," has seen in Marxism, also on this matter, the same limits as exist in hedonistic calculus and the utilitarianism of classical economists. It is strange that he has understood the Marxian conceptions of technology and human work as the residue of a feudal slave psychology. Certainly Marx cannot be counted among the generic exalters of an abstract "joy of work," but in 1844, considering Hegel's position on this matter, he observed: "Hegel adopts the point of view of modern economy. He conceives work as the being of man, which affirms him"; and later, in the *Deutsche Ideologie*: "The nature of individuals coincides with their production."

It is important to notice here that for both Marx and Veblen, "machine discipline" does not contradict "humanism," but is at its origins and constitutes a fundamental condition. When he speaks of mechanization and even the coming of the machine, Veblen's usually cool and elusive prose, full of classical-sounding polysyllabic words, livens, the long sentences are cut and recall the incantatory tone of the *Manifesto*, where Marx and Engels praise the triumphant bourgeoisie, the destroyer of the "stupidities of rural life."

The enthusiasm with which Veblen, Marx, and Engels salute the new "machine discipline" is based upon a singular quid pro quo of scientific nature, which will find its logical conclusion in the thought of Antonio Gramsci. Veblen, agreeing on this with the founders of "scientistic socialism," holds that industrialism, being based on technological development and thus on causality, necessarily leads to the disappearance of, and therefore triumph over, the wealthy class of country gentlemen and country life, which is essentially anthropomorphic and animist. In the same way Gramsci, who, even if he put the accent on the globality of what he called the "historical collision," sees in the modern organization of industrial work the historical moment for the natural developement of a new type of intellectual, the worker-intellectual that is, a technically skilled proletarian, whom the technical process, with its scientific rigor, will have freed from medieval myths and magical superstitions. "In the modern world," Gramsci declares, "technical education, strictly connected to the most primitive and skilled industrial work, must form the basis of a new type of intellectual."[10]

To see the limitations of such a conception, it will be necessary to determine the significant relation, the true inter-reaction, which exists between technology and society, and to delineate the evolution of the factory system from primitive capitalism, which was still largely craftsmanlike, to mass production and the adoption of automatic processes. In this sense Marx's proposal, for a critical history of technology, is important. It is, however, symptomatic that Marxists have not always been able to give us this critical history. Outside the Marxist school there have been many attempts at macro-sociological synthesis. Nevertheless we lack, and it is a decisive lacuna, the essential connection between wide generalizations and field research, towards determining the specifics of the evolution of industrial machinery, and individuating its possible social and human repercussions. That is, we need a critical gathering of the dialectical relation which binds formal institutions and intermediate human groups; this constitutes the effective subject matter of sociology. A critical history of technology cannot exhaust itself in the analysis, as far as it is documented, of certain historico-economics. This implies the conception of industrialization as a global social process, that is to say, as the historical "leap" from the peasant world.

NOTES

1. For some interesting distinctions between various techniques (of "acquisition," "consumption," etc.), see A. Leroi-Gourhan, *Milieu et techniques*, Paris, 1945.

2. This thesis has been especially expounded by Kelsen in his book, *The Communist Theory of Law*, London, 1955, but it runs through most of his writings.

3. Cfr. J. H. Hallowell, *Main Currents in Modern Political Thought*, New York, 1950.

4. It is not too difficult to show how Marx put a new subject in an old plan originating in theologico-cosmogonic thought. This also explains the difficulty of his "determinism," that is, the transposition of his historico-sociological thought to a metaphysical plane.

5. Cfr. Hannah Arendt, *The Human Condition*, Chicago, 1958, p. 105.

6. Cfr. Th. Veblen, *The Theory of Business Enterprise*, New York, 1904; 1932 ed., p. 306.

7. Ibid., p. 310.

8. Cfr. K. Marx, *Das Kapital*, I, chs. 1, and 5 (Eng. trans., *Capital: A Critique of Political Economy*, New York, 1967).

9. The Marxian phrase in *Deutsche Ideologie* is famous: "Men are distinguished from animals when they begin to produce their means of subsistence."

10. Cfr. A. Gramsci, *Gli intellettuali e l'organizzazione della cultura*, Turin, 1949, p. 7.

5

Tradition and Reason in Industrial Society

INDUSTRIALIZATION AS A GLOBAL PROCESS

I have elsewhere observed how the process of industrialization is rapidly becoming the common characteristic of all countries. In present-day conditions, notwithstanding the profound differences of political ideology and institutional character which distinguish them, the process of industrialization, actual or planned, appears as the defining characteristic of modern states from Great Britain to China and the Soviet Union.[1] I use the term "industrialization" in its widest sense: to indicate that type of economic activity which employs variously skilled workers for large-scale production and distribution of goods, such as allows a rapid increase in work productivity and therefore in real per capita income. The objections of classical economists, based upon the opportunity for international work division from which there would have been agricultural countries and industrial countries, have easily been surmounted thanks to new production techniques and to the progress of technology. The physical environment, the lack of raw materials, unhappy locations—far from the oldest centers of production and consumption—and high transport costs are no more than unchangeable "natural" facts as far as technology is concerned. The process of industrialization is a global process announcing the beginning of a new era: it is diverse in its historical origins and in the forces which promote it; it is essentially bound to the decisions of restricted, dynastic elites, to the impersonal and apparently automatic oscillations of the market, and to the managerial classes of newly developing countries, which are pervaded by nationalistic spirit and messianic certainty. Alternatively, the process is rigidly predetermined by a central plan in which the whole country's entrepreneurial capacity is expressed, and which thus coincides with the demands of a "common wealth," which the state is expected to watch over.

Public opinion only sees the more apparent aspects of this process: structural modifications of the environment and modes of work determined by technological change, economic decisions, and financial investments. This is insufficient and deceptive. Economists have recently produced a complete literature on expansion. Sociologists have described the salient phases and common characteristics of it; cultural anthropologists have illustrated the associated evolution of behavior. But we still do not have a dynamic and global interpretation of the phenomenon which is capable of relating the technical aspects, operative instrumentation, and political will that determine the movement, whether at a company level or a general social level. Finally, the cultural basis that makes the phenomenon possible and acceptable needs examination. Following the tradition of Saint-Simon and Comte, Raymond Aron has diligently enumerated several aspects which he considers mark industrial society in an essential manner and distinguish it from historically preceding societies. He remembers in particular that the place of production is radically separated from the family in industrial society and that such a place of production introduces a new method of work division; that this both presupposes the accumulation of capital and implies the notion of rational calculation, and, finally, that this provokes a massive concentration of workers at the place of work.[2] It is a question of ascertainable and meaningful characteristics. But the process of industrialization goes further than the morphological level, biting into the very substance of society.

In the first place the process of industrialization constitutes a break— a break of socio-economic routine and, in its sources of legitimacy, of tradition. Such a break does not limit itself, indeed *cannot* limit itself to the sector of technical, economic, or financial activity. It is an essential break. Through the relevant social behavior it corrodes and transforms basic ideas and values. The specific research so far conducted on this question, fragmentary as it is, allows us to hypothesize three orders of tensions: (1) between traditional practices and the need for rationalization of productive cycles; (2) between a highly personalized type of human relation in which individuals and groups see themselves as "friends" or "enemies" and a depersonalized and psychologically neutral type of relation which is prevalently required in technically and industrially advanced societies; and (3) at the level of the group and social structure, between a modern, functional, and dynamic society composed of groups which are differentiated and active on a larger and commonly recognized front of "public interest" and an incipient developing society, still hardly possessing indigenous entrepreneurial capacity, whose functions do not yet seem to be depersonalized and clearly differentiated with respect to the "private" sphere as compared with the "public" sphere. In the second place the process of industrialization is a self-generated process. When it has found conditions suitable for beginning it shows itself to have its own ideologically neutral logic of development which does not need to borrow external justifications. In the third place the process of industrialism is irreversible. To refuse industrialism is to refuse the modern world. Industrialization is a cumulative and pluri-linear process which cannot negate itself without also negating the modern world, of which it is a fundamental component. The remedy for industrialization, so to speak, can only be an internal homeopathic cure. At what price?

On the micro-sociological or psycho-sociological level industrialization profoundly corrodes fundamental collective notions, in particular: (1) the sense of time; (2) the concept of value and of duration; (3) the prevalent mental attitude; and (4) the motivation of productive activity. On the macro-sociological and structural level industrialization principally touches and influences two mutually conditioning institutional complexes, that is to say: (1) the class structure of a given society, and its level of stratification and mobility; (2) the bases and exercise of power, through its rationalization. The study of these themes is still at an early stage. It presupposes the inter-disciplinary planning of researches, on which sociology, psychology, cultural anthropology, economics, and history combine their respective methodological and theoretico-conceptual resources. Excepting a few sporadic studies of specific cases from whose results it is risky to generalize, we have for the moment only impressionistic notations on this subject, whose validity lies exclusively in indicating the fields for eventual analytical research.

EXISTENTIAL TIME AND MECHANICAL TIME

The contrast between peasant world and industrial society regarding the sense of time is radical. It is in this respect that the "mental change" is most evident. Time, as a mechanically fractionable and measurable chronological fact, has no great importance in the pre-industrial world. The reason is intuitive: the basic activities of the peasant world develop with, and are conditioned by, natural seasonal rhythm, climatic character, and atmospheric conditions. In a word, people are in direct contact with nature and follow the evolutive rhythm. Peasants work from "morning to evening"; Vico mistakes his date of birth in his *Autobiography*. But for a factory worker a mechanical signal from the factory siren, rather than first light, indicates the start of his work, and his first action each morning is to "clock-on." There are noticeable subtle and significant connections between the economico-technical changes and intellectual changes. John U. Nef observes that we do not know the dates of Rabelais' life. It is not an erudite matter. This ignorance tells us that in Rabelais' time people worried less about precise quantities than we do today.[3] Nef goes on: "If contemporary scholars do not succeed in establishing Rabelais' birthdate, we may well ask ourselves whether Rabelais himself knew it. This is one of the queries made by Lucien Febvre in his book, *Le problème de l'incroyance au XVI siècle, ou la religion de Rabelais:* "In Rabelais' time did people know his age?" Lucien Febvre concludes that it was not usual to know one's age in that epoch."[4]

Georges Friedmann also refers to the studies of Lucien Febvre, who affirms that "in general the members of a peasant society are accustomed to being in ignorance of the exact time except when the bell rings (supposing that the bell-tower clock is correct) and otherwise refer to plants, to the flight of a certain bird or the song of another."[5] Friedmann comments sensibly:

It is not strange that men whose intimate life-structure is thus strictly connected to natural rhythms, tuned to the elements, seasons, and collective determinants which have matured slowly in them and have been confirmed by centuries, it is not strange that such men would have a different sense of duration to our own. The lack of precise reference points for measuring the passing of time, the indifference to that lack, the slowness (not to be confused with carelessness) and absence of a sense of speed, only exteriorise the previously mentioned profound sense of rhythm in the execution of everyday life. One can undoubtedly observe similar phenomena in every civilization whose base is essentially rural and artisan. Only particular manifestations have taken on a different character, in relation to geographical, ethnical and historical conditions.[6]

On the other hand, in the technical world and in urban-industrial society, time, as a mechanical, quantitative unit, is an important element. It is the study of time which makes scientific organization and predetermination of work possible. Mumford goes so far as to declare that the clock, rather than the steam engine, is the key machine of the modern industrial epoch.[7] But it is necessary to remember that such importance is not limited to the production world; it also incises the concepts of duration and value. The peasant world is dominated by a consciousness of scarcity, a sense of precariousness and man's final impotence in the face of nature; in this world things which last, and resist time, have value. From this fact derives the fundamental sense of the value of tradition, which cannot be commiserated and cannot be expressed in logical terms. In the technical world, especially in industrially mature society, it is necessary to "create consumption": quality and duration are radically separated. Quality is substituted by interchangeability, and duration takes on a secondary importance. On this matter Nef has noted that substitution is the required comfort, that one forgets in practice that there is another comfort; that of staying in the same place, with the old ideas.[8]

THE LOGIC OF MASS PRODUCTION

But it is not a question of a pure and simple oversight. The second comfort, that of remaining motionless where one finds oneself, content with satisfying real human necessities—which are fairly constant, refusing any showy or superfluous comsumption, however much it is suggested by obsessive publicity—is incompatible with the logic of mass production. This type of production in fact needs an economy of large consumption. The paradoxical aspect of the situation is that large consumption is no longer optional. It has become a moral imperative; it is necessary to keep the wheels of the market and the economic mechanism in motion, otherwise absolute paralysis, endemic unemployment, and poverty will result. Mass production was initially made technically possible by time and motion analysis, scientific work organization, and automatic processes. It constitutes the resultant of a highly rationalized productive organization which has become an end in itself, to its own perpetuation and indefinite expansion—independent of real, specific needs and human groups.

Industrial society has liquidated the "old ways," with no alternative.

Scientific organization of work does not permit nostalgia. The trouble generated by anti-machine literature is largely due to lack of comprehension of this fact, which is usually modified to a gross personalization of tensions determined by large-scale mechanization; the treatment of the real problem is transformed into a parody of judicial proceedings.[9] The scientific organization of work is only really scientific when the principle of work division is pushed to its extreme consequences. The famous example with which Adam Smith opens his researches in "The Wealth of Nations," the eighteen distinct operations with which pins were then made, is more pathetic than illustrative. It is no longer merely a question of subdividing the production cycle, which was traditionally entrusted as a unit to a single artisan-worker, into a series of fragmented operations. The problem is now set by the rigorous, spatio-temporal definitions of such operations. I think that the "industrial revolution" in the correct sense has been made rather by time and motion studies of specific operations or work-phases and their practical application in factories than by the transformation of artisan workshops into factory departments. The "social" importance of the first forms of technical evolution which occurred in the nineteenth century has usually been exaggerated. The conspiratorial and ideological conception of social development, which still seems to prevail in the debate between technicians and humanists today, has undoubtedly contributed to this. In reality, the worker in those early factories still enjoyed considerable freedom, even if he had lost the legal ownership of his means of production, that is, his work-tools and raw materials.

It is in fact substantially correct to derive the birth of modern industry from the moment at which man, renouncing himself to direct manipulation through the use of tools, entrusts work to a machine which is capable of operating tools with pre-established methods and within pre-established limits. It has been noted: "The machine was born historically as a combination of tools operated by a mechanism, which can do a superior job than could be performed by the same tools operated by hand, with respect to quality and quantity. The machine has thus become the normal production tool, and man-operated tools the exception."[10]

But that did not provoke an immediate change of working method, and even less a change of the life style traditional until that time. We must not forget that the first small industries were born within the old order, as activities integrated with the usual agricultural occupations of large landowners. That cannot surprise us excessively. The rich landowner could become the first entrepreneurial figure because he had at his disposal, besides capital, the most widely used raw material (wood), energy sources (water, and again wood—as a combustible) and sufficient man-power. Such early factories, for most of the nineteenth century, were still organized according to the principles of an infant capitalism. New production techniques had not yet acted deeply on the psychology of their protagonists, that is to say, had not yet become new modes of production. They had not corroded and revolutionized the organizational basis of paternalistic industry, in which the machine was certainly used, but with artisan spirit and techniques, without making rigorous measurements of the time needed for a single operation and the workers movements.

THE SCIENTIFIC ORGANIZATION OF WORK

Although they no longer owned the tools of production and were forced to work according to the principle of division of work rather than in complete cycles, the workers could always reconstruct the unity of workmanship in its various stages and grasp the sense of their own work, thanks to the limited size of work places and relatively short production cycles. They avoided a dangerous detachment, if not complete estrangement, from the product of their work. The turning point is found neither in primitive divisions of work, nor in the artisan's lack of autonomy, nor yet in the bankruptcy of their workshop—which had already been, for at least a hundred years, at the mercy of the big merchants who controlled either the commerce of raw materials or the finished products.[11] The real qualitative leap is determined by that complex movement of opinions and practical experiments which goes under the name "Taylorism," after the American engineer F. W. Taylor who theorized and promoted it.[12]

There are three fundamental principles of Taylorism: (1) the "one best way" principle, which states that there is always one and only one "best way" of carrying out any operation of the production cycle; (2) it is only possible to find and fix this method or particular technique through experiment and empirical research; above all through the analytical study of the time needed by a worker for a particular operation (chronometrical valuation of production) and of the quality of raw materials used, one is able to predetermine the cutting speed of tools and then the machine's optimum rhythm; and (3) such study and the relative responsibility are part of the exclusive prerogatives of company managements. These principles constitute the fundamental presuppositions of the scientific organization of work as elaborated by Taylor from 1878, based on his first experiences as a workshop engineer and industrial manager. Later developments, especially as a result of Frank and Lilian Gilbreth's work, brought about two distinct, and occasionally polemically opposed, schools. Some of Taylor's disciples preferred to insist on the measurement of work time needed for each single operation resulting from the fragmentary decomposition of the production cycle, while others underlined the importance of method and movement, that is, of gestures necessary to complete a given operation.[13] Recently the synthesis of the two schools has been attempted and the essential complementarity rediscovered. It has in fact been asserted that in the everyday reality of industrial work the study of time cannot be kept apart from the study of methods and movement. In this way we have arrived at the present phase of Taylorism and factory organization, that is, the M.T.M., or Measurement of Time and Method proceeding. More precisely, it consists of analyzing each manual operation or method into the basic movements necessary to its execution and assigning a standard predetermined time to such movements.

But the new fact represented by Taylor and his followers passes the technical level and affects the psycho-sociological attitude of worker groups and everybody who is part of the structure of a rationalized factory. In Taylor's words, during his speech to the commission of the House of Representatives, the scientific organization of work presupposes a "complete mental revolution" in both workers and industrial managers. A productivist attitude and mentality must replace the restrictivist or Malthusian mentality, which is justifiable with workers through their fear of technological unemployment and with employers by its tendency to earn a lot on every finished product instead of a high volume of production and sales. Taylor, with naive optimism, makes the solution of today's social questions dependent on this productivist mentality. If such matters were dissipated in the conquest of greater welfare and did not instead involve the problem of the power to judge men in an inevitable and direct way, Taylor's optimism could at least benefit from the extenuating circumstances. In his technocratic conviction that the essential problems are organizational and that the rest will follow automatically, Taylor tends to underrate, or simply ignore, the negative consequences of his "system," from a psychological and sociological point of view. It is said that he replied with brutal frankness to certain workers who questioned him about problems of production: "You are paid to work, not to think; somebody else is paid for that."[14] It is certain that, with Taylorism, the fragmented division of work assumes a rigorous nature and starts those organizational experiments which necessarily resulted in the "assembly lines" of Henry Ford's factories about 1913. Assembly-line work can be defined as a type of work organization in which the various operations, reduced to the same duration or a multiple or sub-multiple of such a duration, are executed with no interruption between them, and in a temporally and spatially constant order.[15]

The conception of the production cycle was substituted for a jerky, typically artisan production, which was adapted to and conditioned by the psycho-physical needs of individual operators. This production cycle is like a continuous, uninterrupted, constant, and depersonalized flux, whose rhythm is determined independently of a single operator. The assembly line becomes the dorsal spine of production; all energy supplies, raw material supply, worker skills, and the organizational structure of the factory are conceived and actuated in function of it. It is no longer the artisan-worker but the job, impersonal and rigorously defined in its essential temporal and spatial elements, which is the crux of the rationalized factory. It is even more important than the machine. The job, or, to use Taylor's word, the "task," becomes the nodal point of the whole production structure and must be kept strictly impersonal, interchangeable, and active, precisely to guarantee the continuity and regularity of the assembly line's flow. The most striking sociological consequence, whose repercussions in terms of individual psychological security and professional profile have not been fully explored, is that the planning of work, and the method of actuation and time required for it, are irrevocably out of the worker's control. It is, therefore, only with Taylor that the epoch of craftsmanship—governed by man's unique, irreducible, and natural rhythms—closes and the epoch of rationalized work begins. The latter bears the acquired consciousness of a permanent tension between calculation and feeling, which is destined to remain the fundamental characteristic of industrial society: the hidden cost of affluence.

NOTES

1. Cfr. my book, *La protesta operaia*, Milan, 1955, p. 99.
2. Cfr. R. Aron, *Le développement de la société industrielle et la strati-*

fication sociale, mimeographed edition by the Centre de Documentation Universitaire, n.d., part 1, pp. 54–55.

3. Cfr. John U. Nef, *La naissance de la civilisation industrielle et le monde contemporain*, Paris, 1954, p. 18.

4. Ibid., p. 19.

5. Cfr. L. Febvre, *Le problème de l'incroyance au XVI siècle* Paris, 1942, p. 428.

6. Cfr. G. Friedmann, *Où va le travail humain?*, Paris, 1957, p. 18.

7. Cfr. L. Mumford, *Technics and Civilization*, London, 1946, p. 14.

8. Cfr. Nef, *La naissance de la civilisation industriele*, p. 24.

9. Cfr. L. Duplessis, *La machine ou l'homme*, Paris, 1947.

10. Cfr. S. Leonardi, *Progresso tecnico e rapporti di lavoro*, Turin, 1957, p. 17.

11. Cfr., among others, the book *Der Bourgeois* by Werner Sombart, esp. book 1, ch. 5 (Eng. trans., *The Quintessence of Capitalism*, New York, 1967).

12. F. W. Taylor was born in Philadelphia on 20 March 1856, and died there on 21 March 1915. His writings are collected and published under the title *Scientific Management*, New York, 1947.

13. There is an abundant literature on Taylorism, but of an unsatisfactory average standard. For a critical, though slightly propagandistic biography, see F. Mauro, *F. W. Taylor—la vita e l'opera*, Milan, 1966; see also J. Chevalier, *L'organisation du travail*, Paris, 1946; F. B. Coopley, *F. W Taylor: The Father of Scientific Management*, 2 vols., New York, 1923; P. Devinat, *L'organisation scientifique du travail en Europe*, Geneva, 1927; D. Bell, *Work and Its Discontents*, Boston, 1956.

14. Cfr., against Taylorism's implicit authoritarianism, H. Dubreuil, *Des robots ou des hommes*, Paris, 1956 (Eng. trans., *Robots or Men?*, New York and London, 1930); see also my essay, ''Il taylorismo: fine di una orotodossia,'' in *Il sindacalismo autonomo*, Milan, 1958; *An Alternative Sociology*, New York, 1979, pp. 48–101.

15. Cfr. Friedmann, *Où va le travail humain?*, esp. part 3, ch. 2; cfr. also A. Touraine, *L'évolution du travail ouvrier aux Usines Renault*, Paris, 1955.

6

Man, Mass, and Values

THE CORPORATION AS A META-POLITICAL REVOLUTION

The scientific organization of work is not a purely technical fact. It has made mass production possible but in doing so has necessitated mass consumption and has therefore opened the way to mass society and mass culture.[1] If the problem today were to eliminate scarcity through a constant increase of welfare and an expansion of consumption, it is evident that it would be necessary to agree with R. L. Bruckberger when he affirms the socially and politically significant character of the "Revolution U.S.A." carried out by Henry Ford. I take Bruckberger's affirmations as typical expressions of a series of more or less conceptually and variously orientated mediating positions which, besides all the divergencies and discrepancies in specific details, essentially converge and agree in recognizing in the organization of production the function of a basic "prius" with respect to the development of society and to the solution of its problems.[2] These are points of view particularly interested in the "revolutionary" aspects of technological innovation. But the messianic tone, while often being successfully suggestive, does not seem sufficiently guaranteed as regards rigor. It is true that "revolution" is a common thing in our times, in which change is praised in direct proportion to its gratuitousness. The notion of "revolution" as a sudden and violent break with tradition and established order has no correspondence in the *Politics* of Aristotle. He, as most political thinkers of antiquity, only speaks of gradual change, that is, an organic or evolutionary growth. Revolution is a completely modern invention, certainly connected to what Halévy called the acceleration of history and the emergence of ideologies. But, also in this matter, one must not exaggerate. Bruckberger presents "Fordism" as the *true* revolution of our time. He writes: "The great revolution of modern times, the only one that has essentially changed the form of society, has not been realized in Russia, but in America.... For me, 1914 will always be the year in which Henry Ford, establishing an eight hour working day and more than doubling salaries in one blow, finally freed the worker from "proletarian" slavery and raised him above the "minimum subsistence wage" in which capitalism had thought to imprison him."[3] Bruckberger is not alone in this evaluation. It is necessary to recognize that the Ford phenomenon has always had the power to alight fantasy in students of it. Even Peter Drucker has written in more than one place that the true revolution of our times is not fascism or communism but rather mass production, which is to say, "Fordism."

Stripped of its millenarial, or even messianic, halo, with which ideologists of right and left, prophets of "managerial revolution," and deluded Marxists have wanted to endow it, Fordism is reducible to its natural dimensions as a mundane company policy and as a particular phase of the administration and coordination of the various operations that characterize the modern factory. It would be difficult to deny extenuating circumstances to diligent elaborators of the Ford myth, considering that Henry Ford himself has left a disconcerting document of frequently acritical optimism in his book, *My Philosophy of Industry*.[4] It is a very personal testimony of enlightened faith in "automatic progress," which occasionally seems to recall Smith's mythology of the "invisible hand" and does not avoid an idyllic tone.

Henry Ford writes: "Little by little, under the benign influence of American industry, housewives are freed of domestic cares, children are no longer exploited; soon both women and children will be free to go out to find new products that new industries are making. As industry grows, so we can see the close relation that domestic life has with industry. The prosperity of one is the prosperity of the other. In reality, all problems combine in one big problem. The parts are all interconnected one with the other. The solution of one problem helps to resolve another, and so on. Machinery is fulfilling in the world what man has been unable to do through preaching, propaganda or the written word."[5]

THE LIMITS OF CORPORATE PHILOSOPHY

Apart from this saturnian rhetoric, Fordism has a precise meaning of company administration, which serves to indicate several fundamental stages in the organization of production: the construction of a standardized product with interchangeable parts, which is not changed for years; price reductions to reach and conquer ever new and wider markets; the inauguration of the first "assembly line."

Fordism has institutionalized this process in its various phases and in the innovations it made feasible. It has made a continuous process of this with its own internal logic; it has made of it a new production method, a new rhythm and coordination for human work. The historian Allan Nevins clearly explained the existence of strict coordination and of the harmonious distribution of materials at the base of such a process.[6] In August of 1913 it took Ford twelve and a half hours to assemble a chassis. After the introduction of a mechanical assembly line it was possible to assemble a chassis in one hour and thirty-three minutes, with the obvious condition that coordination between various operations and the supply of various materials were organized in a perfectly synchronized manner. It is evident that this coordination of production processes allows huge savings (it is enough to think of the problems of unsold goods, warehouse space, transport, deterioration, etc.). These savings in their turn allow successive price reductions, further enlargement of the market, and therefore a rise in production. The social questions seem to be resolved. The machine is the "new Messiah."

What has elsewhere been called the "organization myth" is here affirmed with all its weight, that is, the belief that the great social problems of our time are essentially—and only—problems of organization in a technical sense. They can therefore be resolved with purely organizational methods and terms, by the application, case by case, of certain techniques which are offered us by the most advanced stages of technological research. This can help us to understand how "Fordism" necessarily presupposes Taylorism, that is, scientific management, either from the point of view of classification and rigorous definition of functions or from the point of view of work times and methods. Both Taylorism and Fordism, seen as administrative policies, allow incalculable savings and an accumulation of profits that, opportunely reinvested, make a powerful contribution to the expansion of production employment levels, the power to buy and consume, and therefore, in the last analysis the rising of the standard of living and of the general welfare.

In this sense "Fordism" has brought about a profound transformation of the environment, radically and rapidly affecting the economic structure, and in this way changing the way of life and behavioral pattern of individuals involved in the operation. Harry Bennet, for thirty years the controversial adviser of Henry Ford, offers us a picturesque testimony:

In 1916 Ford was probably better known to the majority of Americans than their president. He had made one of the most notable contributions to the modern age; he had the idea of producing a standardized automobile for the man in the street in an age when the automobile was still a rich man's toy. His famous "Model T," a black, ugly, strong, and mechanically very simple automobile, had put millions of Americans on four wheels. Capable of surviving any abuse, built so that it could be repaired with a pair of pliers and a piece of wire, the "Model T" took the farmer's eggs and milk to market and his family to the cinema or to Sunday lunch with some distant relatives. It ran on the city roads, climbed the Eastern or Western coastal mountains and advanced through the slushy plains of the Middle West, revolutionizing the social and economic life of a continent.[7]

It is certainly true, as Bruckberger observes, that "Fordism," indeed America, as he says emphatically, has discovered a new "social organism," that is, the factory as a human organization besides being economic and technico-productive. But such a discovery meets its natural limits on at least two levels: (1) on the general economic level, the economy of hypothetical companies, outside the social system, even if perfectly managed towards achieving maximum production efficiency, is not absolutely guaranteed against waste, cyclic fluctuations, or the eventual crisis of its own system and final collapse; and (2) the factory as a unified organism or collaborate policy; that is well and good, but not everything is so smooth and harmonious as it seems; the reality is that the big modern factory presents a fundamental ambiguity, inasmuch as it is at the same time a system of domination and an organism of cooperation.

TECHNICAL EFFICIENCY AND POLITICAL POWER

The essential and insuperable limit of Fordism and Taylorism cannot be found at the company level; it affects the significant behavior of individuals and the human substance of all society. Humanists like Thorstein Veblen and Antonio Gramsci who loved the machine and are subdued by the technocratic myth had hope in a cathartic and liberating function of the scientific organization of work. Alternatively, as Veblen tends to do with characteristic irresponsibility, they simply omit to point out the final outlet and extreme consequences. In the words of Antonio Gramsci:

When the process of adaptation has occurred, it really happens that the worker's brain has reached a state of complete freedom rather than mummifying. Only his physical gestures are completely mechanized; memories of work, reduced to simple gestures repeated with an intense rhythm, "nest" in the muscular and nervous bundles, and leave the brain free and clear for other occupations. As one walks without needing to think about all the movements necessary to move every part of the body in correct synchronism, in that specific coordination that enables us to walk, so, in industry men have performed, and will continue to perform, the basic gestures of their work without needing to think; one walks automatically and at the same time can think anything one likes.[8]

Things are not like that. What for Gramsci seems to mark the beginning of a richer interior life and constitute its objective premise appears to psychologists and sociologists of industry only as a partial compensation for the worker's loss of control over his own gestures and movements, which defines the condition of "alienation" of today's worker much more than the loss of legal ownership of his tools: "The only relief that we can offer the worker is, we think, to make his work as unconscious as possible to permit his brain to busy itself with other things. The direct stimulus of a happy job, which is destined to disappear in contemporary industrial evolution, must be replaced by an indirect stimulus: a shorter working day, reading, and possibly some music in the factory."[9]

In reality, the case of the worker who, in conditions of rationalized production, succeeds in avoiding the processes of disintegration and estrangement with respect to himself and his own work is rare and extraordinary. The salient aspects of this process as far as they are connected, independently of the structure of the owning classes of global society, to production techniques used in the factory, are heavily underlined by Dubreuil:

One can say that today, for thousands of people working in industry, the movements which they make, minute by minute and for a precise period, are long established without their knowledge—and not by the classical world's "blind destiny" but by the wholly rational spirit of industrial organisation. These men may well believe themselves to be free, while attending to their own affairs outside the factory, but for days and weeks to come the most

important part of their lives is fixed in advance, and without their knowledge
on the rigid planning level. They do not think for a second about what they
will do on such a day at such a time, but the factory already knows. It already
owns the time that has yet to come; it is written there, in the planning stage,
whose execution will reveal it as a well regulated mechanism.[10]

And Dubreuil goes on, stripping the intimately constructive nature of
planning: "It is possible to affirm that in present day industrial conditions the mechanisation of man has reached its highest stage, far
beyond the appearance of repeated gestures, which usually absorb the
attention of the profane. Repeated gestures are visible things, but the
ultimate extension of planning, that is to say, that which comes into
contact with the operator the man, go much further than material acts.
At this point, they bring about a real distortion of the individual by way
of the state of mental passivity into which they induce him."[11]

FROM THE ADMINISTRATION OF THINGS TO
DECISIONS ABOUT MEN

In a world dominated by scientific work organization, the disintegration of the individual and his reduction to a mass, that is, an inar-
ticulate and passive member of an essentially amorphic aggregate which
is incapable of autonomous expression, is therefore a logical result, and
an inevitable one as long as he remains inside the system. Taylorism
and Fordism indicate a particular form of company administration but
are also something more. They constitute a particular allocation of
power, together with particular methods of management and decision
making; in other words, a hierarchical structure which, in the name of
functionability and efficiency—towards the abolition of a "dead" time
and "passive" gestures—conditions human groups in a decisive manner, whether at the place of work or outside. Being an all-invading and
all-comprehensive power structure, the factory system accompanies both
worker and clerk even when they have left their factory and office.
Mass welfare and high consumption are not the answer. Incorporated
into and assumed by the plan, "free time" obeys the recreative, cultural,
and welfare logic of industry. In today's conditions it is only an evasive
pause which allows the restart and the normal development of the process of rationalization. For these reasons Taylorism, notwithstanding
the psychological criticism which has assailed it from its beginnings,

has been able to diffuse itself and develop itself calmly. It corresponded objectively to the structural needs of the existing phase of the evolution of industrial machinery and also satisfied the basic need of dominating groups to have a technical, "meta-political" justification for their actual power. Taylorism must therefore be faced on the level of organizational structure, in those situations in which its chalice is being drunk to the full and which mark the advance positions towards which the whole production system moves; it must be faced through *organic reforms which affect the concentration of power at its roots.* Contrary to the implicit and undemonstrated assumption which underlines the current experience of pure psychology at the company level, management and their prerogatives, as they are conceived and valued, are not outside the problem but in it up to their eyes. De te fabula narratur.

The essential condition, which guarantees the character and potentiality of effective incision into the reality of organic reforms, redeeming them from the constant danger of becoming apparent reforms, or merely legal in the formal sense—deprived of sociological content—is the analysis of Taylorism as an organizational structure and as a system of power allocation from the point of view of the development of production technology. Ideological schemes are helpless here. Marxism reveals its limits. It is a historical task upon which the destiny—development or regression and death—of industrial society depends.

NOTES

1. Cfr. on this question the strictly technical "principles" clarified by F. G. Woollard in *Principles of Mass and Flow Production*, London, 1954. Woollard's first principle is expressed as follows: "Mass production needs mass consumption; production as flux needs continuity of demand" (p. 53). Woollard goes on to produce sixteen other principles. In my judgment the distinction between mass production and flow production does not indicate two qualitatively different modes of production; it is an internal distinction. What essentially differentiates the modern production method from the traditional method is not mass production as such, which is hardly modern—at least for certain products, such as textiles and terra cotta vases—but the principle of interchangeability.

2. I quote only the pioneers, that is, James Burnham, *The Managerial Revolution*, New York, 1944; Adolph A. Berle, Jr., and G. C. Means, *The Modern Corporation and Private Property*, New York, 1933; Peter Drucker, *Concept of the Corporation*, New York, 1946.

3. Cfr. R. L. Bruckberger, "Revolution in USA," *Life*, 3 August, 1959.

4. Cfr. Henry Ford, *My Philosophy of Industry*, London, 1929.

5. Cfr. Ibid., p. 44.

6. See Allan Nevins, in collaboration with Frank E. Hill, *Ford: The Times, the Man, the Company*, New York, 1954.

7. Cfr. Harry Bennett, *We Never Called Him Henry*, New York, 1951, p. 7.

8. Cfr. A. Gramsci, *Note sul Machiavelli, sulla politica e sullo Stato moderno*, Turin, 1949, pp. 336–37.

9. Cfr. L. Walther, *Etude technopsychologique d'une industrie de produits alimentaires*, Geneva, 1928, p. 192.

10. H. Dubreuil, *Des Robots ou des hommes*, Payot, Paris, 1958, p. 145.

11. Ibid., p. 146.

7

The Ambiguity of Technology

THE NECESSITY OF A GLOBAL PLAN

The lines of a global plan in relation to the problem of technology, its evolution, and its social impact are already present in Marx's sharp reply to Proudhon, "the philosopher of poverty." Marx reproaches Proudhon first of all for having made an "eternal law" of the division of work, for having made an abstract category while history does not proceed by categories. To put into practice in Germany that large-scale division of work which determined the separation of town and country, a secular evolution was necessary, a long and complicated dialectical process composed of advances and setbacks, contradictions and moments of balance. Besides, depending upon the different epochs in which it was carried out, the division of work had assumed a particular physiognomy which, Marx observes, "would be difficult to deduce from the one word 'divide,' from the idea or the category." Prisoner of a completely inadequate and abstract explanatory plan, Proudhon claims to individuate a "prius" in the division of work. Marx, for his part, replies that this, in reality, only exists in modern industry. It certainly did not exist at the beginnning of the world. It is not, as Proudhon wants to say, that the factory is born from the division of work and factory wage-earners; neither can the concentration of working tools lead to the negation of the division of work, as Proudhon maintains. Moreover, the contrary is true.

Marx observes that as the concentration of tools develops so does the division of work, and vice versa. This is why every great mechanical invention is followed by greater division of work, and each increase in the division of work brings in its turn new mechanical inventions. In fact, the development of the division of work in England was accelerated precisely by mechanization. The weaver and spinner, until now united in one family, were separated by the machine, and it was in virtue of the use of machines, Marx concludes, that the division of work assumed such proportions that industry, once detached from the national soil, came to depend more on world markets and international exchange.

These brief comments suffice to show clearly that Marx approached the problem of technology in a more articulate fashion than Proudhon. Although a lot of Marxists and exegetes of Marx have proposed various reductionist solutions to account for his stance, which is difficult to schematize precisely because of its articulacy and complexity, there is no doubt that he was conscious of the necessity of a global plan for the problem. For example, according to Hallowell, as we have seen above, it is possible to reconstruct Marxism as technological determinism, recognizing within the system a privileged position for the variables of technology. Following this line one arrives at the conclusion that, for Marx, history is intelligible as far as it is technological history: in fact, tools are made by man, and what man makes is intelligible.

With such interpretations one finishes by misunderstanding the modernity and value of the Marxian position, which consists precisely in the fact that it does not attribute a dogmatic priority to any dimension or component of the social process. On the contrary, Marx insists on the necessity of considering the social system as a system, although not in the vitiated meaning of the term. The social system is in fact conceived as a dynamic and historically determined totality which is susceptible to scientific analysis on various levels. These levels are certainly interconnecting and inter-reacting in each specific historical situation, as we have already seen, but their capacity for reciprocal determination is obviously not the same. To assure the forward thrust of the social process against each total and relative stagnation, these levels are active at a different intensity with respect to the global social structure and have a different incidence with respect to historical development as a whole. Now, only a superficial interpretation could attribute the role of a (relatively) independent variable to the level of production forces in the restricted technical sense of the term. But in such a case it would be impossible to avoid a technocratic tendency, which is essentially foreign to Marxism. For Marx and Engels the basic connotation of defining a society is to define not its technology, but, in the first place, its "social structure," which is to say its "class structure."

With regard to this it is worth remembering a recent attempt to consider Marx as a "technological thinker."[1] I refer to a recent study by Costas Axelos, who clearly declares his intent to analyze Marx's thought as a "descriptive and dialectic interpretation" of technology seen as human, voluntaristic initiative: "Men were naturally drawn to the division of work; in the future they will be able to dedicate themselves freely to social activities, getting over the suffocating horizon of the division of work.... One must never forget the very narrow connection between the division of work and property, and between the various forms of the division of work and the various forms of property." Axelos' attempt has some merits. In a cultural situation in which Marx is usually interpreted and commented on sub specie philosophica, it underlines the peculiar nature of Marxian analysis, which is not deduced from Platonic ideas or from neo-Kantian categories, but is outlined and examined through its everyday contact with practice and the tools of practice: "Neither politics, nor religion, nor art, nor philosophy are for him constituent powers of human (even if alienated) history, or ways of connecting man and the world. Practice is the only source of truth and reality; it unites man and the world."

It is indeed said very well and very eloquently: practice with its tools, that is, with technology; rather than a comment on Marx, it is a happy repetition. In fact we read in the first book of *Das Kapital*:

Technology reveals the active behaviour of man towards nature, the immediate process of production of his life, and with it also the immediate process of production of his social relations and of the intellectual ideas which come from it. No history of religions, however carried out, which makes abstractions from this material base, is critical. In fact it is much easier to find the heart of nebulous religions through analysis than, vice versa, to deduce their celestial forms from the real relations of life, such as they occur. The last method is the only materialistic, and so scientific, method. We have already seen the defects of a materialism modelled on the natural sciences, excluding the historical process, in the abstract and ideological conceptions which its spokesmen create once they leave their specialised field.

MARX AND THE PROBLEM OF TECHNOLOGY

What is essential for Marx is to examine the "practical base" rigorously and firmly, to observe phenomena scientifically with exact heuristic methods and precise methodological controls. There is a vast literature on "dialectical impatience" and the "messianic spirit" which would excite him. But he very rigorously describes industrial machinery and the principal technical methods of the stage of the process of industrialization in his time. It is enough to read Chapter 13 of the first book of *Das Kapital* to be convinced of this ad abundantiam. For example, Marx liquidates the persistent legend of the steam engine as mother to the industrial revolution in one sentence, and certainly does not think to substitute the clock, as Lewis Mumford would have done. He acutely sees that the real revolutionary machine is the "machine tool." "As soon as man acts only as the engine of a machine tool, instead of acting with his tool on the object of his work, the disguise of motor force in human muscles becomes a casual fact, wind, water or steam can take his place."

It is this capacity for empirical observations of fact which gives a sociological sense to Marx's work. And it is precisely this that authors such as Axelos only partially understand. Axelos in particular does not realize that Marx's "techniques" are something more than the external application of an explanatory plan of Hegelian origins. In Marx there is no metaphysical construction of practice. Practice is neither an absolute point of departure nor a pre-categorical postulate; it is simply the specific situation of life, the immediate social process with its manifold moments of interaction. Marx never speaks—as technocrats more or less consciously love to—of technology in general; when he says "technology" or "machine and big factory," he wants to say, and says explicitly, "factory system."

In other words, he sees things in a sociologically meaningful perspective; he does not look at machines as if they were mythical monsters, but as a situation which has resulted from the "cooperation of many homogeneous machines," or from a "machine system." What Marx has in mind here is not abstractly conceived technology but the "factory system," with its rules and its regularities of a social nature, that is, *technology as the power structure which unhinges the traditional social situation* through its peculiar dialectic which Marx intuits, but is not in a position to render explicit. He remarks that heavy industry had to take control of its own characteristic mode of production, the machine itself, and produce machines with machines. Only in this way did it create its own adequate technical substratum and begin to move of itself. In fact, with the growth of the mechanical industry in the first decades of the nineteenth century, machines gradually took over the manufacture of machine tools. Nevertheless, only during the final decades did the enormous railway construction programs and trans-oceanic steam navigation give life to the large machines adopted for the construction of engines. Later, he sees that machines fundamentally revolutionize the formal mediation of the capitalistic relation, that is, the control between worker and capitalist. Until the relation acted on the basis of the exchange of goods, the first supposition was that the capitalist and the worker were free people in respect to each other as independent possessors of goods, one possessing money and production tools and the other possessing work capacity. But now capital acquires women and children. First the worker sold his own work capacity, which he disposed of as a formally free person. Now he sells his wife and children. He becomes a slave merchant.

Here, there is an important lesson for social analysts, especially for sociologists. In the first place, Marx decisively refutes the idea of considering the good or bad use of machines an error. Technology has human relevance as an influx on society and the power structure which it obliges society to adopt, whose rationalization in terms of its good or bad use make it impossible to perceive. In the second place, Marx adduces as evidence the vital connection between technical change, power structure, the worker's family life, internal family relations, work market, and political system. This perception of a connection between the various aspects of the life process tends to be lost, so that what Marx used to observe on the question of political economy in his day is perhaps true for modern society of work: it is a question of a science which uses such rigid and dogmatic concepts that they may well have issued ex capite Jovis, and which are evidently unable to catch the dialectical reality of the social process. Here we find the reason why the suggestion put forward in a famous note to Book I of *Das Kapital* has not had, until today, a satisfactory response. Darwin, Marx observes, has drawn attention to the history of natural technology, that is, of the formation of vegetal and animal organs as tools of production of plant and animal life. Would the history of the formation of the productive organs of social man, the material base of each particular social organization, not merit equal attention?

TECHNOLOGY AS FORMAL RATIONALITY

At present we do not have a critical history of technology. Sociologists of work generally seem wanting in historical consciousness and start from the implicit assumption that the phenomena are the same every-where. Thus the evolution of industrial machinery, for example, as if it took place in a social vacuum; even worse—and it is no surprise, granted that the widest social structures are more or less intentionally disregarded—the problems are resolved in psychological terms. We therefore ask ourselves whether the worker is favorable or unfavorable to technical change, or whether he fears it; whether he thinks that, as a consequence of change, he will have a bigger or smaller salary. In other words, structural problems are reduced to individual headaches, in a way functional to the needs of an ever more formal rationality, always less directed to the satisfaction of the individual's needs. In this way one finishes considering technical progress as an end in itself, as a supreme good which has its own justification and which will be naturally prolific with universal advantages, in the short run or in the long run.

According to the technocrats, machines resolve all problems. The important thing is to construct ever more perfect machines, ever capable of increasing production and making it faster, more standardized, and more specialized. The machine would carry not only the answer to the social problem but also the answer to the problem of man and his meaning in the world. Technical progress and civil progress coincide.

It is unnecessary to discuss this at length in order to show the sim-plicity of such an outlook. It is clear that technology increases production and accelerates development, but it does not possess the tools for re-solving the related problems of development. Technology offers means; it cannot indicate ends. It can promise great things, but it remains to political judgment to decide on the ends in function of which we should use the tools offered us by technology. Technocrats do not seem to recognize this ambiguity. Or perhaps they recognize it all too clearly and hide from the inevitable interference of political judgment behind the screen of the internal needs of technological growth.

We are examining a transparent conjuring trick which should be unmasked; to this end Marx is certainly useful. But we cannot draw a universal recipe from sacred texts. For Marx, the machine is the only work-tool which confers continuity on the working cycle as far as it is based on the application of analyses and syntheses of the entire process, that is, on the application of scientific method, which no longer meets obstacles of principle in the factory system. Unlike the artisan's tool, it is a mechanism capable of indefinite progress, which will eventually restrict the worker's work area and finally dissolve it.

In this perspective, manual and artisan operations are only residuals that can be mechanized when technological innovations are introduced; the machine, progressively absorbing these operations, reserves only managerial, inventive, and purely intellectual activities for man.

Now, precisely through the connection that he sees between technological developmennt and the progress of production forces, Marx finishes by assigning a positive and guaranteed value to such development, seeing the form of cooperation which can push mechanized work to its extreme consequences only in communism. Machines, in other words, do not only represent for Marx a victory for man over nature, but also constitute one of the basic pre-conditions for the elimination of obstacles which interpose themselves on the free and total fulfillment of human activity.

In a certain sense, then, even Marx overrated machines. But the consciousness of the "technical" moment and of the "despotic" moment in production organization remains in the Marxian conception, that is, the connection between the technological element and the politico-organizational element of power. The conclusion would be that, because technology does not itself constitute a control system but favors a shift to a "reign of freedom," it must be imposed on a different organizational base: technological rationality should be subjected to a new use—the "socialist" use—of machines, which, however, implies a radically different conception of economic and socio-political development, based on "substantial rationality."

A NEW CONCEPTION OF DEVELOPMENT

The previous arguments will be no more than an ineffectual prologue if at least two conditions are not realized: (1) the acquisition of an empirically based, more precise knowledge about the real effects of mechanization, and, today, of automation; above all research into the factory, which is the natural habitat of technology; and (2) the conscious initiative and political fight of social classes, not on the basis of mere doctrinal assumptions and constructions, but on the basis of a constant process of verification and transformation of social reality, which springs from participation in the concrete process of decision making.

Several recent studies and researches offer valid information for satisfying the first condition.[2] The works of Woodward, Touraine, and Blauner are, with others, more directly interested in gathering individual social characteristics and relating them to each type of production system. Woodward constructs a plan that includes new stages of technological development and two mixed types of production systems; it is fundamentally based on criteria connected with the complexity of technology and with the degree to which it is possible to exercise control over production systems and reduce uncertainty. Touraine develops a three-stage plan of technical evolution, characterized, in his judgment, by the decomposition and fragmentation of the workers's capacity and, at the same time, by an increasing integration of production operations from a mechanical ponit of view. Blauner, finally, describes four principal types of technology: (1) manufacturing industries; (2) mechanized industries; (3) assembly industries; and (4) continuous cycle industries, based on a growing mechanization and standardization of the product. The attempt to link some technical characteristics problematically to a particular social structure validates these studies. But one must make a reservation with regard to the rigidity of the categories delineated and a certain implicit ideological vision which seems to act as a self-censoring mechanism each time the research must confront the characteristics of work conditions which are specifically connected to the system. Another reservation concerns the lack of a diachronic perspective, especially regarding the passage from a "natural" to a "technological" environment. The fact is that every technological change which influences the workers's everyday activity reflects on his entire working life, family life, and general conception of life. Even at the elementary level of factory or shop, a coordinated analysis is necessary if we wish to understand different levels of experience contemporaneously. A modification of working activity produced by a technical change is always accompanied by a corresponding change in the worker's attitude towards his work, fellow workers, and overseers; that is not to mention the larger implications for the community and society. Such a change necessarily requires a period of personal adaptation to the new situation during which the worker modifies his particular view of his work, the management, the factory, the union, and, finally, the whole of society, as a "system."

It is a question of adaptation "through a modification of one's way of feeling," which is objectively based in the worker's feelings of restlessness and uneasiness, whether they are owed to the objective consequences of technical innovation (for example, modification of his wage packet or potential work mobility) or to the vague feeling of being dragged ever further from a "natural environment" and immersed in a deeper and less manageable technical environment, where stability and security seems to be lacking and change seems to be the rule.

With these three guidelines it is possible to formulate a series of specific working hypotheses, regarding the following aspects:

1. the influence of technical change on concrete working conditions
2. the influence of technical innovation on the psychological security of the factory worker (frustration, sense of alienation, anxiety, etc.)
3. the way in which individuals and work groups adapt to the experience of the process of social change and its consequences, with particular reference to:
   (a) the fragmentation of professional capacity and its increasingly interchangeable nature
   (b) the breaking of former and traditional careers
   (c) the tendency towards the reduction of autonomy in the decision process at work
   (d) the increasingly formal character of relations between workers and employers.

In all these fields researchers must expect to encounter diffuse attitudes of hostility among workers. The rational part of this general hypothesis could be complementary to the class war and could be summarized in the word "isolation," that is, in terms of a physical, mental, and social isolation in the place of work. The worker can feel the physical isolation through the ever decreasing importance of men in comparison to machines; the mental isolation because of insufficient information on the necessity of technical innovation; and finally the social isolation because of the collapse of traditional interpersonal relations and, in consequence, of worker solidarity.

Under this aspect the only way to avoid the lack of psychologism seems to be a new criticism of Marx, even as regards the study of individual companies. In reality, in the modern industrial company, decisional power cannot be assigned on the basis of a criterion of technical work divisions (capacities differentiated in view of a common production process) but rather on the basis of a criterion of authoritarian cooperation (needs differentiated to the management's discretion). The fact that power on the company level is not assigned on the basis of a technical division of functions and jobs makes the manipulative nature of the company, and the radical contrast between who commands and who obeys, extremely clear. The contradictory nature of the factory as a system of cooperation and domination also becomes very clear. As far as the workers are concerned, Davydov, literally following the *Deutsches Ideologie*, has justly observed: "Social power, that is, productive multiplied force, which draws its origins from cooperation by various individuals and is determined by the division of work, appears to these individuals—because the cooperation is not *voluntary but natural*—not as their united power but as an extraneous force; they do not know where it comes from or where it goes; they are unable to dominate it, and, on the contrary, it follows its own succession of phases and its own degrees of development: a succession which is independent of these individuals' will to action, and actually commands this will to action."[3]

On a more general level, one can observe that modern society is technically complex, needful of elaborate connections and coordinations, and, not less, politically quite simplified—from the point of view of interests. In this sense present-day technical society allows the proposal of radical reforms which at the same time revalue the function of utopia and make us understand that the problem of technology cannot be reduced to the good or bad use of machines: it implies rather a new, different way of conceiving economic development, human work, and the relation between work and thought, which is still governed by the Greek dichotomy between practice and theory.

Rousseau's moment of revenge is perhaps close. The progress of productive technique united to the restructuring of social relations (in a solidarity sense) through the overturning of present power relations and their corresponding political institutions could open the possibility, on a historical level, of harmoniously reassembling the functions of man.[4] But it could also open an opposite outlet: that which Samuel Butler sketched in his image of a world of real automatons ruling over a mass of men-automatons. But there can be different concrete possibilities of historical evolution between "man-machine" and "integral man," rescued from automaton to his human dimension.[5] The alternative, far from formulating itself in terms of mutual exclusion, only represents an extreme schematism. *Tertium datur*. The outcome could not but depend on the choices made by social classes and specific social groups made beyond any technological eudemonism or anti-machine lamentation.

NOTES

1. Cfr. K. Axelos, *Marx penseur de la technique*, Paris, 1956 (Eng. trans., *Alienation, Praxis, and Techné in the Thought of Karl Marx*, Austin, Tex., 1976).

2. Cfr. in particular J. Woodward, *Industrial Organization*, London, 1965; A. Touraine, *L'évolution du travail ouvrier aux Usines Renault*, Paris, PVF, 1958; R. Blauner, *Alienation and Freedom*, Chicago, 1964.

3. Cfr. I. Davydov, *Trud i svoboda* (Ital. trans., *Lavoro e libertà*, Turin, 1968).

4. See on this particular point U. Cerroni, *Tecnica e libertà*, Bari, 1970.

5. About this alternative, decidedly too drastic, see my "La tecnica come problema umano," in VV.AA., *L'uomo e la machina*, Turin, 1967.

8

A Critical Look at Industrialization

THE HISTORICAL DIMENSION

It is a difficult and at the same time fascinating undertaking to define the salient characteristics of the process of industrialization in historical perspective and to move from that to a cluster of factors which may plausibly be considered as the economic and socio-cultural framework of the phenomenon. The attempts at explanation traditionally and characteristically waver between an interpretation of a psychological nature based on specific value orientations and special gifts or endowments of the historically dominant type of personality (whose manifestation, however, remains mysterious) and a reconstruction, based fundamentally on structural economic factors to which, as indispensable functional prerequisites, new values and psychological values must be juxtaposed. The one-sidedness of these attempts and their limitations are obvious. On the other hand, it is clear that here there is no question of counterposing Marx and Weber or invoking the Keynesian and post-Keynesian "new economics" to the static analyses of classical economics. The fact is that we do not yet have at our disposal an integrated explanatory theory of social change. I have noted elsewhere that we do not yet have a global, dynamic interpretation of economic development and the process of industrialization. The rare attempts to link the formation of a particular type of personality systematically with specific structural characteristics of the social system by way of average social awareness or the system of prevailing values and previous mental habits for the most part have added to the sorry confusion between analytical schemes and concrete historical contents.[1]

To this one must add the Manichaean tendency to see the social process in its reality developing black and white, on the basis of a series of dichotomous contrasts whereby one passes—without any qualifications—from personalism to contractualism, from mechanical solidarity to organic solidarity, from military to industrial society, from tradition to rational calculation, and so on. The schematicism of such an ingenuous rationalism can be much more negative when incautiously applied to explanations of a generic kind: here, the social process passes from one stage to another like a train on its rails passing from one station to the next. History loses its dramatic character as a human undertaking. It becomes the mere chronicle of the gradualness of the inevitable.[2] In addition to these theoretical problems, the question is made more complicated by the ideological tension with which it is shot through insofar as it concerns the manner of life and world of values of each one of us. At once the terms normally used to identify the historical period in which it began in the West (the process of industrialization) seem ideologically colored. Indeed, one speaks of "industrial revolution." The term suggests sudden, radical upsets. But in which areas of social life? The indeterminacy, in this case, adds to the weight and extent of the catastrophe.[3] This suggestive phrase—"arresting" as Ashton says— has, it would seem, a political origin.[4] Anna Bezanson has managed to trace its origins in France, a country in ferment at the end of the eighteenth century.[5] Unhappy with the origin of the phrase, hastily attributed at times to Arnold Toynbee or Marx, or to J. S. Mill, she saw its first exposition in François de Neufchateau's 1798 proposal for a huge "industrial exhibition" to celebrate the anniversary of the 1789 Revolution.[6] Ashton, and also Hacker, Hutt, De Jouvenel, and above all von Hayek, as well as von Mises, are right: the term has distant Jacobin connections and rightfully belongs more to the rhetoric of the platform than to scientific investigation.[7] Ashton has certainly done well in bringing out the relative ignorance of economic processes and their logic on the part of many historians. It would be more correct and credible to speak of an evolutionary process in the economy than of "revolution," one marked by moments of great dynamism followed by periods of stasis and equilibrium, after which there have been greater productive impulses, according to the normal profile of the economic cycle. This argument is valid, but only by confining it to the technico-economic aspects of the transition from the feudal to the modern world. However, these aspects do not exist in a void, and only by using a heuristic expedient can we isolate them and consider them separately from the rest of the social structure. Undoubtedly technical progress points to an essentially evolutionary, unilinear, and cumulative process; a non-dialectical one. It is also probable that the social significance of the first technical innovations of the initial phases of the industrialization process has been overestimated,[8] but it is hard to deny the existence of a qualitative break when, by expanding the perspective, we take into consideration the political and juridical aspects, value sets, the expectations and new attitudes of individuals and social groups. Precisely for this reason the vocabulary of the politicians, and social writers and economists of a sociological turn who were both describers and actors in the process of transformation, was ultimately enriched by the term "revolution." In fact, while technological evolution and the formation of the capitalist relation of production show a remarkable continuity in the passage between the pre-industrial world and industrial society, the "sociologically important aspects" of social life—that is, the totality of socio-cultural systems linked with technical evolution and the rise of capitalism—appear with characteristics of development less continuous and homogeneous. Here, the basic datum is provided by the transformation of the free artisan into a wage laborer. Other distinctive and typical characteristics of industrially advanced societies are investigated and defined by sociologists, but the formulation of these "analytical" or "ideal typical" schemes is a risky undertaking, wherein traditional prejudice and arbitrary preferences can play a large part.

Examples abound. The argument that economic development and the process of industrialization are necessarily accompanied by a process of reduction in family size, supposed to be transformed from the "extended" or "enlarged" to the conjugal, nuclear one, is subject to serious exceptions, both as regards highly developed societies like the United States (where Paul Lazarsfeld has documented a clear re-emergence of the extended family in recent years) and in underdeveloped, primitive societies, in which M. F. Nimkoff and Russell Middleton have pointed out the complicated type of conditioning between family types and means of subsistence.[9] Furthermore, whereas Aron mentions among the distinctive criteria of "industrial" as against "pre-industrial" society the fact that the place of production is radically separate from the location of the family, equally separate production units are regularly found in the most distant times.[10] In fact, in pre-industrial society there existed what Weber called the *ergasterion*, a work place sharply distinguished from the place of habitation.[11] Its most typical form is the medieval *fabbrica*—at times rented to a group of workers and artisans to carry their work, at others a work place set up by the local lord, the monastery, or guild to use its *corvées* or *banalités*. Another example of a productive unit completely separate from the family habitation is the oriental bazaar, made up of a series of little enterprises linked together into a commercial unit. In many ancient societies, especially in Egypt and Greece, one then finds an industrial undertaking on a vast scale. The concentration of workers in a single work place was thus not alien to the pre-industrial world. The qualitative distinction must be sought on a different level: both the medieval and the Renaissance manufactury were for the most part a simple gathering under the same roof of worker-artisans who *worked in common but not in collaboration*. One must not forget, however, that even in society generally considered as pre-industrial there were workshops which required a high level of coordination of the labor of the individual workers and a certain division of their productive tasks. For example, these were the foundries, the blacksmiths' workshops, the breweries, the bakeries, the mills, and so on. Division of labor, technical specialization, and coordination of tasks carried out in collaboration were already in existence at the end of the sixteenth century. From that time to the end of the eighteenth century there developed a continual, homogeneous technical evolution which first hinged on new types of production and types of products, but later ended up by involving every type of manufacture then extant, giving rise to a huge range of mechanical apparatuses in the workshops of these two centuries by using water and wind power and human and animal energy.[12]

Concentration in a work place separate from the family habitation, division of labor with subsequent specialization of tasks and their coordination, and use of machinery and mechanical devices—all these are established characteristics which, however, would not by themselves make up sufficiently differentiated elements to distinguish industrial from pre-industrial society. One aspect of differentiation traditionally held to be crucial is provided by the use of a specific type of energy, thermo-mechanical, provided by easily dissipated steam power, and which therefore is also called upon to explain the massive urban industrial centers. However, for Marx, the form of energy employed is basically irrelevant. In his view, what marks the "eighteenth-century industrial revolution" is the replacement of artisan tools by the machine. The introduction of this third aspect of industrial machinery, following the mechanical motor and mechanical transmission, is for Marx the initial moment of the transformation of manufacture into factory production in the real sense.[13] For Weber, the crucial element is different: "The decisive factor is that the entrepreneur works with fixed capital, in relation to which a capitalist system of accountancy becomes indispensable."[14] The composition of fixed capital has no special importance for Weber. It can consist of expensive machinery—or not: it can be set in motion by mechanical or natural energy, but it is on the basis of this that we can rigorously distinguish the system of pre-capitalist industrial manufacture from capitalist manufacture. The existence of fixed capital, the system of rational accounting, concentrated in the hands of a single owner-entrepreneur, make up for Weber the indispensable conditions which lie at the origins of capitalism, and the process of industrialization of the Western European countries. He said: "The truly distinctive characteristic of modern industry is in general not the instrumentality of the labor used, but the concentration of the property of the workplace, the means of production, the energy sources and supplies of raw materials into a single ownership, that of the entrepreneur. Only exceptionally can one find this combination prior to the eighteenth century."[15] Weber often stresses that one of the basic properties of the private capitalist economy is the fact that it is rationalized on the basis of rigorous estimates and that it is systematically and soberly structured in relation to the end pursued.[16] However, these two interpretations— the Marxist and the Weberian—are not by themselves alternatives. Technological evolution and the capitalist form of productive relations are linked together by a relationship of interdependence which is still one of the great sociological advances brought out into the open by Marx. Marx stresses technology to the point where some scholars are led to attribute to his system an interpretation along the lines of technological determinism, as it arises from this to identify structure and thus to explain the superstructure. However, along with the technological given, which Marx analyzes with extraordinary subtlety and insight, we note other important characteristics—private property in the means of production and exchange, the existence of classes, the sale of labor power on the impersonal labor market and the production of surplus value. Weber, on the other hand, stresses the form of capitalist organization as he sees in this the result of a rationalizing mentality which in his view is the sole response possible to the unsettling question—why were the basic concepts of technology and generally of the mechanization of production which had already been acquired in classical antiquity only practically applied on a huge scale towards the middle of the eighteenth century?[17]

In fact, it was in England that the process of transition from feudal society to the modern world took off in the second half of the seventeenth century, to be completed in the eighteenth. England inspired and led this process. French, German, and Italian intellectuals looked on with amazement. This was the amazement of one who sees a society renew and re-structure itself without sudden breaks, drawing out from itself the innovatory elements and starting a process which was to make them replace the old almost by a natural force, and in any case without meeting insurmountable obstacles. True, in the seventeenth century there were two revolutions, but these were phenomena of adjustment, restricted in time, which concern more the political superstructure and its adaptation to the new society than the economic structure. The final balance sheet of the English seventeenth century marks the definitive victory of bour-geois society and the premises of the process of industrialization. The ideological, political, and cultural structures of the feudal world were thenceforth destroyed, and bourgeois society was replacing them with its own. The premises were created in every field: the victory of con-stitutional government in the political field; the arrival of utilitarianism on the moral field, and tolerance in the religious one; and finally the sensitizing of the state to the new economic necessities. In fact, the state took on as its own the needs of commerce, on this basis modifying its own customs and policy. Wars were no longer wars of religion or concerned with dynastic politics, but rather increasingly tended to be-come wars for the conquest of markets and economic supremacy. In this sense England involved herself in a hugh colonial policy which allowed her to take over, at the beginning of the eighteenth century, the abundant heritages of Spain and Portugal, which the mercantilist policies of those two countries had never managed to exploit.

Civil society arose from the definitive triumph of the city over the countryside as regards economic supremacy. In feudal society, where alongside the noble there is only the peasant, who, because of his psychology, the monotonous, individual, relationless function he dis-charges, is not organized or organizable into a class, relatively free intermediate social strata simply do not exist, nor is a development for civil society possible. This is born when classes in the modern sense are born—that is, the urban, organized, self-conscious classes, since each individual is daily aware of the sentiments and interests which bind him to others and the need for a common action to attain common ends. With the birth of social class in the modern sense, civil society is therefore born, and with that also the breaking of the traditional, religious, or naturalistic forms of the study of man and society and the new outlook on such studies on a strictly empirical level.

Thus, at the end of the seventeenth century, the urban social class and civil society were already in England a concrete fact and rested on solid economic bases. City dwellers acquired an increasing awareness of their strength. The rich merchant was no longer at the mercy of the whims of the monarchy: now, it was his interests which entered into the royal audience chambers. His economic solidity gave him political security. At that period, the Bank of England was founded, the political parties were born, the system of cabinet government took shape, and the king was no longer above the law, but beside it.

Civil society, however, at its point of take-off, was a phenomenon known to few. This awareness had to be diffused. This was the task assumed by the English intellectuals. The periodical press was born, which found a strong stimulus in the civil wars. It took on the task of underpinning the awareness of the middle class and giving it a critical mentality. The number of publications increased at an impressive rate. There was even ironic comment on the number of books printed in England. From the beginning of the eighteenth century, Swift and Defoe provided authoritative propaganda organs for the political parties. If Pope could complain of the fact that the periodicals lived on "foolishness scarcely born" or "still-born scandal," it accomplished Addison's great ambition of taking "philosophy out of studies and libraries, schools and colleges, to stay in the company, among the tea tables and the coffee houses." Through the periodical press the man of letters no longer wrote for a few but for the great anonymous mass, and he had to be understood by all. He thus tried not so much to make people admire the loftiness of his thought as to arouse sentiments through images of daily life accessible to all. The man of letters thus became the interpreter of the new science for the multitude and the official moralist aware of his high charge in order to fulfill which, as Dryden wrote, he must be "cultivated in several sciences, should have a reasoning mind, philosophical and to some extent mathematical. . .should have experience of all types, humors and manners of men, should be precisely skillful in conversation, and should have a great knowledge of humanity in general."

As has been said, in the new society religion is not an obstacle but an incentive to development. It became rational and often worldly. It abandoned mysticism and fanaticism for rationalism, the problems of dogma for those of behavior. Deism was born, a kind of religion of atheism, a significant symptom of the decadence of the traditional religious spirit. From the end of the sixteenth century the difference between religious principle and economic practice had become so extended as to make a re-elaboration of religious sanctions necessary. This occurred in the seventeenth century when the outlines of the commercial, bourgeois revolution seemed definitely set. The birth of the middle class was by then something to be accepted, and religion had to adjust to the new order. Thus the figure of the Puritan arose, for whom "worldly toil itself became a kind of sacrament." The Puritan reformation was of an unworldly but not ascetic character: it introduced a deep conviction of sin and the necessity of grace for salvation, but re-established salvation in active life and action. Puritanism rejected indolence as a source of temptation and preached abstinence from amusement and pleasure, which can offer only worldly seductions. The Puritans were thus real men of steel, Ironsides in the same belief, who could only succeed in the undertaking to which they set their hands. Hence they devoted all their energy to daily work, so as to obtain the proof of grace from its success. The Puritan moralist was well aware that his teaching must be applied to the nature of man, who is turned towards evil, and to life, which is a vale of tears. However, he was no less conservative than other moralists in preaching strict adherence to religious norms. Yet, paradoxically, the very virtues he was driven to encourage weakened the influence of the teachings. The subtle, dialectical transformation of the *Zeitgeist* began by allowing the introduction of usury: an increasingly differentiated contrast between private and public world was created. Poverty and failure were regarded as lack of grace. The feeling that private benefit was the forerunner of public welfare became widespread. This mental attitude was to dominate the whole of eighteenth-century England: from Melville's work, based on the principle of "private vices, public benefits," to Smith's, in which the analogous principle of the "invisible hand" is set forth. Finally, at the end of the eighteenth century, puritanism already demonstrated two different criteria of moral judgment: one for property owners, the other for wage-earners, and if one notes the dominant position held by puritanism in burgeoning industry the significance of this dualism becomes still more pronounced.

In conclusion, in the first years of the eighteenth century puritanism presented itself as an essential factor for the spread of the lay outlook. Further, as a minority religion, it necessarily had to be individualist. Its old hatred for the state thus was transformed into the doctrine that man must count only on himself, that prosperity is the result of his energy, and that property should be guaranteed in every way. From this viewpoint, puritanism did not remain isolated in its own epoch but slowly became a widespread, dominant viewpoint which rose above the limits of religion and placed itself as a foundation of the new classes and the youthful civil society.

Even though to a less degree and with some delay, in France too the same forces which created the formation of the capitalist spirit in England showed themselves. If France did not manage to stay equal to England it was because French society was less elastic and because administrative and political centralization did not favor the development of autonomous forces with the rapidity possible in England. However, in France too the ties which religion imposed on economic and social development slackened and atheism advanced. Science and philosophy increasingly freed themselves from ideological censorship. As in England, the search for profit and the expansion of the mass of the economic enterprises posed new prospects and problems. The state found itself faced with complex problems of economic policy, and from daily practice there arose economic science. As in England, though to a lesser degree, in France too the origins of the bourgeoisie left their mark on art and literature: public opinion advanced slowly and became sensitive to the new political and social problems. It is a fact full of meaning that a writer of memoirs such as Saint-Simon should lament the rise of "new men" and work out a plan of government aimed at restoring to the nobility a part of its lost authority, fully aware that the royal centralism would not have let this happen.

The political, economic, religious, moral, and intellectual premises presented in the second half of the seventeenth century for the birth of the industrial society bore fruit in the eighteenth century. Indeed, at the end of the eighteenth century modern industry was born and had already found its first theorist in Adam Smith. The English industrial revolution was made under the banner of laissez faire. Government and Parliament welcomed the principle of abstention from any intervention in economic life. This principle was enforced, not without much conflict, both in relation to a law on apprenticeship and to the question of the statutes on wage regulation. The effort of rising industry could admit of no compromises with the world of labor. The defense of the contractual liberty of employers and workers was maintained and applied unreservedly. Towards the middle of the century, when the question was raised, it was widely felt that:

The statutes for the regulation of wages and the price of labor were an absurdity and a great blow to commerce. It seemed absurd and outlandish that a third person should try to fix the price between the buyer and the seller without their agreement, for it was agreed if the journeyman does not sell his labor at the fixed or statutory price, or the employer will not give it, of what use are the thousand regulatory laws? There was a fairly general agreement that these regulations could not be set up so as to provide the requisite and reasonable provision of the abundance and scarcity of labor, of the cheapness and shortages of provisions, of the difference in standards of living in city or country, of fuel for heating, of rent, etc., or of the good or bad quality of administration, the different levels of ability or swiftness of the laborer, of the uneven quality of the materials he must work with, the conditions in which we find the factory or the prosperity or stagnation of business within and without. In the end, there would still be a difficulty: who would make, or how would you make the journeyman work or the employer give him work if they did not reach an agreement between them? And if they reach agreement how would you or I, or anyone else, interfere? Such was the intellectual climate of the time.

It was the attitude of the industrial manufacturers who in the House of Commons maintained that wage regulation must meet with considerable technical difficulties, that solutions should be sought on the individual level, and that it was neither possible nor equitable to assign by law an equal value to human labor. As the industrialists argued, the system did not take into account individual differences in working ability, did not stimulate productivity, and would make prices rise. Also, as regards the regulation of wages, the Commons accepted the industrialists' point of view, as likewise on the apprenticeship law, and reasserted the principle of laissez faire. Political criticism often confirmed the wisdom of Parliament's decisions and its hostility to any system of regulation. The cities where trade flourishes, someone has written, are those in which respect for the laws which regulate trade leave most to be desired. As Burke wrote to his electorate, a great empire cannot be maintained by a system of laws restrictive and limiting both for trade and for government.

In this climate, English industry prospered, and Adam Smith wrote his *On the Wealth of Nations*, published in 1776. The central problem in Smith's work is that of wealth. For the first time, after the mercantilists had looked for the origins of wealth in precious metals, and the physiocrats in the soil, industry was seen as a source of wealth, and the principle of division of labor as an instrument for the increase of productivity was put into theoretical form. This was the first philosophy of industry, which, as a living creation of man, was inserted into the natural and social environment in which man himself lived. Smith started from the principle that each individual in the first instance is propelled to concern himself with himself, and to satisfy his own needs. However, by acting so as to satisfy these needs, he is directed by an invisible hand to pursue a goal which is not part of his own concerns. Therefore, for Smith the multitude of personal actions performed in order to pursue his own private benefit are transformed into a social good. We do more for society through this simple system of natural liberty than if we consciously sought after its advantage. Everything, thus, which disturbs the order of nature contributes to evil, not good. Hence there follows Smith's aversion to any state action. The state is necessary above all to protect us from violence, injustice, and any attack on property. It must intervene in education, in public works, and in that limited area in which the individual does not perform as he finds there no particular benefit; but aside from this, its task is only that of protecting the spontaneous activity of the individual. When that "tricky, cunning animal known as statesman or politician," he wrote, has given us peace from without and internal order, his main work is finished. Once this state of security has been reached, according to Smith, there is scarcely any more need for political action, which would be artificial, unnatural, and opposed to the simple system: it would invade the natural rights of man and constantly work so as to deprive him of the fruits of his labor. The greater part of those who claim to trade for the public good obtain very slender results: leave to each the freedom to pursue his own interest, and the greatest quantity of social good attainable will be reached by the care each takes in his own interests.

Smith is thus a fiery critic of every existing discipline or regulation— protective tariffs, commercial consortia of capitalists or workers, subsidies, labor legislation, and monopolies. He saw industry as a mass of interlined individual actions which would do well enough as long as commitments were maintained and violence prohibited. The public profit would be greater to the extent that competition was greater. By applying a broad system of liberty, everyone felt the more driven to work, as he had the certainty of reaping from it the greatest reward. Providence had created a natural order so that even the owner, in order to achieve his aims, needed to act for the common good. In fact, one must produce so as to exchange; to live one must satisfy the needs of others; there is a reciprocity of intrinsic profit in relations between men whose destruction can only come about through interference from above since this— as Smith attempts to show through historical examples—only helps a few privileged individuals, who deceive the people by making what is their private advantage appear as public welfare.

The influence of Smith's doctrine scarcely needs to be referred to: it contributed to bring out in industry and the business man that almost religious halo which puritanism had provided them with.

Smith's work is simply the scientific codification of a revolution which transformed England in the eighteenth century and the logical expression of a mentality which rooted itself thereby. We have spoken of the foundation of the Bank of England at the end of the seventeenth century, which, together with the consolidation of the public debt in 1697, was the real turning point of the English industrial revolution, to which naturally all the political, cultural, and religious premises already discussed contribute. This innovation allowed an agricultural, still relatively poor island to become the "workshop and financial market of Europe." In fact, just mechanical inventions and mineral wealth would not have been enough to achieve these results. Only a solid system of bank credit allowed the full exploitation of the invention of the steam engine and the mechanical loom, something which would have been impossible had the English financial system been as deficient as the French. English wealth and power in the eighteenth century and its ability to resist the strains of the Napoleonic wars were the work of the banking and financial system. With the setting up of the Bank and the reconstruction of London in brick and stone, and with the introduction of the use of coal—the source of power which was to transform the economic structure of the world—England took on the appearance of a modern industrial state with over half a century's lead over other European states. Agriculture itself began with an act of transformation. The old medieval agrarian system based on crops dispersed in open fields was replaced by the enclosures of paid laborers who, by exploiting the characteristics of certain roots and grains, began to practice the scientific rotation of crops, which, by increasing the production of food, created a strong incentive to increase of population. Hydraulic power and steam power changed the nature of economic life. The iron industry, which during the reign of Queen Anne was on the brink of bankruptcy because of the shortage of fuel, found in the rich coal mines of the center and northern region an unexpected stimulus. Iron replaced wood, miners the charcoal burners. The fairs and travelling markets gave way to the shops of the towns and villages, through which, in the whole country, there ran a highly active retail trade. In little more than half a century (from 1760 to 1821) the population of England rose from 6.5 million to almost 12 million, and the face of the country was wholly changed—rapid communications, factories beginning to pollute the air with their smoke, full of ingenious machinery to increase the productivity of human labor, industries which drew their raw materials from one hemisphere and sent their manufactures to another, huge, almost horrible cities built in a rush, and a population dominated from the earliest age by the sound of the factory whistle.

In part, the English industrial miracle was due to the generosity of nature. The humid climate was suitable for the cotton industry. The northern and northwestern regions were rich in water power. Above all, there was a wealth of coal and iron, disposed in such a way as to be transportable by water. With iron, coal, and textiles, Britain was able to create a model type of civilization later imitated by other countries.

The rationality of the exploitation of natural resources was not drawn from a high level of popular education, but from the atmosphere peculiarly favorable to industrial invention and its swift, immediate exploitation. As against the French nobility, the English aristocracy was concerned with commerce. To get money, unable to exploit public property, it was certainly not contemptuous if the possibilities of a factory, a mine, or a commercial enterprise in India opened up to them, the more so as such initiatives were encouraged by the regime of freedom of which we have spoken.

However, a stable financial system, favorable climate, raw materials, and initiative would not have been enough for the industrial transformation of England had inventions been lacking. Some of these now seem negligible, but then they managed to revolutionize a whole economic system. Certainly, Bacon's inductive method contributed much to inventions, and in fact some inventors were scientists, as was James Watt, who was the first to give the steam engine industrial value.

However, possibly more important than true scientific culture was the idea, strongly promoted by the Royal Society and the periodicals, that knowledge was a force unravelling and that through observation and experiment one could discover new truths. The spirit of curiosity was thus directed towards the object the English people gave most attention to—the conquest of wealth through industry and commerce.

Thus, some great inventors were poor workers, without education, but directed to innovatory applications in the industries in which they worked by a mechanical intuition which bordered on genius.

So Kay, of Bury, in 1733, with his mechanical flying shuttle fully doubled the possibilities of output of the weavers, apart from improving its quality, and James Hargreaves, who with his 1754 mechanical jenny increased the productive capacity of the weaver eightfold. Thus too Richard Arkwright of Preston, inventor of the device (the mule) for obtaining from the spinner threads of all thicknesses and strengths, was founder of the English cotton industry and father of the factory. His influence in the process of industrial revolution was profound. From being a barber's assistant and wigmaker he made possible the production of cotton on a large scale by a series of inventions for carding and spinning, and in the factories he set up to exploit his own inventions, he installed the system of complex, disciplined labor typical of the capitalist era.

The first textile factories, which took their power from water, were built alongside waterfalls, generally on a high, desolate heath, far from centers of population, where even today one can see the ruined shell of an abandoned building with tall chimneys. The replacement of water by steam as motive power in spinning mills made it suitable to group factories in the cities. The isolated factory thus became a memory like domestic industry, and the application of steam to the machine marked the arrival of urban industry.

Watt, inventor of the steam engine, discovered in 1769 the secret of the boiler, which allowed steam power to revolutionize industry. Newcomen's engine had been used as a pump in the mines, but it did not work at a very low level, and at all levels, both because it lost a great deal of heat and for other reasons, it was not very powerful and worked irregularly. Watt eliminated its defects by applying the boiler. This discovery meant control over the mines and thereby more power, machines, light, and heat and a higher standard of life for the whole population. The use of the rotary motion in imitation of the water wheel swiftly brought the steam engine into the cotton factories. Without the financial aid of Matthew Boulton, Watt's inventions would not have had much success. The former, a fancy-goods maker in Birmingham, began to make steam engines with Watt's help in 1775 and put them on the market. His confident energy and indomitable qualities, combined with Watt's mechanical inventions, in ten years brought about a revolution which in other circumstances might have taken a century. The first effective machine left his Soho factory in 1776. Four years later, forty engines were sent to the mines in Cornwall. In 1789, steam was confirmed as the dominant factor in almost all the main industries of England.

In the first half of the eighteenth century the great obstacle to England's industrial development was still communications. Whereas France had streets and canals which earned the admiration of all travellers, English roads, entrusted to unpaid parish officers, were in a shameful condition, and there was not a single canal. As long as this state continued and many roads were passable only in the summer months and others were open to horse traffic only, not carts and wagons, a considerable industrial development was impossible. The revolution in the sphere of communications, by land and water, was swiftly accomplished. Ashton, in his 1816 *History of Manchester*, said, "In 1770 there was only one coach for London and one for Liverpool, and they only ran twice a week. Now we have 70 coaches leaving from here, of which 54 have a daily service, and 16 run three times a week, for different destinations. In 1754 there was talk of an express coach, boasting proudly that it covered the stretch from Manchester to London in four and a half days. Now, coaches normally make this run in only 30 hours, and in various circumstances, as when the downfall of Bonaparte was imminent, and when there was the conclusive news of the victory at Waterloo, the diligences Voyager, Challenge and Telegraph arrived in only 18 hours." This was the short, though golden era of horse-drawn travel, but already in 1829, George Stephenson's railway closed this chapter of English history, giving rise to a great revolutionizing in the area of transport. However, already at the end of the Napoleonic wars, England had all the characteristics of capitalist, industrial society, as was then being created throughout the world.

INDUSTRIALIZATION AS A GLOBAL SOCIAL PROCESS

It is a basic premise of sociological analysis that social systems are wholes—of structures, cultures, personalities, and values—tendentially unitary and coherent. It is their inner, constant tension as regards the coherence of the parts which binds its components into a basic congruence, even though with evolutionary terms and rhythms which were not necessarily unequivocal and mechanically compatible. Furthermore, it is this tension which makes social systems rationally intelligible—that is, conceptually manageable. In other words, the fluidity of social systems which Weber often points to as the "chaos of facts" or the "infinite richness of life" is certainly real, but it should not be understood as a simple gratuitous erroneousness. Let us not misunderstand: the social system may be analyzed and expressed in scientific terms only on the basis of an ordering principle, or a group of premises linked in various ways to the interests—in the widest sense—of the researcher and the historical context to which he belongs and should not therefore be seen as a *given social reality* valid *a parte rei*, basically immobile and understandable *without residues*, at the risk of reifying analytical schemas and their confusion with the concrete historical situation and ultimately the falling off of sociological analysis into a mere instrument for the rationalization and justification of the status quo.[18]

Social systems are thus tendentially unitary, coherent wholes, but in a problematic sense,[19] historically, in that their development recognizes no results taken for granted or mechanically predetermined—rather their development appears as a human undertaking, open, without automatic organizing and rationalizing powers. We do not know on the basis of what logic of combinations the complex game of influences and interdependence between structures, individuals, and primary groups takes place, and by what processes social evolution achieves basic transformations which "change life," or what personality types, what structural characteristics and special value and belief orientations, ideological or religious, are required so as to move on to the mediations and mutual fertilizations which open the way to new historical phases. It is with these basic reservations that we talk of differentiated types of society, and further, it is on the basis of the premise of the tendential coherence of social systems that the process of industrialization appears as a global social process which ends up by implicating and involving the mode of working and of thinking, family life and political structure, religious practice and the ethical bases of power, social exchange and the institutional structuring of authority. Without making concessions to Manichaean standpoints—criticized above—it thus becomes possible to define the process of industrialization first and foremost as a break with the method of working, of economic routine and technique, which was then to resound on the whole of social life and at the same time involve the traditional institutions and the personal fortunes of individuals.

However much assuredly idealized, as the myth of the *saturnia aetas* is removed in time to the psychological past, the overall picture of pre-industrial society clearly contrasts with the urban-industrial mode of life of which we have direct experience. Schematic contrasts are not to be taken literally, but certainly contain elements of undoubted heuristic value. At the beginning of Engels' *Condition of the Working Class in England* (1844), he touches on the idyll, but the pages Friedmann devotes to the "green tree of direct contact" between man and nature are no further distant.[20] Starting off, Engels states, "The history of the proletariat in England begins with the invention of the steam engine and of the machinery for processing cotton." In Engels' view, before this period, "the workers lived quietly through a passably comfortable existence, leading an honest, peaceful life with all uprightness and religious feeling, and their marital condition was far better than that of their successors." Clearly, we cannot speak of the great opponents in principle of the "industrial revolution"—of Carlyle, Ruskin, the English romantics from Coleridge to Wordsworth, who, together with Marx, are the great analysts of the human, economic, and political transformation of European life from the end of the eighteenth century. Still less may we concern ourselves with their countless modern followers, whose analytical incapacity is clumsily compensated by a taste for paradox and a dubious prophetic enthusiasm. However, if we discount the fashionable romantic counterpositions—cohesion as against disintegration, stability against instability, mechanical solidarity as against organic solidarity, participation versus alienation and anomie, affective, personalist relations versus neutral, impersonal ones, qualitative interests and values versus the cult of efficiency, precision, and quantity—there remain the outlines of two different modes of life.

The social framework in which men lived and worked, the village and the neighborhood, was relatively stable and developed slowly; furthermore, it was relatively narrow. Long custom provided that each knew his place, occupied a specific position and enjoyed a certain respect for it. The possibilities for rising were few, but almost certainly hopes and plans for the future were achieved, at least to the extent that they were based on the social structure.... Authority was exercised according to a hierarchy all found natural. Work done well, good neighborly relations, and honesty were the values of a code the group was used to. Life unrolled according to well-defined stages and everyone could easily see from infancy the position they would occupy as an adult.... The obligations each had to fulfill appeared as the logical consequence of the upbringing they received.[21]

The community spirit and the idyllic harmony of a society of this kind, classically traditional, had their price in the "village morality" and iron social control, formal and informal—exercised either directly through politico-juridical and religious normative systems or through ostracism and the sanction of ridicule on the side of the collectivity. Social structures seemed solidly rooted in time. Rarely did the individual live long enough to see them change even slightly. It is probable that psychologically this social and societal condition would produce tranquility, a sense of acceptance, a basic identification with the existing social situation. Then, there was the satisfaction of working on a finished product, and for someone who, even if not known personally, was nonetheless known for what he was. The village cobbler saw the village in his shoes. Social integration was not just a juridical norm: as in Meister Eckhart's song in the finale of the *Meistersinger*, this was a deep existential experience. However, one must not forget that the artisans, as regards the total active population, and especially as regards the slaves and agricultural or house serfs, were few. To see the golden world of the artisan and compare it to the modern industrial worker without taking into account the bondsmen and day-laborers, those who worked in the mines, the workshops, and fields—that is, those who were both motive power and instruments of labor—means giving oneself over to misunderstanding of one's own time.

The society I conventionally refer to as "traditional," distinguishing it from two other types of society—the "cultural" society of elites and the "contractual," pluralist-industrial society in the full sense—is a society in which community and society, individual and function, coincide.[22] Every aspect of coexistence is quite explicitly controlled and seen as strictly interdependent as regards the others. There are slaves because a certain kind of work needs doing, and one does a certain kind of work because one is a slave; the cycle is solely legitimated by tradition: "You and your fathers were slaves." One literally belonged to society rather than being a part of it. The mystique of the artisan can play rude tricks; to refer to the magisterial reconstructions of Weber and Sombart on the figure of the "free artisan" as a polemic against the process of industrialization means to expose oneself to the risk of unfounded and probably untenable generalizations regarding the artisans themselves, free in many cases only to decide their own method and technique of working, but already at the mercy of the merchants for raw materials as well as customers.[23]

Tradition, relative immobility, crystallization of institutions and their mode of legitimization, and social control, very powerful and pervasive, even if hardly perceived given total internalization, affective and personal relations, primary groups, direct, qualitative knowledge—this is the world which the steam engine or the clock with the new sense of time it involved, or, simply, the new technology and its widespread application, came to erode technically, but also from the institutional, political, and religious, point of view. As Halévy said, the great "acceleration of history" had begun—a dramatic phrase which contains a considerable, but not entire, truth. In fact, the premises for the ending of time and the abolition of history are presented.[24]

What is striking is the rapidity of the spread of technical innovation. Watt himself in little less than twenty years installed 289 engines in England alone. The steam engine, said Mumford, became the symbol of efficiency, and by that the rhythm of development began to be marked.[25] As regards the traditional sources of energy, this required a relatively huge investment both at the outset and for its running. So as to achieve rapid repayments, this led to round-the-clock working, rarely to be found in traditional manufacture. The working day was extended to the limits of physical resistance, and beyond. A related invention, gaslight, made night-time production increasingly profitable, making it general with deep repercussions on the life of the community and working families. The cost and power of the steam engine, but also technical and social reasons (steam dissipates easily, and on the other hand discipline among the workers is more easily assured by putting them together) gave the impulse to the greatest possible concentration of productive units under a single roof. The modern factory was born. With this, once and for all, there ended the divorce between ownership of the means of production and the direct producer. In conjunction, economic motivation and personal responsibility for production weakened. On the other hand, no longer determined by waterways, industry could arise anywhere. In fact, it initially tended to concentrate in the areas rich in coal. Once cooperative barriers were overcome, it became urban, too, assisting a rapid, massive urbanization. In 1685, Liverpool had 8,000 inhabitants; at the start of the period of industrialization it had 40,000, and in 1891, 517,000. The social and psychological consequences of urbanization are well known: the prevalence of *secondary* (transitory and anonymous) relations, no one knows us anymore, the "lonely crowd," a phenomenon also known in classical antiquity, but now generalized; the breaking of social controls and "village morality"; the segmentation of interpersonal relations and the fragmentation of social roles; the worker is a laborer in the factory and a citizen at home, between the two roles there is a break in continuity and there seems to correspond to that segmentation a feeling of no longer being able to participate meaningfully in community political and social life.[26]

The urban concentration of manpower at the same time made possible a more perfect division of labor. In other words, what Smith called "the friction of space" was lessened. Precisely because it was concentrated in the city, the working population offered the assorted needs of the entrepreneurs a more specialized variety of professional attitudes and skills. Elements of production massed territorially lend themselves better to an efficient productive combination. The old unitary trades had suffered a first blow with manufacture, which had given rise to the inevitable downgrading of professional skill. For the ex-artisans, this meant the diminution of the sense of creativity in working activity. For those with neither art nor craft—that is, for most—this meant once and for all giving up the development and intelligent use of their own abilities. There did, however, remain some kind of apprenticeship. This was no longer the total formative apprenticeship of the classical artisan; the apprentice no longer lived with the workshop owner, the example of technical skill but also of morality of life. However, it was a technical qualification which gave the ex-peasant a new, important basis of social identification and prestige. We are now in the period of universal, flexible machines, that is, of machines which could be used for a whole range of operations of a particular kind—lathes, milling machines, boring machines, drills, and so on. We are not dealing with special machines, machines specialized in the production of a single element, thus requiring of the operator only a few motions, always the same, to feed them. Universal machines require intelligence and responsibility; the work cannot be predetermined in detail; the speed of the machine is decided by the operator, and it is he who has to take care not to "burn out the tool." Thus he has to know the speed of the cutting rate of the tools and the relative hardness of the metals they deal with, and he must furthermore plan the best way to execute the design of the product, decide the time required, take care of the specific unforeseen difficulties in production.

The social, rather than technical, differences were not slow to show themselves very clearly. As one moved on from artisan qualification— which was formative in the total sense—to technical qualification, so one moved on from the master craftsman to the supervisor, the foreman, the overseer. The gap between executive functions and directly productive or operational ones, which was basically determined by the division of labor, does not merely demonstrate a break or difference defined in technico-functional terms. It rapidly took on the sense of a psychological distance and a social breach which were hard to reconcile. Respect and admiration for the artist-artisan tended to change to antipathy, if not fear, for the supervisor. The "natural" hierarchy, or that based on ability and skill mutually recognized, tended to be replaced by a military-type hierarchy based on the regimentation of the labor force. Historians have traditionally given the same recognition to the "inventors" of military discipline applied in industrial establishments as went to those responsible for technical innovations. Thus Arkwright, in Mumford's terms, "was not responsible for a single original invention," in opposition to what people have continued to believe and recount, but rather he should be remembered as the man most responsible for setting out a code of industrial discipline which was exemplary for decades. "Three hundred years after Prince Maurice transformed the military arts, Arkwright perfected the industrial army."[27] The arbitrators thenceforward took on the responsibility of making this discipline respected and keeping alive in popular imagination the link between factory and barracks.[28]

Once the affective atmosphere and the communality of the artisan workshop had disappeared, and the gap between management and productive power had been eliminated, it was the market's turn to undertake the essential integrative function which guaranteed the social system against involutory and disintegrating trends. However, the market was impersonal and abstract and inexorably followed the laws of demand and supply, and its balance was not necessarily compatible with the daily needs of working-class families. Its fluctuations might mean unemployment and poverty for whole populations—and on the other hand, the wage received when working did not see an adequate recompense for the effort expended. To the feeling spreading among the workers of being the object of exploitation, at the mercy of uncontrollable and incomprehensible forces, there corresponded the laborious, difficult organization of workers' societies for mutual aid, trade associations, and brotherhoods of various kinds which were moreover in total agreement regarding the attempt to correct the fluctuations of the market by restricting its influence, and protecting those at work against their employers' power. We are not yet dealing with unions in the real sense, that of class. We are dealing with organizations in which a certain charitable ambiguity remained, often under the patronage of a saint and presided over by those very employers, but there is no doubt, as we shall see hereafter, that these were the historical and psychological premises for the rise of real associations of resistance and workers' struggle.

With the adoption on a vast scale of special machines, prepared solely for a given operation on a given product, technical qualification itself also disappeared, and there remained only *mechanical specialization*. With increasing mechanization, we see the levelling out of the hierarchy based on the differentiation of professional skills. The division of labor proceeded, becoming more differentiated and specific. There was no longer a need to know the machine; others "set it up"—and these were few. Others again repaired it in the event of breakdowns or malfunction—the specialists expert in maintenance. The control of quality also was wholly removed from the worker. His only responsibility now lay in performing a few simple movements, already clearly laid down and specified in the instructions. Time, like motion, was precisely measured and rigorously enforced. The operative, no longer the "workman," became the tool of the planning and methods department.[29]

We have arrived at the logical conclusion of the "industrial revolution," marked in its most mature phase of development by two basic characteristics: (1) the application of a new source of energy, electricity; (2) the transformation of productive organization according to the principles of the scientific organization of labor—scientific management, presented as a real social invention, or a new mode of allocating and justifying decision-making power over human beings. Here, clearly and decisively, the break with the past occurred. With the scientific organization of labor, the mass market, required by the capitalist form of production based on a continually evolving industrial technology, expanded at an extraordinary rate. Consumption became a necessity independent of real needs. Needs were solicited, induced, and created. Locked into a spiral with production and wages, the need for consumption tended to hinder, or make more difficult, the formation of stable social values. Technology and productive relations had changed the appearance and essence of society by modifying professional activity, and family roles and by affecting religious beliefs and practice, contributing to political change. However, now the contrast regarding the pre-industrial world emerged as something more radical, as a different vision of life and the position of man in the universe. Feudal society drew its cohesive strength and the source of the legitimacy of its own institutions from immobility in time. Modern society ended up by finding the path of its own survival and the condition of its own welfare in the unceasing change which involved values, personality, and structures.

THE ACTORS IN THE PROCESS OF INDUSTRIALIZATION

Entrepreneurs

However strange it may seem, if indeed it is not downright incomprehensible, only recently has the question of economic development and the process of industrialization been posed in terms not strictly, or exclusively, economic.[30] Economists themselves, urged on by psychologists, sociologists, and cultural anthropologists—not to mention historians—ended up recognizing the impossibility of an exhaustive and scientifically tenable explanation of the phenomenon of development, and especially of its origins, so long as these were restricted to factors of production narrowly conceived, as the classic land, labor, and capital, with the unspoken understanding that the discussion concerning values, attitudes, and cultural and political norms and systems was really superfluous, as one assumed in a manner really rather hasty that in any society and culture or historical epoch the individual always and necessarily tended to maximize his own individual benefit.[31] That this crude psychological generalization, secretly introduced into the majority of economistic treatments of the problem as a base or general conception of "human nature," never explicitly viewed as such, is both inadequate and misleading is now almost universally admitted. The economist

Nicholas Kaldor writes, "In my view, the much accelerated economic development of the last two hundred years—that is, the rise of modern capitalism—can only be explained in terms of changing human attitudes regarding risk and profit."[32] Other authoritative testimony abounds, but systematic attempts to connect the formation of a particular type of personality with a specific culture within the framework of a particular social system are still few and fragmented. The results are clear: the process of industrialization is studied as though it arose ready-made, *ex capita Jovis*, a product of mechanical forces and their impersonal articulation, a drama without actors. Questions of great interest, rather embarrassingly, remain open: Why, with equal resources and demographic conditions, do some countries develop and others not? How do we explain the fact that specific countries, already economically developed, tend at a certain point to stagnate and eventually decline and fall back into a state of underdevelopment, while other countries, without natural resources and unfavorably located as regards the major centers of production and consumption, manage to take the path of rapid industrialization?[33]

Clearly, we are dealing with classical concerns, reflected in Marx's work and still more in that of Weber. However, only in relatively recent times have the actors in the process of industrialization—the entrepreneurs and the organized working-class movement—been taken as the object of systematic analysis, outside the schemas of doctrinal ideological preferences.[34] By this I do not mean that the analysis of the entrepreneurial function lacked the now classical research of Joseph A. Schumpeter and the Research Center in Entrepreneurial History at Harvard, which for ten years, from 1948 to 1958, continued and critically elaborated Schumpeter's teaching.[35] Already in the *Essai sur la nature du commerce en general* by Richard Cantillon, which dates back to before 1734, we have an interesting attempt to determine the basic character of entrepreneurship, which Cantillon, English by birth and French by adoption, saw in the lack of a fixed income, in not being dependent on anyone and therefore living in a state of relative uncertainty.[36] Apart from the occasional remarks on the entrepreneur by Quesnay and Turgot, it was only in 1803 with the publication of J. B. Say's *Traité d'économie politique* that we find a new attempt to make an explicit theorization of entrepreneurial functions. The entrepreneur is not considered as one of the factors of production, traditionally reduced to three—industry, capital, and land. By industry, Say understands industrial labor in the broad sense, insofar as it includes both workers and employers. However, in his view, the entrepreneur is to be distinguished clearly both from the capitalist and the provider of work, while occupying a key position in economic activity. In fact, he should be seen as the great intermediary between seller and buyer, producer and market. In this sense, he is not a productive factor. He stands outside the process of production in that he is its motive power which articulates its elements and determines the distribution of income. Similar views are repeated by German economists of the time. For example, Hufeland, while not recognizing the basic importance attributed to them by Say, sees in the entrepreneurs a connecting link between the two sectors of production and consumption, while for von Jakob the *Unternehmer* is the means whereby the technical knowledge of the scientists finds its practical application on a huge scale.[37]

However, the major interest of Say's approach is for us polemical and is to be found in the criticism he levels primarily against Adam Smith, and then against "almost all the English economists." Not having clearly established the distinction between interest and profit, Smith can only see the entrepreneur in the clothes of the capitalist or proprietor. In *On the Wealth of Nations*, there is no lack of comment on the figure of the manager or employer as distinct from that of the owner, but the distinction between the two roles is not carried through, and even the terminological equivalent of the terms "entrepreneur" and "*Unternehmer*" diminishes—even though the term "undertaker," which today has quite a different meaning, may have had some popularity for a time.[38] In Smith, as also in Ricardo and Marx, the systematic aspect clearly prevailed over those aspects we may call voluntaristic. The role of the actor as regards the structural characteristics of the system and its logic of development does not stand out. For Smith, the employer is just a capitalist. His function is clear and limited; it lay in the use of capital, owned or borrowed. But it is capital itself, rather than the activity and the projects connected with its use, which produces income. With Ricardo and in general the economists of the classical school, interest in systematic theoretical analysis grew, and there declined in direct proportion interest in the voluntaristic, motivational, psychological, and cultural (i.e., historical) aspects of the economic process. The possibility of drawing therefrom gain from the rational exploitation of specific situations certainly is explicitly recognized in Ricardo. For example, he who first adopted a technical invention would have an undeniable advantage from the lowering of production costs, but this, for Ricardo, would be of small importance because it would be temporary and destined to be cancelled out by competition. It is typical that in the *Principles of Political Economy* there is no real distinction between inventor and innovator and that he spoke of "he...who made the discovery" and "he...who first usefully applied it" in the same sense.[39]

The new productive methods and generally the technical aspects of the factory system had an important role in Marx's system, and the fine thirteenth chapter of *Capital* would suffice ("Maschinerie und Grosse Industrie") to eliminate any suspicion concerning an ideological treatment, yet the figure of the entrepreneur, his role, the value orientations, and the aims which determine his specific activity have no special importance for Marx. The capitalist, technically equipped and driven by the acquisitive urge, supposedly a common feature, arrives on the social scene, destroys the "idiocy of rural life," and seems to perform no special activity save that of accumulation. His activity is thus simply a function of capital. The personal element in entrepreneurial activity has no substance here. One cannot even say, in fact, as with Smith and Ricardo, that the figure of the entrepreneur ends up by embracing and becoming mixed with that of the owner of capital. It simply does not emerge, is not specifically envisaged, save for the anthem of praise Marx never tires of generically dedicating to the bourgeoisie as revolutionizing the traditional productive apparatuses, and for which Weber's severe and detailed critiques are still valid.[40] For Marx the process of investment derives spontaneously from the pressure of the needs of survival of the system: it is not linked to any charisma of worldly asceticism, as for Weber; nor does it owe its dynamism to "titanism"— half heroic, half sporting—of some "superhuman individual," as later in Schumpeter. As for Smith and Ricardo, we are probably dealing with a theoretical limitation deriving from the lack of historical data to be analyzed. The concept of the entrepreneur was to be taken up as object of specific theoretical discussion when the methods of financing themselves tended to stress the distinction between owner and operator, that is, between being a capitalist and the activity of the entrepreneurs.[41] This distinction was produced with difficulty and once solidly founded, then tracked between two poles which we may respectively call the conception of the entrepreneur as simply a capitalist and the conception of the entrepreneur as an organizational whole. Between these two poles there is a whole series of concepts of entrepreneurship, which probably arrives at the most suggestive—if not logically based—point in Schumpeter's conception of the entrepreneur as "innovator"—an ambitious concept which hoped to embrace the level of historical explanation of economic development along with that of individual will and psychology, without diminishing its basically economic character. It is this which clearly distinguishes the explanatory argument for the development of modern capitalism set out by Schumpeter from Weber's. Schumpeter wrote: "Economic activity can have *any* aim at all, even a spiritual one, but its meaning is always the satisfaction of wants. Hence derives the basic importance of those concepts and propositions which derive from the fact of wants, amongst which the concept of marginal utility is pre-eminent, or to use a more modern term, the 'coefficient of choice.'... Production on one hand is conditioned by the physical properties of material objects and natural processes.... On the other hand, the one that we can enter into more profoundly—into the essence of production rather than in the physical and social aspects—is the concrete aim of every productive action."[42] Schumpeter has no need, in order to explain the break in routine, to invoke the prophet, the charismatic leader who has, aside from other things, the disadvantage of being highly exceptional. In order to pass from the "circular flow of economic life," or a basically static and traditional phase, to that of "economic development," he did not need to refer to external religious, cultural, political, or other forces. Here, the entrepreneur was no longer the simple capitalist, as in addition many, besides Say and Cantillon, had already seen clearly—from von Jakob, Hufeland, and K. H. Rau to G. Ramsay, who analyzed the function of the "masters," to Nassau W. Senior, and to Walter Bagehot, for whom the activity of the capitalist was described as "the action whereby he not only preserves his capital and does not consume it, but indeed uses it for the accomplishment of other ends."[43] Nor is he always the simple "coordinator," as Cannan and Mill, in England, and Francis A. Walker in the United States believed.[44]

The conception of the entrepreneur as "coordinator" can be strongly backed by Marshall's contribution; he initially seems to press it beyond its bounds with the introduction of a fourth factor of the process of production, described as "organization"; however, on closer inspection, this is simply the recognition of a more articulated and specific division of labor.[45] Marshall's contribution should rather be linked with the question of the remuneration of the entrepreneur—a question which takes on importance following the distinction between capitalist-owner and entrepreneur-organizer, for whom the remuneration of the entrepreneur cannot be equated with earned income, but at the same time does not either have the character of a wage, the typical remuneration of the subordinate worker. According to Mallock and many other writers, this concerns rather an income sui generis, intended to reward a "particular skill" which the entrepreneur clearly demonstrates in carrying out his functions and which concerns the public interest. In fact, the "skill," in the view of these scholars, is the principal factor of wealth, and the very well-being of society and the workers appears thus closely linked with the prosperity of the class which actually exercises this "skill," that is, the entrepreneurs.[46] However, in essence the entrepreneur, however exalted and glorified, is no more than a high-grade worker, entrusted with special responsibilities, and we are thus very far from the full recognition of a specific, autonomous function regarding the productive and distributive process. Hawley and Davenport—in fact, with little success—attempted to review the by now traditional theories of entrepreneurship, the former by seeing in the entrepreneur the sole economic factor animated by economic aims insofar as he is motivated to collective action, whereas the other three factors are supposed to be motivated only by individualist aims, and the latter by providing so broad a conception of the entrepreneurial function that it included doctors, lawyers, and houseowners, thus destroying any attempt at definition.[47] J. B. Clark restated the "pure" conception of the entrepreneur as "coordinator," who can also be a capitalist when he invests his own money, which is indeed a benefit as he will in general be led to act with greater caution, managing to take on a multiplicity of functions and related roles. As entrepreneur he is a "reducer of risk" and finally as capitalist a "bearer of risk."[48] The polemical aspects of Clark's position are particularly directed towards Hawley's argument, which views risk as connected with property, while for Clark the dimension of risk is wholly absent in the concept of property, just as later Schumpeter was to argue against the connection of risk with the entrepreneurial function in the strict sense, claiming that this concerned a mere residue of the conception of the entrepreneur as capitalist. In other words, risk in the true sense was run only by the person who provided the means of production, that is, the capitalist: if the entrepreneur runs some risk, that means he too is a capitalist.[49]

The concept of risk as a basic aspect of entrepreneurial activity, and its insertion into the dynamic of the economy, are classically set forth in the work of Frank Knight, who managed to escape from the criticisms commonly levelled by the Schumpeter "school"[50] by way of the connection, often stressed, between the processes and initiatives of innovation regarding the "circular flow" and the occasions for risk.[51] In Knight's analysis and distinction between "risk" as quantitative and measurable, and thus also ensurable, and "uncertainty," as a special dimension neither quantitative nor measurable, is basic. Uncertainty cannot be assured beforehand; on the other hand, where uncertainty is less, the raison d'être of the entrepreneur himself disappears. Indeed, with a perfect knowledge of the situation, only management functions of a simple, routine kind would be needed. On the other hand, given uncertainty, "the task of deciding what should be done and how it should be done takes on a predominant importance as regards the responsibility of execution."[52] The fine line, which, however, allows of a certain convergence between Knight's and Schumpeter's positions, is provided by the fact that Knight sees the service of the entrepreneur explained not so much in "bearing" the risk as rather in the way he faces up to uncertainty. His function lay in identifying objectives and managing the course of an economic activity in not precisely foreseeable conditions. Profit, thus, is the reward not for a coordination accomplished or a sacrifice borne, but rather for a more or less precise foresight.[53] From risk to innovation, once the confusions of a juridical nature which underlie the confusion of capitalist and entrepreneur are clarified, the transition is relatively easy. Naturally in Schumpeter the perspective is much broader. Knight's entrepreneur seems to be restricted to a function of choosing, which may certainly be dramatic, but does not imply really "creative" gifts. Schumpeter's entrepreneur however is really demiurgic, if not titanic. He is not only the one who faces up to the uncertainty which generally but not always and not necessarily, accompanies change, but the very producer of change. In Schumpeter's theory, the entrepreneur brings about the transformation of the situation from within and interrupts the "circular flow"—close to Walras' "state of equilibrium," Marx's "simple reproduction," and Clark's "static situation." It is the demand of the entrepreneur which gives rise to the transformation of credit and creates the capitalist. The entrepreneur is further clearly distinguished from the industrial manager. He too is a coordinator, but a coordinator of a special kind, who has nothing to do with the current terminology and meaning. He coordinates by establishing new combinations, combinations not inherited from the past and which nonetheless do not make them the copy of the inventor. His is a completely new function: "between producing new projects and behaving according to custom there is the same difference as that which lies between making a road and travelling on it."[54]

In Schumpeter's view, the entrepreneurial function is thus highly dramatic: it has no precursors and leaves no heirs. Entrepreneurial activity ceases at the moment the new combination is achieved: it is not only atypical but transitory. To think of the group of entrepreneurs as one thinks of the class of landowners or capitalists is a logical contradiction. It is clear that the entrepreneurs and their families were part of the "upper" classes, the wealthy elite, but this manifests no tendency on the entrepreneurial side to become routinized. In Schumpeter's view, "the upper strata of society are comparable to hotels always fully booked, but we are dealing with individuals who are constantly renewed."[55] As regards the entrepreneurs, we are dealing with people who owe their success not to ascribed, hereditary roles, but rather to "decision-making ability" and the necessary foresight "to evaluate forcefully."[56] The family group counts for less than the individual gifts and psychological drive, which cannot be reduced to a search after one's own benefit or a philistine maximization of one's own happiness. Schumpeter postulates the need for a non-hedonistic psychology to explain the behavior and incentive of entrepreneurial activity. This does not mean just recognizing, with Veblen, a generalized "instinct of workmanship" which would end up by driving a wedge between the captain of industry, predatory and speculative, ready to buy and sell according to the logic of the market, wholly indifferent to productive and technological values as such, and the kind of lay saint who for Veblen is the engineer, the socially conscious technocrat. The desire for technical perfection, like that for profit, would not explain the tenacity, the extraordinary and absorbing dedication, of entrepreneurship. It was not for nothing that Weber invoked religious motivations, deaf to daily consciousness, but still active in the depths of awareness, on the basis of the *Beruf* which is both profession and vocation. For Schumpeter, it is a matter of "worldly passion," for which pursuit of wealth becomes the moment for proving oneself, before oneself and others. It is an exploit of the sporting kind, the satisfaction of "achievement" gratified not so much by gain as by the success which marks the distance between oneself and the rest, a special variation of Veblen's "antagonistic confrontation."

The "provocative" aspects of Schumpeter's view emerge fully, and the critical demands are not slow in coming even from those who most immediately experienced the influence of his thought and teaching. Leaving aside the consideration of interesting attempts to mediate between Knight's view and that of Schumpeter,[57] I shall limit myself to a summary recapitulation of Arthur A. Cole's criticisms and suggestion of a plurifunctional definition of entrepreneurship.[58] These help us in fact to clarify the emergence of the notion of the entrepreneur as "organizational whole" or as a "corporation actively oriented towards profit." From the entrepreneur-capitalist, we have thus arrived at entrepreneurship as the institutional function of productive and distributive organization, by moving through the concepts of entrepreneur as coordinator, as risk bearer, and finally as innovator. For Cole, too, the innovatory function is crucial, but for him the concern is that of defining the indices which permit empirical definition outside any cliché of superhuman voluntarism. In this regard, Cole stresses the importance of the size of the enterprise. The firm (or corporation) marked by entrepreneurial behavior, open and able for innovation, is one whose dimensions seem to grow more rapidly than those of competing corporations. However, one is not restricted to this indicator as, moreover, one no longer sees in entrepreneurship an isolated fighter, a "great individual" intent on the "construction of his own personal empire," but rather an "entrepreneurial term," which faces up to a multiplicity of functions. These last may be variously identified and defined. Elsewhere, I have pointed to the following basic moments of entrepreneurial function as self-perpetuating and institutionalized.[59]

1. the moment of combination or innovation—conceptualization and foresight
2. planning
3. combination of productive factors
4. execution
5. trial and checking-supervision
6. distribution

The point to stress here is the process of depersonalization and deindividualization of the entrepreneurial function. This becomes a permanent characteristic of the corporative organization as "processual," in A. Sauvy's term, or that corporation which acts upon nature instead of submitting to it and gives rise to processes of development whereby the increase of productivity must not be separated from the increase of labor power employed. The concrete methods of realizing this process have long attracted the attention of industrial sociologists. The common stages of management decisions (information, decision, action, checking) have been analyzed in different economic, historic, and ideological contexts for comparative purposes, and a typology of entrepreneurs from the point of view of social origins, religious upbringing, value set (if not ideological), leadership styles, and psychological motivation in management activity may in the future be elaborated on this basis of the empirical research conducted up to the present and still underway. As against some people's expectations, it is probable that the "managerial revolution" will not take place. However, there is no doubt that the institutionalization of the entrepreneurial function lies at the root of the creation of the great corporation as social institution and that the great corporation itself today is a reality of major importance which the working-class movement and the basic structures of society, from family to state, must face up to.[60]

Workers' Movement

Before becoming an ideology and particular organizational structure, the workers' movement was an existential experience, an act of solidarity. In the enterprise it discovered a level continual, daily battle. However, its activity involved—away from the strictly technical and company level—the community in which the factory arose, the intermediate organisms of professional and political representation (such as municipalities, political parties, and the variegated undergrowth of pressure groups) so as ultimately to involve society itself and the political order which expressed its basic attitudes, structural characteristics, and values. The birth and development of the working-class movement as an autonomous one, aware of the non-negotiability and specific nature of its interests as representing a social and human condition, historically unrecorded, pointed to a journey and process of definition which would be slow, complex, and troubled, but whose aim emerges clearly from its origins. The end of the securely organized labor movement and its social function is, from the first mutual aid societies, the neutralization or at least the containment of the negative effects of economic crises, and generally the oscillations of the capitalist market, more or less dramatic.

Once the trade corporations and the medieval guilds disappeared—the former through a complicated system of regulations and controls ensured an adequately harmonious relation between producers and consumers—the market was now involved in discharging this integrating function. However, the connection the capitalist market provided was no longer the direct personal link between artisan and customer and within the productive process, between masters and journeymen. Rather, this took place in the abstract, impersonal, automatically self-adjusting relation between demand and supply. Seen as a whole, both as professional organization and as political movement in the strict sense, the working-class movement appears as a systematic breaking action as regards the mechanical working of the capitalist market and as a co-ordinated reaction to the simple unravelling of the law of demand and supply. Naturally, this is an interpretative explanation. In historical reality, things were much more complex, and the positions adopted by the workers' movement itself should not be seen as endowed with abstract ideological principles, but rather as "responses"—adequate to various degrees—to specific circumstances in specific historical and cultural contexts. A "non-dynastic" history of the working-class movement, one not concerned with a priori salvaging of a given orthodoxy, but able to see in it development in relation to the responses of the entrepreneurial counterpart (in the terms of available economic resources and legally codified institutional structures, connected with a specific technical equipment and a specific historical heritage, a specific political regime and geographical position) has yet to be written.

This must not be seen in the sense that the working-class movement is by definition a dependent variable, incapable of actions not determined a priori, as is often understood. Rather, we are dealing with a recall to the heuristic need not to consider the workers' movement in the abstract, in a perspective which, claiming to be analytical and metahistorical, seldom manages not to be changed into mythology. These same interpretations of the workers' movement which I shall here just record very briefly, and the variety of its attitudes and evolution, would in that event be incomprehensible.

The fact that the working-class movement generally appears as an action of solidarity and an attempt at protection against the "laws" of the capitalist market should not be confused with an invitation to paradise. The "victimized" attitude and the dolorous tones of so much literature regarding the birth and development of the workers' movement as an important social force in the process of industrialization have a rhetorical and merely persuasory value. From the start, the workers' movement presented itself as an undertaking dominated by the need to guarantee its own survival, to be recognized and accepted, and ultimately to win a certain degree of "social respectability" and decision-making power, both on the level of the firm and on that of society at large. However, the view of the workers' movement as one of poor proletarians, without a trade and supplied only with idealistic enthusiasm, corresponds much more to Pellizza da Volpedo's painting the "Quarto stato" than to historical reality. However disturbing this may be, it was not the poorest and most defenseless workers who were first organized, but the wealthiest, those in possession of a precise, stable trade, able to grasp the mechanism of the expanding industrial system and determined to neutralize, at least to some extent, the logic of the market—printers, cigar-makers, weavers, and so forth.

Thus, in Italy, in a situation where—given belated industrial development in the modern sense—the organization of the workers' movement also started late, we find the printers in the front line in the difficult transition from the general mutual aid associations to the setting up of "workers coalitions," determined to make a clear, systematic resistance to the employers. The textile industries were certainly the oldest and also the most celebrated as regards hours of work and the intensity of exploitation, but for the first example of a permanent association of union resistance we must wait for the project of the workers' elite which gathered together in the "federation of books." Soon copied by their comrades in Genoa and Milan, and then by those in the most important Italian cities, on 7 May 1848, forty workers in Turin proclaimed themselves as the "Society of typographical compositors." The "Society" set itself no revolutionary aims, nor did it base its program on ideological platforms. It presented and concerned itself through a minimalism which was later characteristic of business unionism—that is, of an important trend of the world working-class movement—of defending a "tariff of labor," shortly before gained from the employers.[61]

The results of the breakup in the various Italian states of the corporations were certainly serious for the workers. They were protected by statutes which provided them at least with job security and assurance of the means of subsistence. Once this defense had fallen, they fell under the unbridled power of the capitalists at the moment in which the use of machines and need to economize in the expenses of production drove the new captains of industry to the total exploitation of labor power. As has been eloquently remarked, labor was declared free; thus the law, for fear that the old corporations be revived, forbade workers' associations. However, this freedom, so useful for the bourgeoisie, for the workers without means of subsistence and instruments of labor, is no more than the freedom to become a slave.[62]

With the laws suspending associations, not all were in fact abolished. Mutual aid societies were tolerated. Indeed, the members of the dissolved corporative associations asked to be able to maintain forms of association even though with responsibilities to simple assistance. These organized and managed welfare savings banks, recreational clubs, courses in professional training, and cooperatives. This was generally permitted by the Italian states for fear that the great mass of the Italian people would give themselves over to violent conduct as response to the need for common defense. Moreover, governments were guaranteed of the absolute, apolitical nature of the "friendly societies" (societies of mutual aid) by the presence within them, in a predominant position, of people extraneous to the working-class world—professionals, nobility, and police officers. However, quickly in Italy—especially with the victory of the Mazzinians over the moderates after the 1861 congress, the friendly societies began to decline both for internal reasons (excessive diffusion of responsibilities, conflicts of interest, etc.) as well as because the very gravity of the terms posed by the "working-class question" in Italy made clearly inadequate organisms whose basic aim was ever that of simple assistance. What was then pressing was the movement to associational forms which could organize the defense of labor in new terms as regards the old corporative organs.

It is in this socio-economic and political context, and that of social awareness, that primarily we can explain the fall of Mazzinian influence on the organized labor movement, an influence too closely tied to nationalist concerns—by tendency inter-classist—and a vague sentimental socialism, in origin paternalist, and thus, after the widespread but basically erratic influence of Bakunin, the clear dominance of Marxist teaching. From the point of view of the sociology of knowledge, the spreading and influence of Marxism in Italy, in a cultural situation on one side dominated by the anarchoid myths of Bakunin and Mazzini's

intransigent republicanism and on the other broadly derivative of evolutionary and positive elements from Comte, Darwin, and Spencer,
through whose development and dialectic it was believed one could
cheerfully go arm in arm, this diffusion is still an open question. It lies
at the origin of the historical and cultural hybrid which we might call
Italo-Marxism and which neither Labriola's great work of clarification
nor even Croce's brilliant insight into "how theoretical Marxism in Italy
was born and died" have managed to unravel.

As regards the worker's position, one may however state that in Italy,
as also in other countries of continental Europe, especially France and
Germany, Marxism appeared at the start of the present century as a
realistic interpretation and an explanation which, if not really scientific,
was at least psychologically plausible, of the problems facing the subaltern working classes. The Marxist interpretation, essentially victorious
as regards others, had rapidly to provide the doctrinal basis for the
creation of class workers' parties and in particular to justify the different
position and function attributed to the union and the political party—
the first as defender of short-term interests and subaltern as regards the
party, whereas the latter was the interpreter of the historical situation
and the power relations between classes and guide in the practical
struggle to overthrow these relations—the status quo—to end exploitation, the prehistory of mankind, and finally launch a new human
condition optimistically directed towards a *saturnia aetas*, in which the
free development of each would be the condition for the development
of all.

Historically, to the decline of mutual aid societies there corresponds
the increasingly vigorous assertions of the "resistance leagues" (*leghe
di resistenza*) (defense organizations of the economic and professional
interests for industrial and agricultural workers) and the development
after 1891—the year of the foundation of the PSLI (Partito Socialista
dei Lavoratori Italiani [Socialist Party of the Italian Workingmen]) of
the *camere del lavoro* (chambers of labor), which the socialists were
setting up in the main cities of Northern Italy. The *camere del lavoro*
were set up in imitation of the French *bourses du travail*, with the aim
of creating more efficient and broader forms of workers' protection.
They were made up of as many sections as there were trades, crafts,
and professions of those registered in the friendly societies and the
members of cooperatives. The main function of the *camere del lavoro*
was certainly that of coordination, but they were also especially effective

instruments for the spreading of socialist ideas throughout broad strata
of workers, for whom professional economic defense of their own interests ended up as being only the immediate aspect of a class consciousness which tended to see the resolution of the "workers' question"
through the transcendence of capitalist society.

For this reason, at once doctrinal and political, the *camere* were
opposed by the Catholics as a protest against the occupation of Rome
and the papal state. The Vatican had forbidden the formation of a
Catholic political party, as instead had taken place in France, Germany,
and Belgium. It was, however, concerned to organized the working
masses so as to join together Catholics and their associations . . . in Italy
in common and agreed action for the defense of the rights of the Holy
See and Italian religious and social interests, in full conformity with
the vows and encouragement of the Supreme Pontiff and under the
tutelage of the bishops and clergy.

This desire of the Church led to the setting up of the *Opera dei
congressi* (1875), through which Catholics faced in an organized fashion
the social life of the country, and the encyclical *Rerum novarum* (1891),
which established the Church's position as regards the social questions.
We must remember that the *Opera dei congressi* fostered the idea of
promoting neo-corporative associations inspired "by the statutes of our
old arts and crafts wherein were laid up real treasuries of religious,
social and civil wishes." We can see how this conception, so outdated
as regards the objective needs of the working-class position, was destined to failure, just as the attempt to found confessional *camere del
lavoro* also failed. Union organization which, following the French
example, produced in 1906 a unitary organization of laborers named
the Confederazione Generale del Lavoro (CGL), remained basically
under socialist influence, and within it there duly were repeated the
ruptures and ideological polemics between reformists and anarcho-syn-
dicalists which troubled the Socialist party in the first years of the
century. The conflicts between the two tendencies were resolved by the
abandonment of the CGL by the syndicalists. This led to the formation
of a new organization—the Unione Sindacale Italiana (USI) (Modena,
23 November 1912).

The relations between the Socialist party and the CGL, despite the
formal homage to the Charter of Amiens, which defined the ties between
socialist parties and the working-class movement as of mutual inde-
pendence, were very close. Indeed, though the task of controlling dis-

cipline in the working-class movement, and appeals to proletarian solidarity, lay with the Confederation, organisms for permanent understanding between party representatives and those of confederal proletarian organizations were created—even for deliberation concerning electoral, parliamentary, and civic activity, and for the choice of candidates. These relations were to become still closer with the alliance agreement, ratified 12 September 1918, which increased the degree of subordination of the Confederation to the party. The parties in fact agreed on the following points:

1. Strikes and demonstrations of a national political nature shall be proclaimed and directed by the leadership of the party, once the view of the Confederation has been expressed, which in all events undertakes not to hinder the carrying out of the decisions of the party.

2. Strikes and demonstrations of a national economic nature shall be proclaimed and directed by the CGL, once the view of the party has been expressed, which in all events undertakes not to hinder the carrying out of the decisions of the Confederation.

3. As there are questions which may be considered mainly political by the party and mainly economic by the Confederation, and vice versa, and as there may thus arise doubts and conflicts of competence, it is agreed that every time the party leadership meets it will send in good time its agenda to the Confederation, which if it sees fit will have the right to intervene through its representative in the sessions of the party leadership. The same will hold for the sessions of the managing council and national council of the Confederation, which will send their own agenda to the party leadership so that the latter, if it believes it useful and necessary, may intervene by right in the sessions of the managing council and national council.

4. So as to preserve the best relations between the two organisms, the secretaries of the Confederation and the party leadership shall stay constantly in touch.

We have briefly referred to the tie of interdependence which traditionally links the union to the party in certain countries of continental Europe, especially in Italy and France, so as to provide a point of reference with socio-economic, political, and cultural situations such as those in England and the United States, where the union appears as a powerful organizational reality which reaches the heart of production, into the factory, with no mediating organism of the "internal commission" kind, and which, as regards the organ of political representation in the strict sense—that is, the party—maintains and preserves a basic autonomy and proceeds, maneuvers, and makes decisions according to an outlook of open-minded experimental pragmatism. This obviously did not happen by chance, but corresponds to actual conditions and to cultural traditions and value systems which are readily identifiable.[63]

In England and the United States, too, the first workers' groups to provide themselves with a permanent defensive organization, limited but efficient, were the relatively privileged ones, the "workers' aristocracies."[64] It is probably useless to make a point of this. In this sense, the American case is most instructive. As I have elsewhere noted, no national organization of workers of national significance arose in the United States before the Civil War. However, after the war, given the rapid expansion of industry, there did appear in the Union some organizations which explicitly aimed at improving the contractual position of workers by organizing them on a national scale. Among these, we should pay special attention to the National Labor Union (1866), the Knights of Labor (1869), and the American Federation of Labor (1866). With the exception of the latter, no union organization could survive. That the leaders of the Knights of Labor, for example, lacked clear ideas seems certain. Their program was a strange mixture of doctrinal idealism with strong utopian emphases and very short-term demands. One point was, however, quite clear: their organization was open to all workers, skilled or not, without distinctions. This was the root of their organizational and contractual weakness. Not only did they enroll workers who did not pay dues, they took on—contractually—in the face of the employers, responsibilities for highly mobile laborers, easily absenteeist, for whom in fact they were able to guarantee nothing. The American Federation of Labor rapidly learned the lesson. From the start, around 1880, the AFL based its fortunes on the fact that it was solely open to skilled workers able regularly to pay their dues and, with a realistic business sense, concerned itself with immediate and concretely monetary advantages. Rather than specific global social policies or reforms, its aim from the beginning was the achievement of "social respectability" in the institutions which as a whole made up American society, and the achievement of "collective bargaining"—that is, a social power universally recognized. The rift which in 1936 gave birth to the Congress of Industrial Organizations (CIO) reflected an organizational, not an ideological, one (industrial versus craft unionism) and was moreover to be easily absorbed during the first Eisenhower administration. In my *La sociologia industriale in America e in Europa* I have tried to outline some of the more important attitudes and viewpoints of the American unions, on the basis of the sociological studies made to date.

The attitude of the American unions is basically decided by the needs of the power struggle in a situation of relatively full employment and a dynamic economy. First, the American union tries to keep itself apart, to preserve its own homogeneity, entrench itself territorially, fight for short-term interests with the complete disinterest which is allowed to whoever is not a prisoner of a pre-established plan. This is true to the extent that even today the American union world, after the organizational marriage between the AFL and CIO, cannot be marked out as a solidly centralized movement but must rather be seen as a grouping of large interests each with its own structure and in which the source of real power lies in the base, the locals, the union organization in the firm, rather than at the top, from which a function of bland coordination is requested.[65]

Furthermore, there still exists a very powerful and pervasive anti-legalistic prejudice which stopped Gompers, the founder of the AFL, seeking the aid of the federal government to clean up the unions of gangsters and profiteers, and which generally, while it tolerates no assumption of co-responsibility, tends to scent in any scheme of participation the trap of the bosses' manipulation. The process whereby the struggle for power is carried on and, on the other hand, the reciprocal power relation is tested is collective bargaining.

The main characteristics of collective bargaining are decentralization and flexibility, basically non-ideological, bargaining realism, a struggle for prerogatives, and the homogeneous and exclusive contract between organizations.

Regarding the first characteristic, decentralization and flexibility, the bargaining process in the United States relates to individual, different, corporate situations, by counterposing management and union without any mediation by "internal commissions" or other types of committees from the base, formally distinct from the union. In Europe, the dualism between the union, extra-corporate organism, and the internal workers' commission active among the workers of a given factory has traditionally produced friction, inconsistency, and even real breaks which have put at risk the contractual power of the working-class groups. On the one hand, the bureaucratised nature of the union made it insensitive to the ever new and different problems of specific realities of the enterprise;

on the other, the internal commission, without organic links with the workers' movement as social reality, autonomous politically and organizationally, was easily co-opted and assimilated as a second-rank partner in the employers' management system, and at most gave rise to the formation of enclaves of "workers' aristocracy."[66]

Second, with respect to collective bargaining's basically non-ideological, bargaining realism, one may doubt if the absence of ideological platforms which help to direct the activity of the various international unions and to coordinate it in view of common ends of the whole workers' movement can be maintained and defended indefinitely without grave difficulties. In the long term, the piecemeal approach, or the "issue by issue" approach, set in motion by mere economic-productive pressure without concerns of a greater significance and without theoretical rationalizations, may be seen as incapable of expressing the increasingly complex reality of a world of growing interdependence in the new "organic" era we are moving towards.[67] However, it is an historically established fact, and one daily confirmed by the everyday practice of U.S. union life, that the ideological "radicalism" and doctrinaire formulations—which are not lacking—have left no lasting traces in the American unions. Both the brilliant De Leon, in his *Socialist Trade and Labor Alliance*, and the Western Federation of Miners, which later took up again his attempt at a new socialist, ideologically orientated syndicalism, were without success. In 1905, in a famous meeting in Chicago, under the pressure of William D. (Big Bill) Haywood, the two branches of heterodox unionism were reunited so as to launch a new revolutionary union federation on the national scale, the Industrial Workers of the World,[68] but the attempt was already in decline before 1914. Apart from ideological schemes, the American unions were faithful to a collective bargaining solidly based on individual firms' situations.[69] Beyond purely wage-claiming unionism, the latter had attempted a permanent connection with production which often meant the thrusting of competition between capitalist products back on the same workers' groups themselves, with clear results of union atomism, the weakening—if not the disappearance—of class solidarity and unitary consciousness, and "job consciousness" as a necessary substitute.[70] Decentralization and fragmentation of the "level" of bargaining arose to the extent that the vast majority of American workers still today work on the basis of contracts negotiated and signed at the local, or enterprise level. Clearly, what may seem an excessive bargaining "localism" is in fact mediated by the fact that there are "pilot" industries and groups; that is, the contracts they propose, though they concern for the most a single enterprise or corporation, take on value as a point of comparative reference for other industries in the sector and therefore become pacesetters also for those contracts—still at the firm level—drawn up in less "advanced" situations. The general economic and structural conditions for this are clear: high mobility and polyvalence of labor power; a dynamic economy with fringes which allow for the development of the "more and more"; a basically balanced labor market; an interconnected unionism which strikes out in different ways and not doctrinally and acts as a productivist factor, not a retarding one. As regards European unionism, and especially Italian, still making wage claims in the generic sense, ever ready to look for an excuse in a situation of general freezing (for which it too, at least partially, is responsible), the American unions provide a lesson to be pondered.[71] The real problem of the American unions lies in their removing themselves from the inescapable contradictions of the "marketing union," which, as against the wage-claiming union, may in certain conditions represent a necessary, but not sufficient, step forward. Indeed, to overcome the closure and contradictions of corporationism, inter-corporate contacts are not enough, even if these are extended to a whole productive sector. There has to be an organic coordination which can be provided only by common goals, or a clearly *determined* activity, which moreover must know how to avoid the danger of ideological doctrine. In this sense, it is exact to note that the current union crisis which affects Europe and the United States and probably also other countries is not only caused by a lack of representativeness but also, and mainly, by a lack of power, and with this—when power exists as in the United States—a lack of objectives able to rise above and give direction to the bargaining process.[72] The question of coordination, which arises from the content of the ends in sight from which it comes, poses a specific problem in the sociology of organization which should be dealt with by itself with specific criteria.

Third, there is in collective bargaining a struggle for prerogatives, or for managerial prerogatives and their defense against their "erosion" by the unions on the part of managements, and for the expansion of the area of jurisdiction of bargaining on behalf of the unions. This aspect of collective bargaining has been especially studied by Chamberlain, who notes that issues and problems once considered as the exclusive concern of corporate management are now instead the field for discussion and negotiation between managers and workers' representatives. Chamberlain ends his survey by noting how "first of all, the authors of management prerogatives must explain to the unions, with arguments different from the simply juridical ones, why 'authority and freedom' should be the exclusive privilege of modern industrial managers. Secondly, and as a result, they must admit that the whole process of collective bargaining is undesirable as it limits 'authority and freedom' in industrial managers, or else they must explain how collective bargaining may be permitted in certain areas of corporate activity with no risk, but not in others."[73] Clearly, corporate managements tend to restrict the jurisdictional area of questions of routine administration and of immediate interest to the labor force (working hours, wages and salaries, conditions of employment) to prevent the unions breaking out, by refusing them any chance of discussion of questions directly concerning the productive and commercial policy of the corporations, investment plans, etc., which in conventional opinion, even though they touch very closely on the future of the labor force, lie beyond its competence. From this position there derives, to a great extent, the resistance to the unionist-manager.[74]

Finally, collective bargaining is a contract between organizations, homogeneous and exclusive. Homogeneity and mutual exclusiveness are the guarantee of bargaining power on the organizational level. In other words, the union is efficient and has effective power only if it is the *sole, exclusive* controller of *all* the labor power available on the market. In this context, the tenacity with which the clauses regarding the union shop and the closed shop are defended by the unions is made clear, even though now with the Taft-Hartley Act we are dealing with illegal practices, and one sees how and why the same Taft-Hartley Act with its subsequent "right to work laws," enacted in many of the states of the Union, represents a mortal threat to the unions. This specific aspect of collective bargaining poses problems which specifically involve the internal dynamics of the organization as such and evade both the ideological or doctrinal treatment as well as a summary of the historiographical kind. These only bring us back to the "sociological dimension" of the organization as a social phenomenon (which also thus demonstrates the uselessness of many therapeutic prescriptions) by re-emerging obstinately as a series of basic problems for any organizational structure, or by arising out of the public, private, or mixed institutional context in which the organization operates, as well as from the values or social aims which justify it. Not having solved, or still less faced, these in their own terms explains also the relative fruitlessness of the purely juridical perspective as regards social reforms (for example, nationalization in the United Kingdom, which to many seemed destined to have magical results) as well as the phenomenon of bureaucratic and police involution afflicting the countries of Eastern Europe and the USSR.

To conclude, unionism in the United States operates in the framework of a dynamic economy, a technically advanced one. For this reason, its problem lies in obtaining (normative) conditions of labor and indefinitely better wage levels, higher, more copiously accompanied by fringe benefits. Its motto is so simple as to appear deficient—*more and more*. Faced with the disappearance of simple manual labor and with the expansion of the service sector, the most urgent question before it is how to organize the swollen white collar strata, those who seem to possess the future and for whom on the other hand the traditional rhetoric of proletarian solidarity (solidarity forever) means little.

For those countries which find themselves in a position similar to that of Italy, the problem is different. Here, the union has always been hard-pressed by the need to find work for the unemployed rather than thinking of fighting to improve the position of those already employed. The three basic doctrinal interpretations of the labor movement (the Marxist, based on the premise of class consciousness; that of S. Perlman, which refers to "job consciousness," and lastly, the Webbs' notion)[75] should be continually related to individual, historically determined situations. To say that we are dealing respectively with left, right, and center interpretations would mean using crude parliamentary indicators which in modern conditions are no longer able to point to really well-distinguished prospects and contents and moreover run the risk of being seriously misleading. A particular policy which may in certain respects be "attached" to the right may in reality produce results at various lengths which are profoundly revolutionary and leftist, while a certain verbal leftism often acts as a cover—quite convenient, if not quite an alibi—for positions of basic immobility and indefinite conservatism. These same formulas of "class consciousness" and "job consciousness" are only understandable on the basis of the various data regarding specific socio-economic, political, and cultural contexts. It is on these that a conceptually well-directed sociology can throw light.

THE CORPORATION AS SOCIAL SYSTEM

The industrial corporation is one of the focal centers of modern sociological analysis. In developing societies, and in those industrially advanced, it is perhaps the most important. One might say that the very analysis of the capitalist and industrial system reached a higher critical and penetrative level when one went, with Marx and Weber, from the isolated individual of the first economists to the consideration of the productive unit organized as a whole. This central position of the corporation in sociological analysis arrived by way of a multiplicity of elements which ended up by defining it as the nerve center of the modern industrial society. As we have seen, first of all it was the natural point for the convergence of the activities of the historical actors in the process of industrialization. Furthermore, as a organization of productive activity as a function of the needs of the market it presented itself as the innovatory and stimulating element of societal dynamics itself.

It is hard to doubt that the industrial system is in modern society the dominant one, or that which tends to influence decisively the rhythm and mode of development of all others. The very physical presence of the industrial corporation is an element in the transformation of community institutions. It contributes to the break with the forms of traditional behavior, while we should not allow ourselves to elaborate light-mindedly to real inter-cultural generalizations, given the paucity of available comparative data. There is no aspect of community life which does not undergo a precise, identifiable influence from industrial organization.[76] However, this influence, it has been noted, is reciprocal. Apart from the corporate economic aspects, which most clearly reflect the structures and circumstances of societal economic development, every aspect of corporate life reflects the social and cultural conditions of the community in which it arose and developed. The observation as regards the constant, complex *interaction* between factory and community is pertinent, but does not fully explain the problem posed by the presence of large industrial corporations in modern society. Interaction does not take place according to a basically harmonious scheme of counter-balanced forces, as if it were an intrinsically ''constitutional'' system of checks and balances which by itself would guarantee mechanically and thus indefinitely through time a condition of social balance.

The Corporation as a Formally Codified Structure

As an organization of goods and people in terms of a productive goal, the industrial firm is above all a formally codified structure and a juridically defined reality. We have seen in dealing with the transition from the feudal to the modern world how capitalist and industrial enterprise took on their own shape on the basis of specific types of legal relations. On the one hand, there are those related to goods—that is, their concentration of property into the hands of the entrepreneur. On the other hand, there are those related to persons, that is, relations not of slavery or serfdom but rather contractual, based on the offer of labor power. We have further seen in dealing with the formation and function of entrepreneurship that property relations do not fully explain the nature of the industrial corporation, as beyond the capitalist form in a juridical sense the constant exercise of the organizational function of goods and people is required, or the daily flow of communications in the light of the productive goal.

At the outset, the capitalist was the same as the firm manager. There was then the form of entrepreneur seen as "classic." Later, with the growth in the volume of business, the multiplication of production due to technical innovation and increasing mechanical complexity, and the increase of the work force employed, the entrepreneur ended up by losing contact and direct control of the firm he owned. Increasingly his functions were reduced to those of accounting and a subsequent withdrawal from direct technical supervision and supervision of personnel. Industry and business began to become distinct. In Veblen's epigrammatic phrase, the "captain of industry" became the "captain of solvency."[77] This change helped to produce the rise of big industry and the dominance of the joint-stock company. The circumstances which produced these phenomena are many and too complex to be here developed in detail. However, beyond them there was a very precise need: that of the orderly control of an ever-increasing industrial production which indiscriminate production at the outset had transformed into a considerable financial danger. In other words, there was a need to reduce competition and limit production by relating it not to the productive capacity of the industrial system but rather to the capacity on the part of the market to consume it.

From about 1890 to the First World War, monopolistic concentration managed efficiently to face up to indiscriminate competition by resolving the huge potential for production of goods permitted by technological innovations simply to the benefit of profit. However, monopoly concentration was not only "horizontal" but "vertical," too, that is, it developed along a double line—as the convergence of small firms into a broader, complex "general company," and as a concentration of the various phases of the turning of raw materials into a finished product.

This concentration aided the two basic aspects which mark the formal structures of contemporary industrial organization. On the one hand, this required the rise of an industrial bureaucracy, that is, a differentiated group of technicians and clerical workers who, under the direction of the professional plant manager, could undertake the responsibilities of supervising the productive process, supply of raw materials, maintenance of machinery, management of staff and promotion, sale, and distribution of the finished product. On the other hand, this very concentration made the finding of the considerable capital required harder. Already at the start, a good part of the "captain of industry's" investments had been basically family capital. Indeed, the family was the prime source of the initial capital and of the close associates of the "captain." The extended family, as a clan, provided a broad possibility for choice of manpower proficient in the various aspects of industrial production. In any case, when manpower was lacking, the development of the firm was set back. The enterprise was thus wholly owned by the family group, which was its only source of power. Indeed, in the management structure, there were rarely to be found people from outside the family. However, with the decline of the extended family and the intensification of specialization in entrepreneurial and management tasks, recruitment of management personnel from people linked by family relationships became increasingly difficult. Thus there was an attempt, through the institution of dynastic marriage,[78] to preserve the inalienability of the family entrepreneurial patrimony, and by involving outsiders in family circles, to maintain absolute power in management of the firm. However, these attempts did not always assist the competitiveness of the enterprise and its very economic survival.

Following the numerous economic crises between 1880 and 1914, due mainly to the imbalance between accelerated productive development and the slow expansion of the market, reorganization of the firms, with the concentration here remarked upon, was undertaken by the world of finance and banking. Family heritages were saved only on condition of diversifying their investment portfolio and rejecting through the joint-stock (limited) company the total possession of the family fortune in a single firm. The captain of industry, it was said, became a captain of finance, and family fortunes were no longer tied to a single industrial enterprise but rather to financial institutions.

With the intervention of bank and credit capital the formula of the limited company became typical and widespread. The risks connected with industrial investment diminished, and it was easier to gather together on the financial market the considerable capital needed by big industry. The juridical personality of the enterprise assured it of a continuity over and above the men who managed it and those who were co-owners. Thus the industrial enterprise became an institution endowed with relative autonomy. Thanks to its central position as regards the entire societal economic system, it took on a more public than private aspect, more one of community interest than one tied to the interest of a single family, even though remaining juridically defined as a "private residence."

With the transformation of the juridical relations concerned with the organization of goods, the very concept of property changed. The patrimonial autonomy of companies and the basic attribute of the share, not so much as a real property right as rather a right to the income produced by an autonomously constituted patrimony, had little in common with the traditional concept of property (*Jus utendi et abutendi*), which had its most typical resemblance in landed property. On the other hand, the arrival of the professional manager and industrial bureaucracy helped to change the profile of the organization of the *persons*, and thus that of the relations between capital and labor. Marx had already noted that the setting up of limited companies led to the dissociation of owners and producers. Among the latter now the corporate managers were to be counted. Marx, however, had not foreseen that with the fragmentation of shareholding participation, the elasticity of the share market, and above all the possibility of company self-financing one would have arrived at a still clearer divorce between ownership and control, extending excessively the decision-making power of the managers, who, rather than moving forward the—by definition—subaltern position of the workers, appear increasingly as the real holders of corporate power.[79]

Industrial bureaucracy came to satisfy the two basic characteristics on which modern industry is based: the rational planning of the productive process, and the coordination of the specialization of responsibilities brought in by industrial technology. To the need for iron discipline required by manufacturing and industry at the beginning there was later added the need for a planned coordination of the increasingly complex division of productive responsibilities in the firm. This first need was confronted by the paternalistic and authoritarian "boss," with his hierarchical organization based on criteria borrowed from the military. The second need was confronted by the professional manager with a hierarchical-functional organization, which F. W. Taylor had put forward as the only one able to oversee the complex web of the new forms of industrial production.

With the hierarchical functional type of organization, there was explicit recognition of the role of the experts, the so-called staff, as against that of those employees being managed, the so-called line. This differentiation of management roles which marks the corporate organigram that is, the definition of relations of equivalence, super-, and subordination which link the various positions in the corporate organization) end up by dividing the adoption of decisions by ability and by specific technical knowledge. In other words, it ends up by differentiating the power of the bureaucrats from that of the technocrats. The former is legitimated by the needs of disciplined coordination of jobs and the latter by the needs imposed by the technological and economic structures.[80] However, here we are faced with a process of great interest. While the decision-making power of the technocrats in practice is systematically subordinated to that of the bureaucrats, the latter is forever less restricted by the juridical bonds which at least theoretically regulate the relations between the corporate administrative structure and the property form of the enterprise. In other words, contrary to many people's expectations, entrepreneurial decision-making power, separated from and increasingly less restrained by the tie and authority of ownership, not only does not appear to be in the hands who claim this capacity in strictly technico-functional terms, but tends to become the property of those who wield it on the basis of merely organizational imperatives. Indeed, in the modern industrial corporation, decision-making power is given not so much on the basis of criteria of the technical division of labor (abilities defined according to the common productive process), but rather on the basis of criteria of "imperative coordination" (requirements defined so as to operate with discretionary power). Weber's insight, that the crucial aspect of the modern industrial corporation was really to be found not so much in the technical as in the organizational process, is still valid and appears today still more

important after the changes which have occurred in the system of capitalist enterprise and the rise of state enterprise.

The fact that corporate power is not allotted on the basis of a technical
division of responsibilities but rather on the basis of organization imperatives clarifies the inherent manipulatory reality of the company and
the ineliminable contrast between superiors and subordinates. Not only
this, it makes clear the problematic element of workers' participation
in corporate power, that is, the taking of *important* decisions concerning
the life of the firm. Indeed, if giving and obeying orders were a function
of strictly technical imperatives, and authority were based on the recognition of technical qualifications and knowledge, the distinction between the manager and the worker would remain on the level of a mere
division of responsibilities to which there correspond different *technical
roles*. In this case, the problem of participation would not even be
posed, as it is intrinsically incompatible with the technicist criterion of
the distinction between responsibilities. However, if corporate differentiation and the allotment of powers is not a function of the respective
technical roles but rather of *organizational roles*, then the right to
participate in this power, invoked on the basis of the societal value of
"democracy" may seem obvious. That is, just as it is unthinkable that
it is possible to participate in the decision of a technician without having
his competence, and thus an equivalent role, so, in the light of democratic tradition and values, it seems unthinkable that organizational
decisions be taken without those who are the object of them participating
in them.

If the corporation were simply a technical reality and company power
simply power over *things*, related, that is, to the administration of goods,
to talk of corporate participation and industrial democracy would have
no meaning. However, once one realizes that the corporation is a social
reality and corporate power essentially power over the men who form
part of it, related, that is, to the administration of *persons*, then the
problem of participating in this power by defining the social role of
those who, on the basis of their technical role, already "participate"
in the life of the firm, becomes one of crucial importance.

In the reality of corporate life, to distinguish between merely technical
decisions and organizational ones, those involving things and those
involving human beings, is difficult and often impossible. As we shall
see further on, the technological environment and social structure in
the corporation are so closely connected that there is no technical de-

cision which does not affect the vast range of organizational and human problems. On the other hand, the technical roles are highly differentiated at all levels of the corporate structure so that a technical decision has meaning only if placed in relation to the diversification of tasks which the various professional groups are called upon to discharge on the basis of the common end. Technical and organizational decisions, in the short or long term, affect these different professional groups differently, producing conflicting motivations and interests. By superimposing those on the structural conditions for the exercise of corporate power, these differences make the practical enforcement of the "right" to corporate participation difficult, and obscure its basic terms.

One must thus clearly distinguish the subjects and the forms of this participation. First, there is the problem of participation through representation in the institutional centers of power of the corporate structure, whose most typical forms are to be found in the experiments in co-management and joint consultation (*Mitbestimmung*). Examples of these institutionalized forms of participation in the formation of corporate policies and high-level decision-making are the "comités d'entreprises" set up in France in 1945 and modified in 1950, the "Betriebsraete" created in Germany by law in 1951 and 1952, and the English "joint councils" which existed in England after the end of the last war. However important, these experiments showed the ineliminable limits of participation through representation. In general, these forms of participation leave the majority of employees indifferent. Once the choice of their representatives has been made, they do not in fact feel part of the decision-making process. Those elected to the joint, or mixed (bosses and workers) organs do not manage to avoid the conflict of responsibilities which their dual position as representatives of the subordinates and wielders of decision-making power involves. By the very nature of the technological industrial process, decisions taken by *representatives* charged with long-term economic responsibilities are often unable to win the consensus of those *represented*, who are exposed to the direct consequences of the policies planned. Faced with this conflict of roles, the representatives of the employees often take on so-called employers attitudes, or, when insisting on the workers' position, thus stall the joint organism by standing firm on intransigent political lines which might also threaten the very economic survival of the enterprise and ultimately imply a reform of the economic political and social (cultural) system as a whole, or as totality.

For this last reason, these joint organs end up by restricting their own decision-making sphere to the aspects which are not strictly corporate and economico-productive, such as accident prevention, health and recreational, and generally social policies. The unions themselves are not averse to this solution, in that they are afraid of losing their prerogatives of bargaining for economic (wage) conditions and those of work (normative) to the representative, joint organisms. If on the other hand, the union were to be involved in the joint formulation of corporate policies, it would risk losing its function as "claimant." This would distance it from the working mass, which, by daily submitting to industrial technico-organizational reality, would certainly not stop protesting against its frustrating conditions.[81]

On the other hand, however important participation may be in the working-out of corporate policies, it is undoubtedly of little value if thereafter there is no participation in the execution of those policies at all levels of the corporate structure. This is the problem of the *direct* participation of the subordinates in decision making in the course of management routine. This participation can rarely be institutionalized and thereby resolved in various ways with empirical expedients. These efforts and their theoretical expression lie in the human relations systems as they have developed in recent years in the United States. However, precisely for this reason one often is dealing with a "management device" as a function which is often purely productive and basically manipulatory. Once the intrinsically autocratic reality of the industrial corporation has been discovered, North American managers are not slow to note that, in accepting it (participation), it was necessary still more to limit its negative effects on productivity and dilute its substance through the cultural forms of their societal "democracy."[82]

This awareness and the applied aspects which followed began with the research of the school of social psychology of Kurt Lewin, so-called group dynamics.[83] Of particular importance was that concerning group behavior as a function of autocratic-style management and of the permissive and democratic kinds. The discovery that the democratic type of management could be efficient and at the same time lower the level of group tension and raise its morale[84] started off a complex series of investigations into the kind of supervision exercised by low-level management. It turned out, in the light of empirical data, that the employee-oriented foremen, rather than the production-oriented ones, were basically those whose teams were most productive,[85] that the autonomous group decisions favored high productivity,[86] and that if it was desired to introduce changes in the organization of the technico-productive process without arousing fears and resistance on the part of the employees, it was necessary to anticipate their reactions and solicit their approval.[87] From these studies by Lewin, Lippitt, Kahn and Katz, Bavelas, Coch and French, now classics in their field, the usefulness of the participation by employees in the decisions which concerned them became evident.[88] In particular it was said that participation properly used in the right conditions can be an effective means for allowing employees to satisfy their own egotistical needs, and to motivate the employees to improve their working activity and increase productivity.

We are therefore not dealing with a right to participate in corporate organizational decisions on the basis of the technical role performed for the ends of the common enterprise. That is, it is not an end dictated by an essential and existential condition of the worker in the company, but rather a means derived from a productivist end whose teleological value is a "datum" beyond discussion. However, also as a means, participation must be "properly used." This correct use consists not in making the action to be taken jointly decided by their (the subordinates') own premises, but rather to explain to them and make them accept the decision already taken by their superior as correct and reasonable. At best, the superior gathers suggestions from his subordinates regarding the advantages and disadvantages of the different alternative decisions among which it will be his exclusive prerogative to make a choice.[89]

The Corporation as a System of Machines and Technical Reality

It is the technological apparatus of modern industry that is the corporate aspect which most directly strikes the imagination. From the first upsurge of the industrial phenomenon, intellectual analysis—especially in a century which mythologized mechanical progress, and thence a hopeful resolution of many problems—saw in the phenomenon of industrial mechanization the key element of the new forms of economic production. Whatever the historical judgment regarding the role played by mechanization in the evolution of the capitalist industrial firm, it is beyond doubt that in the modern corporation technological structure has a basic position. There is no aspect of the organization of the productive process, from that of the administrative-financial to that of prestige in informal organization (to mention two of the most disparate corporate features), which does not undergo a modification—often decisive—from the technological structure.

The most direct and crucial effect is that which the technological apparatus exercises on the technical division of labor and thus on the professional corporate structure. With the introduction of flexible machines, that is, with machines using instruments similar to those used by man, the traditional artisan structure underwent a basic change. The artisan who worked with hand tools was a specialist in terms of the product of his labor. As the instruments he used were rarely specialized, the skill lay in his job and personal abilities rather than in the type of labor performed. Professional hierarchy was partly based on experience and seniority in the trade, which often determined the gradual initiation into professional secrets, and partly on his talents and personal skill. Apprenticeship was long and required the digestion of knowledge of the trade to which a cultural education was conjoined. With the introduction of machines the professional ability tended to pass from the man to the machine. In those same artisan workshops the specialist and the specialized began to become distinct—the former, who still knew all the trade secrets which led up to the creation of the finished product, delegated responsibilities to the "specialized" and coordinated their activities. The latter were masters of specific skills which were defined as professional qualifications only insofar as they were linked to the use of one or more machines. Apprenticeship was still long and directed towards a general technical qualification, but the craft was no longer unitary as regards the product, and the technical role no longer managed to coincide with the social role in a clear way. The person specialized in work on the lathe had no social position—a status and role in his community—in the way the carpenter did.

In manufacture, machines were the essential condition for concentration into the "factory." However, in this first phase, the machines were still polyvalent and flexible. They were prepared for a huge, variegated series of operations. With a good lathe one can do many things, and even some finished products. However, one must know how to "set it up," know the cutting rate, evaluate it in terms of the material and quality of the tools, estimate the play and confines of the acceptable calibration, etc. Indeed, one must be qualified on that machine through an often long and difficult apprenticeship. Thus we have the industrial craft, which once learned is an inalienable "art" of the individual and a capital of future professional security. One may change "boss," city, or industry with relative tranquility, as one has a trade, one is still a professional.

However, the trade declined as soon as the flexible, polyvalent machines were replaced by special ones, those built solely for a given operation on a specific product. The replacement by special machines of the universal ones, as we have seen, took place as a result of production line working according to the dictates of the scientific organization of labor. The interchangeability of parts making up a finished product was in this regard the decisive technical aspect. Later, transfer technology, like convectors, the belt, the turntable, which permitted the use of increasingly large volumes of production produced by line production, pushed it to extremes and diffused it. So as to obtain a swifter mass production process, flexible machines were at first used for a specific purpose and used for uniform production and then finally replaced by special machines which were built for a specific type of work on a given product.

Thus, for example, as against the old-fashioned turner who "could do everything with the lathe," there then arose specialized operatives who worked on special lathes, performing a few operations in predetermined periods of time. This special lathe was often no longer called a "lathe." It was a machine, like the others, and the worker working at it was not a lathe-operator/turner but rather a machine operative. The total ignorance regarding the machine on which he worked was the result of the subdivision of productive activity and the specialization of tasks. Without apprenticeship anymore, trained in a few days and then in a few hours, the specialized operative (or common worker, as he was generally called) was not required—indeed, was discouraged—to know how to set up the machine, how to maintain and repair it, how it worked. The relation between himself and the machine was a mechanical one, not technical; he did not use the machine because he did not even know how to "use it"; he made it work for a purpose which others—the technical officers—knew. It was the machine which required his presence, and did this in a mechanical way, in a relation more or less between equals.

Thus, from technical qualification we have moved on to mechanical specialization. The results of this transformation in the structure of professional abilities are many. First of all, the impoverishment of professional skills, now reduced to the precision and automatic character of gestures, created a reason for deep dissatisfaction at work and tended to stimulate the atrophy of intellectual qualities and a sense of inner hollowness. The repetitive and fragmented work to a determined rhythm both individual and collective, by being depersonalized, produced boredom and disinterest and gave rise to forms of exhaustion more dangerous than the merely physical kind. We are dealing with industrial sadness, made up of neurosis and disquiet. The very separation of the physical series of gestures from the mental series of ideas and images, required by this type of repetitive and fragmentary work, fed this disquiet by permitting daydreaming and reverie. At times this mental sequence of ideas and images was set in motion by conversation, when the noise and physical arrangement of working places allowed it. In these instances, the life of the work group finished up by being the sole satisfaction the worker had at his work place.

The system of subdivided labor furthermore created blockages in corporate vertical mobility. Though the move from worker's to white collar qualifications was always rare, the extreme technical division of fragmentary labor was not even favorable to the internal mobility of qualified workers. It does not seem that there can be a worker's "career" where there even lacks the shadow of an apprenticeship and where work is fragmented and timed.[90] Those who have dreams of success, perhaps nurtured by societal stereotypes, have to give them up quickly. The hope for the future is at most that of changing profession—of getting away from the line.[91] The company job structure, in this phase of the development of machine industry, is remarkably rigid and marked at lower levels by hierarchies based not on ability and professional skill but on the mechanical functioning of the man–machine relation. From disciple to laborer, from the worker to the operative; even skill and professional capacity are together disappearing.[92] Now, for the loss of the craft, marked by a relative security for the future, the replacement is the awareness of having only a "job" with all its related insecurity, both economic and psychological, which derives therefrom. There is no longer a concomitant of knowledge and skills to be transferred from one place to another, to bargain with knowledge of the same case, to pass on to someone, to use, even with one's own capital. One is at the mercy of a wholly impersonal labor market in which personal abilities have no great, decisive value. Trained in a few days by a particular firm, one can be replaced by it in the same time, and meanwhile one has not gained an experience which can be used elsewhere, for other concerns. In these conditions only the monopoly over supply of labor can provide a limit to the complete arbitrary power of the employer.

The evolution of the industrial mechanism and its results on professional roles, qualifications, and class consciousness does not stop with special machines. A new phase has already begun, which marks a form of accelerated mechanization: automation.[93] Only in certain cases were specialized machines similar to universal ones, different solely through the fact of having been built for a specific purpose. Rather, one was normally dealing with more complex machines which combined the principles and forms of different machines for a specific product. The operative was partly responsible for the functioning of the machine and partly for its loading and discharge. This "attendance" on the machine is a mechanical relation, clearly and precisely predetermined as regards movement and time. To replace even this human element—which had by then very little of the human, who had only to perform a few, simple judgments regarding choices often already taken for granted and foreseen—the passage was a small one. The servo-mechanisms replaced men's hands in making the machine work, while an electronic interpreter (generally known as the controller) replaced his brain. Certainly there is also a need for feedback circuits and devices and a series of planned information and specifications which allow the controller to direct the servo-mechanisms, that is, to develop a brain–hand coordination. Ultimately, through other servo-mechanisms, which supervise loading and unloading, the machine is linked with another used in the same way. Thus we have what is generally called a machine transfer, that is, a group of several specialized machines operated, loaded, and unloaded in a continual process corresponding to a cycle of the manufacture (through this transfer) of the product. When one adds to machine transfer the electromechanical devices for quality control, automatic mechanisms for accounting and inventory, and automatic maintenance devices which point to possible faults and furthermore look after normal lubrication, we have an "automated" complex. Man seems to have been forgotten. In reality, the workers, though in reduced number, are not only present but also on a different level see the function of the intellectual abilities and professional skills re-evaluated. With automation, fragmented and repetitive, timed tasks disappear. The machine no longer determines the rhythm and intensity of human labor, which instead basically becomes one of supervision. The responsibilities for the checking, maintenance, and repair of automated machinery come to be the new workers' jobs, with high responsibility and technical specialization. There are barriers to be removed, difficulties to overcome, but there is then the possibility of expressing one's own intellectual abilities with a subsequent greater professional and working satisfaction. Technical specialization tends again to appear as a trade, by virtue of the theoretical knowledge which now must go together with personal skill and experience. Apprenticeship, no longer to be estimated in terms of length, again involves a joint cultural and technical formation and becomes once more analogous to that of the artisan.

As human working activity is only indirectly connected with production, if we except the transitional phase, it is a function of the whole productive system. The technical and the organization roles tend to coincide. Indeed, as the contribution to the productive enterprise can no longer be evaluated in terms of the results of technical activity (there being absent a direct connection man–machine–production), professional qualification is no longer the product either of technical competence, as it was in the first phase of the industrial revolution, or of mechanical skill, as in the second, but rather of technico-organizational responsibilities. In other words, the quality of human labor and professional qualification becomes now capable of evaluation only in relation to the organizational system whereby the corporation coordinates the technical, automated whole.

The passage from the man–machine relation to that of the man–corporation basically modifies corporation social relations. Reactions on group relations at work are still scarcely predictable, but an empirical study of a highly automated auto plant in Detroit brought out a substantial fall in the possibilities for social interaction as regards what occurred in the traditional auto plant.[94] Informal social relations only took place within small groups, and even in these the identification of individual workers with the work group was of lesser intensity and sometimes nonexistent.

In conditions of total automation, in some cases there will not even be the possibility of forming work groups because of the need for individual jobs spread out and distant from each other. The informal organization of the employees, in the light of the first studies in this respect, seems to have lost the importance it had till now in the corporation equipped with pre-automated technology. On the other hand, in the automated plant there seems to emerge an increasingly close relation between the operative and the planning technician. Supervision is further made more frequent and direct and intense. Discipline itself can now be better ensured thanks to the very techniques of production which end up by producing a rigid social structure in the heart of the corporation. Research on corporate mobility in these conditions is still lacking, and it is clearly not fair to anticipate their conclusions, but everything makes one think that once we arrive at the re-qualification of the working-class mass as white collar operatives, from the start, in a completely automated corporation, there will not be granted much chance of a career. The rigidity of the corporate professional and organization structure together with the most intense, frequent supervision and discipline will challenge ever more strongly the sources of legitimacy of corporate power. The very fact that professional qualification lies in organizational responsibility rather than in technical capacity, in the organizational role rather than in the technical, makes it foreseeable that the problem of a working-class, non-manipulated, and non-convenient participation would have a basic priority in union claims and a remarkable impact on laborers' motivation and expectations. When later one generally introduces automation in the various industrial sectors and in companies, given the need to reduce the risk of economic fluctuations to the minimum—a risk that production will no longer be able to absorb by adjusting itself to them—and further, give the need of capital investment and constant employment levels in relation to a market which should be highly predictable and expanding—it would not seem improbable that the problem of coporate power in relation to societal economic power and political power should come to present itself as a basic one. From its solution there depends the future—the meaning or the involution, stagnation and ultimately the fatal contradiction, of industrial societies.

The Corporation as Social System and Real Community

The corporation is thus before everything else a juridical reality, economic and organizational. It shows itself as a formally codified structure of service, sections, offices and positions. Every corporate organ is defined in its responsibilities and tasks, power and authority, by the corporate organigram. This organizational structure, officially defined and codified, represents from the sociological point of view the formal organization, which I shall define with Barnard as "a system of consciously coordinated activities by one or more persons.''[95] This is essentially impersonal and characterized by abstractly codified reciprocal relations, in the sense that the social context is not specifically defined. We have earlier pointed to the development of this formal organization in relation to the demands produced by the evolution of the industrial enterprise, by emphasizing the basic aspects of corporate bureaucracy, and especially the hierarchical-functional relations, or those of staff and line.

At the directly productive level, formal organization and technological structure determine interpersonal relations and group relations which oversee the coordination of working activity. However, alongside those formal relations other social, spontaneous relations arise and develop. These relations, not envisaged by the explicit organigram and not required by needs tied to technological structures, are informal relations. Men at work joke, talk, express opinions and judgments, are friends and enemies, as anywhere else. This can only appear natural to us, and yet one must ask if these spontaneous relations are such as to make up a network of sufficiently stable and organized relations as thereby to influence those required by the organization. The answer to this question—not posed, as it is forgotten in a narrow Taylorist and physio-psychological view of the corporation—arose from the failure of a series of experiments in physiology and industrial psychology which a group first of engineers and later of psychologists carried out between 1924 and 1943 in the Hawthorne works of the Western Electric Company.[96]

The experiment, planned and conducted by the engineers of Western Electric, concerned the effect of the intensity of illumination on individual and group productivity. It involved a carefully planned experiment with rigorous controls over the multiple environmental variables in the work place. There were two groups of women workers, a control group and the experimental group. The working hypothesis assumed a rise in group productivity with the intensification of lighting. This hypothesis was supported in the experimental group, in that its productivity indeed increased with the intensity of the lighting. However, extraordinarily, the control group too showed an increased productivity of the same proportion of that of the experimental group, although the lighting remained constant. Not only this, but following the traditional canons of experimentation, when the lighting of the experimental group was lowered while that of the control group stayed the same, productivity, instead of staying the same in the latter and falling in the former, increased in both. Clearly an unknown variable was working unchecked.

The Graduate School of Business Administration at Harvard then planned another controlled experiment so as to examine such other variables as the coffee break, hot meals, working hours, etc. On the other hand, factors such as temperature, humidity, the hours of sleep of individual workers, external atmospheric conditions, and physical and health conditions were accurately controlled with a precise, rigorous record. All seemed ready to manage to identify the mysterious factor which made the first experiment of the engineers fail. This new experiment, directed by doctors, psychologists, and economists is known in the publicity of industrial society as the Relay Assembly Test Room.

The results of the experiment, which lasted five years, were discouraging and surprising: none of the variables, minutely checked, seems responsible for increase in productivity. The latter, at any time of the experiment, tended to rise and remain at a certain level whatever the type and strength of variation in the variables checked. Working hours, pay, and all the various psychological, physiological, and environmental variables did not appear logically associated with productivity. New hypotheses were thus required, and fortunately in the course of the experiment Elton Mayo was associated with the group of investigators. A doctor, psychologist, and teacher of "social logic" at Queensland University, Australia, Mayo had the insight, already touched on in an earlier experiment, that the social environment or work must be the real culprit for the distortion found in the relations among the variables examined. In fact, he stated as his hypothesis, that up till then the investigators had not studied the relation between fatigue, monotony, lighting, working hours, etc., and group productivity, but had rather created a new social working environment. The fact of being the object of an experiment, and thus of special attention for five years, had stimulated in the six workers a group attitude which in post-experimental terms was then called "high morale."

The material gathered was re-examined in the light of this new hypothesis and it was then discovered that the group of six workers was not only a numerical but a social group. They had a direction, norms of behavior, a communications system, and a structure of positions with status and roles. Always in retrospect, one discovered that the failure of the first experiment concerning lighting was due to this: during the meal break the members of the experimental and the control groups ate together and passed on information, opinions, and above all mutually "motivated themselves." The control group was thus linked through a system of informal communications to the experimental one, with which it formed a single informal group.

However, in order to arrive at this complete sociological vision of the working environment, other experiments and above all a huge investigation with open-ended, controlled interviews was needed. Among the experiments, that of the Bank wiring observation room is regarded as the most important. (This room was a special sector of the Hawthorn Works in which cables were produced.) At this time, the investigators, aware of the problem, devoted especial attention to social aspects and the search for the "informal group structure." In the observation room there were nine wirers, four solderers, and two inspectors. After a time it became clear to the investigators that apart from the relations dictated by the organization and technology, those workers had developed a network of reciprocal relations, many of which seemed stably structured. It was possible to identify two subgroups which demonstrated forms of leadership, communications systems and role, status and role structures, norms of behavior.

The informal life of the company organization thus seemed also carefully structured according to the same criteria which underlay that officially codified in the organigram. However, it should be noted that the distinction between formal and informal organization is an heuristic, basically analytical one. Formal organization itself cannot be said to be wholly covered by the codification of the explicit organigram and job classification. Innumerable relations, wholly formal, are not consciously described and codified, although they arise, and have a function, solely in view of the aim of the productive organization. On the other hand, many informal relations, at the level both of the employee and of the worker, are really directly functional for the good running of the formal organizations.[97] Further, one cannot strictly speak of the informal organization in the same sense as the formal. The latter, indeed, is an organic, conscious coordination of corporate activity as a whole and in all its complexity, while the former is limited to groups of employees with little inter-group coordination. In other words, considering both formal and informal organization as the total of small units which comprise the work groups (and office groups), the distinction between formal and informal organization lies in the fact that the first is structured in its inter- and intra-group relations, while the second is only structured in intra-group relations.[98] It would thus be more suitable to speak of the informal group life which is overlaid on the formal one as defined by codified organizational relations and those required by technology.

The function of the informal group is still an open question.[99] Some corporate managements see in it an aspect of the "natural idleness of the workers," their intolerance of discipline and tendency not to co-operate with corporate management. Others see in it the natural result of innate human sociality. The unions interpret it as a palliative in the absence of the assured protection of union organization, and at any rate as the spontaneous expression of the need the workers have of defending themselves against the arbitrariness of management power. Psychologists tend to emphasize its necessity as a function of the general expression of feelings in the emotional life of the workers. The sociologists see it as a function of formal organization and technological structure. We are not necessarily dealing with alternative interpretations.

Sociologically, the informal group arises as a protest—often unconscious—against the impersonality and rationality of modern industrial organization. However, it is born as a function of the personality of the laborer as well as his role. It is a protest formulated by way of the natural channels of human sociality, and we can say that it departs from a stimulus of intolerance of corporate discipline and the constriction of current man–machine relations. In short, it is a protest and attempt at defense which derives from needs of the personality and presents itself in the face of the corporate system as it is structured overall. To use a formula perhaps too psychologistic, organization tends to frustrate the individual and place him in conflictual situations.[100] The unity of management, the specialization of tasks, and the power and authority relations which mark formal corporate organization demand dependency, passivity, and supine subordination of the member of the organization. Spontaneous association at work is a reaction to this industrial bureaucracy and its formal rationality, basically irrational. Faced with this, the worker perceives the discrepancy between his own technical role and the organizational role, his position in the company and his aspirations. Clearly, the more one descends through the levels of formal organization, the more this gap and the frustration which derives from it are sharpened by the increasingly less tolerable conditions imposed by technological structures.

The informal work group provides the individual with the occasion for acknowledgment of a status and role which the formal organization cannot adequately define. Indeed, the informal group provides the worker *autonomously*—by removing himself from the power of management, felt to be pervasive—to alter the formal definition of group roles and status. Though often unconscious, this claim for autonomy is plain and defines the relation between subordinates and superiors. The instance of the attribution of a very low informal status, just by being esteemed by the shift boss or foreman, is not uncommon.

This desire to protest against organizational rationalization and defend oneself against the frustrating conditions of the modern technological process becomes apparent in the norms of behavior the informal group develops, and to which it requires the greatest conformity at the risk of ostracism, ridicule, and at times violence. Already in the first Hawthorne studies at Western Electric four basic norms which systematically reappear in the formation and life of informal groups can be identified[101]:

1. not working too hard; if you do, you are a rate-buster
2. not working too little; if you do, you are a chiseler
3. not to report anything that may be harmful to a workmate to the boss; if you do, you are a squealer
4. not trying to maintain distance and act officiously; if you are an inspector, do not act like one

This is a defensive code, above all of defense against incentives of an individual kind which corporate management introduces so as to increase productivity. It is a code which allows relations between workmates which are relaxed and friendly, promoting a solidarity whose origin lies in the shared condition. The limitation of productivity may also be seen by the workers themselves as the attempt to "get even" with the company, not to let themselves be "exploited" by management, to guarantee one's own or one's fellow's job, but as *social practice* it functions latently as a reaffirmation of informal group loyalty and productive autonomy in regard to the corporate organizational system.[102]

However, even if clearly a protest and anti-management, the informal work group can also be a source of job satisfaction, thereby stimulating high morale and ultimately higher productivity. Yet this is not always the case. It is, however, well founded to believe that often a protest of this kind is open to co-option and may be won over to the complete advantage of the corporate organization. The recovery action has been attempted through a wholly management interpretation of the systems and practices of "human relations in industry." This is not the place to go into the problematic which concerns them, and which in part belongs to the history of industrial management ideologies and partly to sociological deontology. Rather, I shall point to the problem of job satisfaction, in which there are focused a multiplicity of aspects relevant to the corporation as social system.

At many points dealing with the corporation as a formally codified structure and system of machines, we have emphasized the frustrating aspects of the rational organization of the industrial productive process and its technology. Making use only of one's own working capacity, now reduced from craft skill to a simple mechanical dexterity, the modern industrial worker feels deeply insecure and dissatisfied. Alienated by the objective conditions of the modern productive structure, in that it has been made impossible to control the labor–wage relation adequately, to give meaning to his own working activity, and to rediscover on the basis of his own productive role a social one in the broader community, he attempts to find a defense and compensating satisfaction in the informal life of the group, which always runs parallel to the forms of organized, union protest. However, the dissatisfaction remains and appears at the company level in the form of absenteeism, rotation of personnel, sabotage, and wildcat strikes.

Dissatisfaction involves almost all aspects of working life, but the importance these have on the scale of priorities of the industrial worker does not reflect the economic assumptions of traditional company management. The research carried out since 1930 has shown that concern over the wage level, if still understandably important, is not the one which mostly bothers the worker.[103] Even before a high wage, the worker wants job security for the future. The worker's attitude towards arbitrary firing and denial of rights of seniority is always one of intransigence and a fight without compromise. Awareness of the job and its scarcity is the most vital stimulus to the tendency of workers to associate together and their desire for struggle. The reason cannot but be obvious from what I have said: the modern conditions for the exercise of the technical role, stripped of all professional character, and thus of the security which is its own by rights, linked to the evolution of industrial machinery which increasingly replaces human skills, are a constant source of dissatisfaction for the present and insecurity regarding the future. On the other hand, the organizational role, which leaves to management the prerogatives of decision over the possibilities and forms of employment and career, is perceived as an unsatisfying definition of the real contribution to the common productive undertaking.

Linked to these concerns of the industrial worker for his organizational role are attitudes related to the recognition of his status, his relation with the company, the appreciation of his work, the nature and styles of command, the possibility of expressing one's own opinion and making suggestions, the need for being informed about internal company policies which directly involve him, and possibilities for transfers and promotions.[104] In this regard, one should stress that the more the technical role is deprived of meaning and interest by technological development, the more crucial the organizational aspects become in the evaluation and meaning of working activity on the part of the modern worker. The typically Taylorist conception of labor as an essentially instrumental fact finds no effective point of correspondence in workers' attitudes. It does not in fact seem that one may state, after half a century of empirical research in this regard,[105] that once a fair wage is ensured for the worker he will prefer "not to think," accepting his own condition at work as a necessary evil, the price he must pay in order to gain in life outside the company the "true satisfaction" which a consumeristic economy or an affluent society can offer him.[106]

THE SIGNIFICANCE AND PROBABLE DEVELOPMENTS IN MAJOR ENTERPRISES

The last part of this essay more directly reflects personal experiences and insights, working hypotheses, which have yet to be tested and thus have not been critically placed on the theoretical field. They are connected with the purpose of understanding and explaining the structure of power and the prevailing means of exercising it in a society which seems involved in a process of development or which is departing—it does not matter by what paths—from the peasant world, or that of passive acceptance of history as an external, "imported" fact, and which on the other hand tends to approach a model of urban-industrial society, basically marked by rational calculation and the functional division of labor. The enterprise appears very complex for two levels of reasons. First, as there are currently underway qualitative movements of power, these make analytical identification objectively difficult. Second, power in industrial society at all levels (political, administrative, economico-corporative) tends to be depersonalized formally, yet it is able to develop to the highest degree the ability to conceal itself—*deus absconditus*. It is certain that as regards the problem of power in industrial societies, their structural characteristics and the decisive factors which underlie their attitudes and decisions, we find ourselves lamentably underinformed. What we do know is that in industrializing societies, with greater or lesser swiftness, the *locus* of real power is highly mobile, basically ambiguous, and essentially irresponsible in the sense that the rationality it is based on is a formal, procedural, not substantial, one. That in a state of this kind there should be no effective, normative utility for the letter of positive law, or that it does not manage to work upon the reality of the social process, should not be surprising. A second proposition which may be expressed in terms of a group of working hypotheses to be tested is that the *locus* of real power in industrial societies, or in societies marked by a high consumption dynamic economy, tends to be transferred to the great corporation. These societies, which we may define as mass industrial societies, have in common the characteristic of tending to organize and move around—as it were—in the large productive and distributive complexes.

When in 1949 I proposed the "return to the corporation," the misunderstandings and mistakes seemed almost inevitable, and the accusations went from the really easy one of "corporativism" to other more insidious ones, on different grounds, of "yellow unionism" and "breach of class solidarity." The meaning of my proposal was clearly different and had nothing to do with any intellectualistic *vue de l'esprit*—that is, of "Lorian" irresponsibility. It reflected theoretical and practical experiences in a *processual* factory, as Olivetti's was in those years as regards a community—the Canavese—typically static and self-enclosed in an evocative, peripheral balance of artisans and peasants, in which the personnel director and the employment officer had real power over the fate of the population larger and more decisive than that of the mayor and the deputy. What I wanted to refer to was the need to rediscover, behind the formally codified juridical facade, the essence of things.

From that time on, I laid out certain methodological and programmatic points, which afterwards had a broad—if discontinuous—verification in the development of the socio-economic process of the countries of Europe and which I can quickly summarize:

1. company bargaining at all levels, not to break the collective contract which remains as the guaranteed minimum on the national level, but to unleash

workers' initiative at the base, attacking the different, contradictory world of capitalist interests at the points of least resistance;

2. a new kind of struggle—or at least a different one—not for massive wage claims, generic ones, which end up flattening out pay levels and ''distributing scarcity,'' but rather;

3. struggle for power, coordinated in such a way as little by little to eat away the autocratic prerogatives of company managements through joint mixed-base commissions which can involve all the important aspects and problems of factory life or that of the agricultural district (from social services to employment, to the tax assessment of the labor force, etc.), and thus

4. qualified collaboration of a non-corporativistic type, institutionalized and organic, not juridical and rigid, but with broad margins for maneuver, such as was objectively demanded at one time and is now required by the new demands which accompany the evolution of industrial machinery and the obvious incapacity of capitalism to go on by itself;

5. further, the linking together—organic, structured through the requisite institutions of coordination outside the corporation—with the real community as a whole to prevent the formation of closed areas of privilege or other kinds of imbalance, with the aim of channelling and making use of workers' protest as a dynamic factor, one of real democracy or redistribution of power both within the company against the dynastic absolutism of the bosses and in the community and the broader society on the national and international plane, against the entrenched interests of the big monopolistic groups.[107]

As can be seen, this is an ambitious and difficult project, based, however, on an empirically valid insight, that is, the identification of the great corporation as nerve center and fulcrum of developing societies. We are not thus dealing with launching a union action on the criterion of ''apolitical politicization,'' to use Touraine's somewhat extravagant phrase. Rather, we are concerned to discover, set down empirically, and interpret the new objective situation in which the actors in the process of industrialization move and make history, or, put another way, we are dealing with linking together dialectically global society, organization, and intermediate groups and motives, individuo-psychological personality types, by recognizing and defining the points where the innovative break occurs. These points today concern the corporate environment, not only in the so-called market economies, but also, if no longer crucially, in rationally planned and centrally managed economies, which find they have to face the problem of the fall of traditional incentives and the void which opens up given the absence of motivational models and behavioral models to replace them.

This suggestion is naturally purely indicative and in no way adequate for purposes of prediction in the middle or long term for the future of the firm. The pessimism of Veblen, who believed the conflict between "dynastic policy" or predatory speculative-financial policy and the rational needs of production right at the level of the large corporation was inevitable in the future, is becoming manifestly more a personal projection of principles of preference or secretly moralistic postulates than a scientifically based forecast.[108] The same may be said about the famous cry of alarm from Weber regarding what he saw as the inevitable tendency, all-inclusive, towards bureaucratization. In fact, by means of a logical schema, in reality too linear to do justice to the multidimensional and essentially "magmatic" nature of the concrete social process, he linked the ability for dynamic development of great industrial enterprises to their formal, bureaucratic character, that is, to the rationality of their procedures. In other words, to Weber, not only was the modern world "disenchanted," it was also one fatally destined to increasing bureaucratization, at the risk of a fall in productivity and hence of gross social product and hence of well-being. There is now a substantial body of sociological research on organization which shows the opposite: not only is a progression *ad infinitum* to formal bureaucratization not required to guarantee ever-increasing productivity in the great productive and distributive concerns, but it has been shown that a certain deviation as regards the explicit organizational organigrams and a series of informal practices—or official ones—not foreseen and even in conflict with the formal rational organigram help the efficient functioning of the organization and assist it in reaching its goals. This actual functioning of the big corporation has, as regards the natural and human environment, reached such a degree of incisiveness as to make it a kind of private government which now has behind it a definable genetic evolution marked by at least three quite specific types of organizational structure: (1) a decentralized structure, corresponding to the need to win a rapidly expanding market; (2) a vertical and at least tendentially centralized structure, when stagnating demand prompts processes of consolidation and merger and altogether stricter coordination; (3) a structure of operational blocs, functionally autonomous and interchangeable when as in the current conditions of technically advanced countries, in order to keep up the level of profits, it is necessary to diversify products and to work with a structure flexible and coordinated at the same time.

What must be borne in mind and emphasized is the growing importance of the big corporation as a social and political reality, that is, as locus of real power and center of decision making which by its logic crosses over the technical or merely administrative level and takes on a clearly political meaning. In other words, the coming of the big corporation requires the redefining of the relation between public and private, two concepts whose essence has been profoundly changed in the last forty years. Corporations, even where they are still considered simply "private concerns," perform a public role, in the sense that their decisions and conduct involve, often, thousands of individuals and hundreds of families. By contrast, the individual finds himself having to face, in order to pursue his private ends, responsibilities and tasks which lie beyond his concrete possibilities as an individual and can in reality only be confronted effectively at the level of the meta-individual social structure. The question clearly does not concern merely the internal changes in corporate power (from the capitalist-owner to the professional manager; from the power of engineers directly linked to production to that of sales managers linked to the market and finally, today, the rise of accounting specialists or financial controllers whose power is drawn from the global vision they have of all the corporate processes). Rather, it concerns basically the motivation and bases of legitimacy of that power.

Here there opens up a problem of unusual complexity which we shall glance at only rapidly. As nerve center and fulcrum of developing societies, the corporation tends to acquire and exercise a "political" power whose sources of legitimacy appear nebulous. These refer to a threefold series of controls of corporate power in its reflection on the wider society: (1) corporate power is controlled "homeopathically," so to speak, by competition between corporations, by consumer taste and by the needs of suppliers of various kinds, and ultimately by government intervention; (2) control appears in the delegation by shareholders to managers which are in all effects legally responsible to the shareholders; (3) control is decided by a relation of fiduciary trust in regard to industrial managers, based on the value orientation and the implicit consensus of the global society. Around the effectiveness of these controls and thus the validity of the sources of legitimacy, serious critical questions may be posed. There is no doubt that the separation of property from function, that is, the passage from power based on juridical ownership of property to power based on the functional exercise of decision-making prerogatives, is an important fact which is moreover far from resolving the problem. The conversion of de facto power into legitimate authority through the criterion of competence against that of possession does not free corporate power from a halo of ambiguity: Competence for what? For whose advantage? The future of the big corporation depends to a major extent on the answer to such questions.

NOTES

1. Cfr. for example, N. J. Smelser, *Social Change in the Industrial Revolution: An Application of Theory to the British Cotton Industry, 1770–1840*, Chicago, 1959.

2. For a clear example in this regard, see W. W. Rostow, *The Stages of Economic Growth*, New York, 1960. However, also in Weber, Sombart, and Schumpeter we sometimes note the use, which I call "doctrinaire," of certain basic categories, such as, for example, that of "rationality" a real *deus ex machina* for the explanation of institutions and of behavior not simply reducible to them. In the same vein, as a recent critique of "social change," see C. Tilly, *Big Structures, Large Processes, Huge Comparisons*, New York, 1984.

3. Cfr. my *Macchina e uomo nella societa' industriale*, Turin, 1963, pp. 70–72.

4. Cfr. T. S. Ashton, "The Treatment of Capitalism by Historians," in F. A. Hayek, ed., *Capitalism and the Historians*, Chicago, 1954, p. 54.

5. Cfr. P. Mantoux, *La révolution industrielle au xviie siècle*, Paris, 1905 (Eng. trans., *The Industrial Revolution in the Eighteenth Century*, London, 1961), p. 1, note—(Le mot est, croyons nous, d'Arnold Toynbee). Of the same opinion is Henry T. Wood, *Industrial England in the Middle of the Eighteenth Century*, London, 1910. On the other hand, W. E. Rappard *La révolution industrielle*, Paris, 1914, p. 4, attributes the term to the first socialist writers of the first half of the nineteenth century, noting that it is found in Marx, *Das Kapital*, and that it was used contemporaneously by Mill in the first edition of the *Principles of Political Economy of 1848*.

6. Cfr. A. Bezanson, "The Early Use of the Term Industrial Revolution," *Quarterly Journal of Economics*, 36, February 1922, pp. 343–49.

7. Cfr. esp. L. von Mises, *The Anticapitalist Mentality*, Princeton, N.J., 1956.

8. Until there did not exist a real "factory system" in the textile industry, for example, the distinction between home workers and entrepreneurs was not clear; cfr. Smelser, *Social Change*, p. 110. As regards the family nature of the enterprise, with its community of interests between workers and employers, for

the whole eighteenth century, see S. and B. Webb, *The History of Trade Unionism*, London, 1894, p. 39—"Their occasional differences seemed more like family arguments than conflict between different classes."

9. Cfr. M. F. Nimkoff and R. Middleton, "Types of Family and Types of Economy," *The American Journal of Sociology*, 66, 3 November 1960; see, too, S. M. Greenfield, "Industrialization and the Family in Sociological Theory," in ibid., 47, 3, November 1961. For a thorough study of the material, cfr. William G. Goode, *World Revolution and Family Patterns*, Glencoe, Ill., 1963.

10. Cfr. R. Aron, *Le développement de la société industrielle et la stratification sociale*, Centre de Documentation Universitaire, Paris, n.d., 54–55.

11. Cfr. M. Weber, *Wirtschaftsgeschichte* (Eng. ed., *General Economic History*, F. H. Knight, ed., New York, 1927, pp. 127–28.)

12. Cfr. ibid. Weber insists on explaining that the industrial system of production did not develop within the artisan, but parallel and in relation to new products such as cotton, brocade, porcelain, etc.

13. K. Marx, *Das Kapital* (Ital. trans., Rome, 1955, Vol. I; Eng. trans., *Capital: A Critique of Political Economy*, New York, 1967).

14. Weber, *General Economic History*, p. 129.

15. Ibid., p. 224.

16. Cfr. especially Weber, *Die protestantische Ethik und der Geist des Kapitalismus* (Ital. trans., Rome, 1945; Eng. trans., *The Protestant Ethic and the Spirit of Capitalism*, New York, 1958).

17. Cfr. Pierre-Maxime Schuhl, *Machinisme et philosophie*, Paris, 1938; V. Chapot, "Sentiments des anciens sur le machinisme," *Revue des études anciennes*, 1938; John U. Nef, *Cultural Foundations of Industrial Civilization*, Cambridge, 1958. For an explanation of the failure to apply mechanization in terms of social structure (the existence of slaves, etc.) rather than as "mental bloc," see V. de Magalhaes Vilhena, "Progrès technique et blocage social dans la pensée antique," *La pensée*, 102, March–April 1962, pp. 3–20; and P. Rossi, *I filosofi e le macchine*, Milan, 1961.

18. Cfr. my *Max Weber e il destino della ragione*, Bari, 1965, esp. ch. 3, "Il sistema concettuale," pp. 72–86; Engl. trans., *Max Weber and the Destiny of Reason*, Armonk, 1982.

19. One might recall here Schumpeter's remark that structures, types, and social attitudes are coins that do not easily melt; J. A. Schumpeter, *Capitalism, Socialism and Democracy*, New York, 1950, p. 12.

20. G. Friedmann, *Où va le travail humain?* (Ital. trans., Milan, 1955, esp. pt. l).

21. G. H. Sabine, "Beyond Ideology," *The Philosophical Review*, January 1948, p. 135.

22. For a brilliant résumé of the process which distinguishes between social function and individual personality, see L. Trilling, *The Opposing Self* (Ital. trans., Turin, 1962).

23. Cfr. Weber, *Wirtschaftsgeschichte*, esp. chs. 8–11. Werner Sombart, *Der Moderne Kapitalismus*, Munich and Leipzig, 1928, esp. "Die Vorkapitalistische Wirtschaft."

24. For an introduction to this cluster of problems, which should be expanded, see my *Dove va la societa industriale?*, Trento, 1964, pp. 16–19.

25. L. Mumford, *Technics and Civilization*, New York, 1934, p. 162; Mumford, to avoid any misunderstanding in terms of crude technological determinism, stated, "The clock, not the steam engine, is the key machine of the modern industrial era" (p. 14).

26. I restrict myself to mentioning among the extensive literature on this subject, W. H. Hellpach, *Mensch und Volk der Grosstadt*, Stuttgart, F. Enke, 1952; and G. Simmel, *Die Grosstadte und das Geistesteben*, in *Gesammelte Werke*, Berlin, Dunker und Humblot, 1958; Eng. trans., *Metropolis and Mental Life*, Chicago, Syllabus Division, University of Chicago Press, 1961.

27. Cfr. Mumford, *Technics and Civilization*, p. 174.

28. Daniel Bell referred to Jeremy Bentham's attempts to build a perfect prison, the panopticon, in which every prisoner could be constantly surveyed by a single warder in the middle, without seeing him, and thus be totally isolated. The plans for such a building were passed to him by his brother Samuel, a naval architect in the service of Catherine the Great, who had developed them for the purpose of building a factory. D. Bell, *The End of Ideology*, Glencoe, Ill., 1960, p. 223.

29. For an examination of the typical ambivalence of many writers regarding the division of labor, a factor for welfare, but at the same time of worker dequalification, see N. Rosenberg, "Adam Smith on the Division of Labor: Two views or One?", *Economica*, 32, 126, May 1965, pp. 127–39.

30. Cfr. my *La protesta operaia*, Milan, 1955, esp. ch. 1, "Sviluppo economico e movimento operaio," and ch. 7, "La fabbrica come comunita reale."

31. Cfr., among others, Bert F. Hoselitz, *Sociological Aspects of Economic Growth*, Glencoe, Ill., 1960; and Everett E. Hagen, *On the Theory of Social Change*, Homewood, Ill., 1962. Hagen rightly complains (p. 37) that one deals mainly with purely verbal recognition. However, this is not to be conspiratorially attributed to ill will on the part of the economists. The fact is that once the inadequacy of the economic explanation of economic growth is admitted, together with the process of industrialization, the very autonomy of economic science is itself put in peril, and one demands the setting up of a new social science capable of providing an integrated explanation of phenomena in their economic, sociological, and anthropological-cultural dimensions.

32. N. Kaldor, *Essays on Economic Stability and Growth*, London, 1960, p. 236.

33. An interesting though basically one-sided attempt to answer these ques-

tions can be found in D. McClelland, *The Achieving Society*, Princeton, N.J., 1961.

34. Cfr. my *Il rapporto sociale nell 'impresa moderna*, Rome, 1961, esp. ch. 1, "La funzione imprenditoriale: dalla proprieta' all'organizzazionè."

35. For an exhaustive treatment of this theme, cfr. A. Pagani, *La formazione dell "imprenditorialita"*, Milan, 1964, which is also an excellent bibliographic guide, especially for studies of the Schumpeterian school; cfr. too for important critical judgments and original insights on the problem, G. Demaria, "Studi sull'attivita' dell'imprenditore moderno," *Rivista internazionale di scienze sociali*, 38, 11, 1929, pp. 39–53.

36. It is hardly required to stress the interest of this insight, which foreshadows the conception of the entrepreneur as innovator—a factor of rupture with economic and social routine—and elicits, however ingenuously, the tie between deviant individual, marginality, and creativity.

37. Cfr. G. Hufeland, *Neue Grunlegund des Staats-Wirtschafstkurst*, Metzlar, 1870; L. von Jakob, *Grunesatze der National Oekonomie*, Halle, 1805.

38. The term "undertaker" now describes the funeral director; according to Cannan it was much used before the adoption of the corresponding French term "entrepreneur." Cfr. E. Cannan, *A History of the Theories of Production and Distribution*, 3rd ed., London, 1917.

39. Cfr. D. Ricardo, *Principles of Political Economy*, P. Straffa, ed., Cambridge, 1951, pp. 91 ff.

40. Especially in the *Protestant Ethic* and the *General Economic History*, Weber brought out this very important fact, in that he indicts the historical constructs and explanations and dialectical, abstract schemas of the coexistence and parallel development of new modes of production and exchange and wholly traditional modes of production.

41. Cfr. J. A. Schumpeter, "Economic Theory and Entrepreneurial History," in *Change and the Entrepreneur: Postulates and Patterns in Entrepreneurial History*, Cambridge, 1949. This was the first publication of the Research Center in Entrepreneurial History (pp. 65–66) divided into three, with contributions by Chester I. Barnard, G. A. Smith, R. A. Gordon, C. H. Danhof, K. W. Deutsch, F. Redlich, W. T. Easterbrook, P. D. Bradley, H. Whidden, D. B. Shimkin, R E. Duworms, D M. Wright, R. R. Wohl, J. A. Schumpeter, A. H. Cole, L. H. Jenks, T. C. Cochrane. A. Pagani rightly sees this as a basic reference text; *La formazione dell "imprenditorialita"*, pp. 9 ff.

42. Cfr. J. A. Schumpeter, *The Theory of Economic Development*, R. Opie, ed., Cambridge, 1951, pp. 10–11 (original emphasis).

43. W. Bagehot, *Works*, vol. 5, Hartford, Conn., 1889, p. 466.

44. Cfr. Cannan, *History*, p. 314: "The power to manage an industry does not concern capital, dumb or inanimate, nor yet the owners of capital, but rather a specific class of laborers, the entrepreneurs." Cfr. too, F. A. Walker, *The*

Science of Wealth, 5th ed., Philadelphia, 1871, pp. 311–12: "The employer is a factor of production who fulfills the function of arranging a fruitful union between labor and capital." Walker, in his *Political Economy*, 3rd ed., New York, 1888, p. 233, states that the basic factor of the productive process is not capital but entrepreneurial skill which is the "condition without which the industrial enterprises of modern society could not exist."

45. Cfr. A. Marshall, *Principles of Economics*, 8th ed., London, 1897, pp. 240–41, 293.

46. Cfr. W. H. Mallock, *Labor and the Popular Welfare*, London, 1893, p. 145, *passim*. One need scarcely mention the polemic between Mallock and Shaw, in G. B. Shaw, *Socialism and Superior Brains*, Fabian Socialist Series, no. 5, London, 1910.

47. Cfr. F. B. Hawley, *Enterprise and the Productive Process*, New York, 1913, p. 57.

48. Cfr. J. B. Clark, *Essentials of Economic Theory*, New York, 1907, p. 86.

49. Cfr. Schumpeter, *Theory of Economic Development*, p. 137; "Economic Theory and Entrepreneurial History," in *Change and the Entrepreneur*, p. 66.

50. I use this term, which seems appropriate here, while knowing how little congenial it was to Schumpeter.

51. F. H. Knight, *Risk, Uncertainty and Profit*, Boston, 1921.

52. Ibid., p. 268.

53. Cfr. Knight, "Profit and Entrepreneurial Functions," *Tasks of Economic History*, supp. to vol. 2, *Journal of Economic History*, 1942, pp. 126–32.

54. Cfr. Schumpeter, *The Theory of Economic Development*, p. 85.

55. Ibid., p. 156.

56. J. A. Schumpeter, *Imperialism—Social Classes*, trans. H. Norden, New York, 1955, p. 121. For Schumpeter, "forceful evaluation" is that which concentrates on the elements of the situation which lead to success while at the same time managing to ignore all the others.

57. Cfr. especially Maurice Dobb, *Capitalist Enterprise and Social Progress*, London, 1926. Though he does not refer directly to Schumpeter, Dobb notes that economic change, by introducing new elements, creates entirely different perspectives from those traditionally known; hence, uncertainties which are not precisely calculable arise, and in addition there arises the task of the entrepreneur "to adopt and innovate."

58. Cfr. A. H. Cole, *Business Enterprise in Its Social Setting*, Cambridge, 1959; for the discussion of the development of Cole's idea, cfr. Pagani, *La formazione dell'"imprenditorialita"*, pp. 56–62; and G. Mori, "Premesse ed implicazioni di una recente specializzazione storiografica americana: l'Entrepreneurial history, Studi storici," 1, 4, 1959–60, pp. 755–92.

59. Cfr. my *Il rapporto sociale*, p. 31.

60. The literature in this respect is huge. A first systematic treatment of the bibliography can be found in Pagani, *La formazione dell "imprenditorialita"*, pp. 309–48; and cfr. my *Il rapporto sociale*, pp. 109–34.

61. Cfr., among others, G. Candeloro, *Il movimento sindacale in Italia*, Rome, 1950, p. 11.

62. Cfr. G. De Ruggiero, *Storia del liberalismo europeo*, Bari, 1926 *passim*.

63. For an attempt at an overall comparative review, see the collection *Comparative Labor Movements*, ed. W. L. Galenson, New York, 1953.

64. For a satisfying clarification of the term, see E. J. Hobsbawm, *Laboring Men*, London, 1964, p. 273, which considers five factors or aspects to try to define the phenomenon: (1) level and regularity of earnings; (2) social security; (3) working conditions; (4) relations with higher and lower strata; (5) general conditions of life and prospects for social improvement for oneself and one's children.

65. For a detailed, rich analysis of the structure of American unions, see Philip Taft, *The Structure and Government of Labor Unions*, Cambridge, 1954.

66. For an analytical treatment of collective bargaining in the United States, see, among others, Neil W. Chamberlain, *Collective Bargaining*, New York, 1951; R Dubin, "Power and Union–Management Relations," *Administrative Science Quarterly*, June 1957; C.S. Golden and V. D. Parker, eds., *Causes of Industrial Peace under Collective Bargaining*, New York, 1955; F. H. Harbison and J. R. Coleman, *Goals and Strategy of Collective Bargaining*, New York, 1961; J. Shister, "Collective Bargaining," in *A Decade of Industrial Relations Research, 1946–56*, New York, 1958; G. W. Taylor and F. C. Pierson, *New Concepts in Wage Determination*, New York, 1957.

67. This is the essence of the "dilemma of the American unions" I spoke of in 1953. This dilemma, which was then alive in the awareness of a few advanced pockets of American opinion, now seems to have become—by measuring the at times dramatic intensity with which a new dynamic and definitely oriented leadership, capable of propounding a coherent policy on the internal and still more the international level—a dilemma for the whole American nation.

68. In this regard, see my *Il dilemma dei sindacati americani*, Milan, 1954, pp. 8–11. See, too, D. J. Saposs, *Left Wing Unionism*, New York, 1926.

69. Concerning the organizational framework of collective bargaining in the United States, see E. W. Bakke, *Mutual Survival: The Goal of Unions and Management*, New York, 1946; J. Barbash, *The Practice of Unionism*, New York, 1956; G. W. Brooks, "What Will Collective Bargaining Look Like in Twenty Years," in *The Next Twenty Years in Industrial Relations*, Cambridge, 1957; J. S. Bugas, *Industrial Relations, 1957*, Ford Motor Co., Dearborn, Mich., 1957; R. Dubin, *Working Union–Management Relations*, Englewood Cliffs, N.J. 1958; J. T. Dunlop and J. J. Healy, *Collective Bargaining: Prin-*

ciples and Cases, Homewood, Ill., 1953; R. R. Franee, *Union Decisions in Collective Bargaining*, Princeton, N.J., 1955; F. H. Harbison, "The Politics of Collective Bargaining: The Post-war Record in Steel," *APSR*, September 1954, pp. 705–20; A. Kornhauser, R. Dubin, and A. M. Ross, *Industrial Conflict*, New York, 1954; R. A. Lester, *As Unions Mature*, Princeton, N.J., 1958; E. Marting, ed., *Understanding Collective Bargaining*, American Management Association, New York, 1958; A. M. Ross, "Collective Bargaining and Common Sense," *Labor Law Journal*, June 1951, pp. 435–43; A. Wesenfeld and M. Berkowitz, "A New Look in Collective Bargaining," *Labor Law Journal*, August 1955, pp. 561–66.

70. For elaboration of the concept of job consciousness, see Selig Perlman, *A Theory of the Labor Movement*, New York, A. M. Kelley, 1928; Italian trans., Florence, Nuova Italia, 1956.

71. In Italy, too, for some time there has been discussion of the "new" in the union field; however reading the great majority of the contributions in this area, one is struck by their not always intelligent character of distracting rhetoric. They want to take into account the "new" but by preserving intact, and indeed changing nothing of, the old. The same thing happens with the neoscholastics of Marxism. The very development of industrial machinery and their effects on the labor force, which Marx literally could not guess at in their specific reality, may have made Marxism in certain aspects erroneous, incomplete, or simply outdated. But woe to whoever says this! One must know how to read between the lines and saddle Marx with the reflections of the latest disciples of ideal Marxism.

72. Cfr. for the United States, A. R. Heron, *Beyond Collective Bargaining*, Stanford, 1948.

73. Cfr. N. W. Chamberlain, *The Union Challenge to Management Control*, New York, 1948.

74. For the definition of this "type" in relation to the actions and thought of Walter Reuther, see my *Il dilemma dei sindicati americani*. For questions related to jurisdiction, see L. H. Hill and C. R. Hook, *Management at the Bargaining Table*; New York, McGraw-Hill, 1945; J. T. McKelvey, ed. *Management Rights and the Arbitration Process*, Washington, D.C., 1956; J. F. Morton, "Limitations upon the Scope of Collective Bargaining," *Labor Law Journal*, October 1956, pp. 603–6; F. H. Harbison, "The General Motors–United Auto Workers Agreement of 1950," *The Journal of Political Economy*, October 1950, pp. 397–411; M. Lerber, W. E. Chalmers, and Ross Stagner, "Collective Bargaining and Management Functions: An Empirical Study," *The Journal of Business*, April 1958, pp. 107–20; S. A. Cook, "The Right to Manage," *Labor Law Journal*, March 1958, pp. 187–217.

75. I refer the reader to my *La protesta operaia*, Milan, 1955.

76. Cfr. W. H. Form and D. C. Miller, *Industry, Labor and Community*, New York, 1960, *passim*.

77. Cfr. T. Veblen, *Absentee Ownership and Business Enterprise in Recent Times: The Case of America*, New York, 1923.

78. A typical case is that of the Krupp family: when there were no male heirs, Gustav von Bohlen married a Krupp and took her surname.

79. On the separation between ownership and control, and on corporate power based on the right of property and that instead exercised in the name of functional-operational criteria, see A. A. Berle and G. C. Means, *The Modern Corporation and Private Property*, New York, 1932. On the problem of managerial power, see J. Burnham, *The Managerial Revolution*, New York, 1941, which marks the starting point of much of the modern debate on the power of industrial managers.

80. Though a large part of top management of corporations in the different industrialized countries is recruited from the ''line'' and has specific technical qualifications (in Europe, for example, engineers predominate), both the criterion of choice and the functions bestowed have little or nothing to do with that type of experience and those specific qualifications. What predominates in the selection of the men called upon to manage the destinies of industrial corporations are considerations based on organizational ability rather than on technical competence, which is provided rather by the ''staff'' and the study units.

81. One can find a summary of this activity in *Human Relations in Industry*, European Productivity Agency, Project 312, Paris, 1956. For France, see H. Desroche et al., *Etudes sur la tradition française de l'association ouvrière*, Paris, 1956; and for England, *Joint Consultation in British Industry*, London, 1952; and W. H. Scott, *Industrial Democracy*, Liverpool, 1955.

82. Cfr. R. Tannenbaum and F. Massarik, *Participation by Subordinates in the Managerial Decision-Making Process*, I.I.R. U. of California, reprint no. 14, Los Angeles, 1950.

83. For an exhaustive examination of this school, see D. Cartwright and A. Zander, *Group Dynamics: Research and Theory*, 2nd ed., New York, 1960.

84. K. Lewin, R. Lippitt, and R. White, ''Patterns of Aggressive Behavior in Experimentally Created Social Climates,'' *Journal of Social Psychology*, 10, 1939, pp. 271–99; and R. Lippitt, ''Field Theory and Experiment in Social Psychology: Authoritarian and Democratic Group Atmospheres,'' *American Journal of Sociology*, 45, 1939, pp. 26–49.

85. Cfr. R. Kahn and D. Katz, ''Leadership Practices in Relation to Productivity and Morale,'' in Cartwright and Zander, *Group Dynamics*, pp. 554–70.

86. Cfr. A. Bavelas, ''Morale and the Training of Leaders,'' in *Civilian Morale*, G. Watson, ed., New York, 1942, pp. 143–65.

87. L. Coch and J. French, ''Overcoming Resistance to Change,'' *Human Relations*, 1, 1948, pp. 512–32.

88. For a critical approach to the problem of participation, see my *Sociologia come participatione*, Turin, 1961, esp. pt. 2, ch. 1, "Evoluzione tecnica e partecipazione operaia," pp. 101–19.

89. R. Sutermeister, *People and Productivity*, New York, 1963, p. 44.

90. On these aspects of industrial mechanization, see G. Friedmann, *Problemi umani del macchinismo industriale*, Turin, 1949 (Eng. trans., *Industrial Society: The Emergence of the Human Problems of Automation*, Glencoe, Ill., 1955); *Dove va il lavoro umano?* Milan, 1955; *Lavoro in frantumi*, Milan, 1960.

91. E. Chinoy, *Automobile Workers and the American Dream*, New York, 1955.

92. In our discussion of the evolution of mechanized industry, the most important aspects are brought out for an understanding of the modern industrial corporation, but one should not think that in every type of working activity and industry there are, in the generalized form I have adduced, these technological phenomena and the latter psychological consequences. The production line itself, which in publicity material is now taken as a prototype of modern industrial labor, now uses in the U.S. auto industry only 15 percent of the total manpower.

93. The literature in this regard is now infinite. See, e.g., "Proceedings of the Carnegie Study Group on the Basic Principles of Automation," *International Social Science Bulletin*, 10, 1958, pp. 83–120; J. Diebold, *Automation: Its Impact on Business and Labor*, Washington, D.C., 1959; F. Pollock, *Automazione: dati per la valutazione delle conseguenze economiche e sociali*, Turin, 1956 (Eng. trans., *The Economic and Social Consequences of Automation*, Oxford, 1957).

94. W. Faunce, "Automation and the Automobile Worker," *Social Problems*, 6, 1, Summer 1958.

95. C. I. Barnard, *The Functions of the Executive*, Cambridge, 1947, p. 73.

96. Cfr. E. Mayo, *The Human Problems of an Industrial Civilization*, New York, 1933; *The Social Problems of an Industrial Civilization*, Cambridge, 1946; F. Roethlisberger and W. J. Dickson, *Management and the Worker*, Cambridge, 1939; T. H. Whitehead, *The Industrial Worker*, 2 vols., Cambridge, 1938. See too my contribution on "Sociologia industriale," in *Antologia di scienza sociali, campi di applicazione*, ed., A. Pagani, vol. 2, Bologna, 1963, pp. 175–244.

97. Cfr. D. C. Miller and W. H. Form, *Industrial Sociology*, 2nd ed., New York, 1964, p. 282.

98. Informal intra-group relations are not generally *structured* in the same sense in which inter-group relations are (roles, status, communications, norms, command system, etc.), but they nonetheless exist, especially in the case of

informal groups which present themselves as pressure groups for a particular goal (cliques of employees linked with career interests and distribution of power not officially bestowed).

99. E. V. Schneider, *Industrial Sociology*, New York, 1957, p. 193.

100. Cfr. C. Argyris, *Personality and Organization: The Conflict Between System and the Individual*, New York, 1957.

101. Roethlisberger and Dickson, *Management and the Worker*, p. 522.

102. R. K. Merton, *Social Theory and Social Structure*, 2nd ed., Glencoe, Ill., 1957, p. 66.

103. Cfr. R. Hoppock, *Job Satisfaction*, New York, 1935. An exhaustive treatment and bibliography may be found in M. S. Viteles, *Motivation and Morale in Industry*, New York, 1953. For more recent studies, see F. Herzberg et al., *Job Attitudes: Review of Research and Opinions*, Pittsburgh, 1957; and D. C. Miller and W. H. Form, *Industrial sociology*, 2nd ed., New York, 1964.

104. A. Zalenik, C. R. Christensen, and F. J. Roethlisberger, *Motivazione, produttivita' e soddisfazione nel lavoro*, Bologna, 1964; D. Katz et al., *Productivity, Supervision and Morale among Railroad Workers*, Ann Arbor, 1951; W. F. Whyte, *Money and Motivation*, New York, 1955; G. Friedmann and P. Naville, *Traité du sociologie du travail*, Paris, 1961, esp. J. Frisch-Gauthier's contribution, vol. 2.

105. See the works of Viteles and Herzberg cited above. It is worth stressing that though the research conducted up till now has helped to change many of the "rabble hypotheses" of corporate management, first of all the work of Mayo, there is still a basic divergence between the management and worker's conceptions of industrial labor. The first sees wages as an expense, the latter enjoys it as income. In the first view, labor is something one buys, in the second it is not necessarily the equivalent in a buying–selling relation. Perhaps the strangest aspect in this non-understanding is that at every level of the corporate hierarchy each seems to perceive the importance of not strictly financial factors in the evaluation of their work, but with serious illogic tends to believe the reverse for those at a lower level in the hierarchy, as cfr. N. C. Morse and R. S. Weiss, "The Function and the Meaning of Work and the Job," *American Sociological Review* 20, April 1955.

106. For the limits of Taylorism, see my *Sindacalismo autonomo*, 2nd ed., Milan, 1958. For a general comparative overview of the current state of the sociology of labor in the United States and Europe, see my *Sociologia industriale in America e in Europa*, 2nd ed., Turin, 1960.

107. Cfr. my *Sindacalismo autonomo*, pp. 170–71.

108. For a balanced examination of Veblen's position, see W. C. Frederick, "Was Veblen Right about the Future of Business Enterprise?", *The American Journal of Economics and Sociology*, 24, 3, July 1965, pp.225–40.

9

Social Information and Human Development

SOCIAL INFORMATION VERSUS COLLECTIVE INFORMATION

Though the shadow cast by our own subjectivity may seem to be both objectionable and intrusive, we must have a clear picture of the cultural weight and historical significance of our own work. Information, in contemporary terms, means power. If power implies control and if it is impossible to control something we know nothing about, then information is a necessary, though not the only, condition underlying all exercise of power. But what information? Not any information, not the all-devouring information which serves in its superabundance as the ally of manipulation, not that information which instead of developing awareness serves to nip it in the bud—nor even that kind of information which under the guise of public relations serves merely to involve either groups or individuals, utilizing their support for practical purposes, or which serves to indicate objectives which, even at the moment they are named, have already been decided or else are irrelevant. Our concern is social information.

In the first place, *social information is not to be confused with collective information*. Unless this confusion is avoided we immediately lose all chance of identifying a precise problematic setting: We move in a world of collective signs and messages, of mass communication media, of explicit indications which involve the whole of our everyday experience, from meteorological variations to traffic signs. *Social information is that type of information which covers all socially and politically relevant themes regarding relations between citizens and institutions*. In this sense it can be correctly affirmed that social information relates to, and invests, the very heart of power.

The deeper implications of this statement can only be grasped by examining the transformations which have taken place in various nations and cultures, in the grand scheme of history; and at the same time it is necessary to understand the new ways in which social groups and classes, within the framework of individual nations, conduct their relations.

Though the most important fact of the century is neither the splitting of the atom nor the landing on the moon, the importance of these technical and scientific achievements is unquestioned. They also serve the purpose of making a deep impression on the popular imagination, so that they can easily be claimed by different and competing political regimes as signs of qualitative superiority. To this extent the great inventions of the nineteenth century and recent achievements in nuclear and space physics are indications of the typically "modern" and "Western" tendency to reduce all values to calculable data, to exact measures, or, in current jargon, to the technical-productive potential.

The problems of human co-existence are in this way transformed from problems of values to problems of organization. Instead of dealing with problems raised by the necessity of significant choice in relation to alternatives organically linked with human needs in a given setting and in a given historical situation, they become merely problems of "social engineering," or problems which can be solved by the importation and mechanical application of techniques (technological know-how) from those countries and cultures which have reached a higher stage of technical advancement. The *quantification of the qualitative* gives these countries and their essentially scientific-technical cultures a social and political standing which is, in my opinion, hard to accept and which, in any case, if it is to be accepted uncritically, bristles with danger.

The crucial and decisive characteristics of our time, however, are neither technical nor scientific factors. *The most important fact of this century is that for the first time peoples and entire continents which had been cut off from the mainstream of human life have made their entrance into history.* They are no longer so much lifeless matter, firewood waiting for kindling, the object rather than the subject of historical action. That is to say, these peoples have hitherto figured in history, but without playing any active part. Traditional societies, whether pre- or paleo-technical, are characteristically supposed to consider history as a given fact, as a "natural situation," by definition outside human initiative. These peoples, in other words, rather than playing an active part in history, are passively subjected to its results. It has long been the practice of certain currents of Western culture to regard this passive state as the logical and practically inevitable outcome of a natural, mental, and civil inferiority of such races, which they regard as human only in the zoological sense of the word and not in the spiritual sense. By projecting onto other human civilizations and groups its own particular values and especially its technical achievements, Western culture has set itself up as the touchstone and normative ideal for all other races, which are indiscriminately reduced, even while in effect they are being exploited, to the rank of "subjects to be educated." But this is just where we run into a fatal contradiction. Just at the moment when Western culture puts forward its way of life as the only and exclusive ideal, in effect it prevents, just because of this ethnocentric attitude, any real communication with the other cultures. The flow of information is blocked, or, at best, it functions only in one direction, from above downward. It is a culture which is moving toward its own historical destruction insofar as it makes it impossible to understand others just because they are others.

This extraordinary and novel fact of the entry into history of peoples and nations which were excluded until the present day gives a peculiar connotation to our time. Something profoundly significant has changed not only in the relations between different nations and cultures on the international plane; the epoch of vertical imperialism has begun, the age of interior colonization. Within single countries new forms of exploitation of man by man are to be found. Our mental schemes, the images which support like a strong and invisible scaffolding the conceptual structure of our reasoning, have fallen hopelessly behind the evolution of the objective situation. A new "political demand," and the request for participation which corresponds to it, lies at the basis of the contemporary institutional crisis. The crisis marks the moment of anguish and indicates the breaking point, but it is also a moment of epiphany. The crisis tears things across, but at the same time it opens and lays bare.

We are living in an age when the link between men consists of a constant flux of explicit communications, politically relevant on a planetary scale, a synchronic world in which anything happening in Southeast Asia has a direct influence and effect on North America, a word whispered in Pekin re-echoes in Rome, in New York, in Tokyo, in Paris. The things we used to learn by rubbing shoulders with our neighbors are learned today through specific messages. But we have still to realize this. We know it with our minds, but we have still to *realize* it existentially. We are still thinking of the exploitation of man by man, of one social class by another, in nineteenth-century terms. At this rate we shall only move into the twentieth century when in fact it is drawing to a close.

Nineteenth-century exploitation rests on certain basic assumptions. It invents the autonomy of civilized society, both in respect to the economic system and in respect to political institutions. On this basis it constructs the notion of the individual as a formally free agent, capable of making his own contracts. It sees all as equal in the market, whether as capitalist or proletariat—the one as the buyer, the other as the seller of his labor. Nineteenth-century exploitation exists on the basis of this purely juridical and formal equality. "As Christians are equal in heaven but not on earth," Marx has written in *The German Ideology*, "so workers are equal to the middle classes in the heaven of legal definitions, but not in actual relations of economic and social forms." The difference between the modern worker-slave as compared with the classic slave of Graeco-Roman times is purely juridical in kind. The slave of the past belonged physically and effectively to the family of his master; he was the *famulus*. The modern worker is formally free, he belongs only to himself, he can work and bargain, he is part of a formally free and impersonal market. But in fact he is heavily tied down in all his attitudes; he cannot survive except by selling his labor, and the fruit of the labor he has sold corresponds exactly to the disadvantage in which he finds himself in relation to his employer in terms of bargaining pressures, of urgency, of direct and indirect influences which can be brought to bear. This is the origin of the nineteenth-century picture of the proletariat as a poor class, modestly dressed, receiving a humble and precarious wage, forced to be sober and simple along the lines of the populist image emblematically represented in Pellizza da Volpedo's painting, "The Fourth Estate," in Henry George's book *Progress and Poverty*, and in the novels of Charles Dickens. As compared with present-day exploitation, nineteenth-century exploitation was direct and genuine. It was immediately observable. It dealt with measurable quantities in terms of physical force, muscular energy, rhythms and times of operation, working hours, and so on. In effect, it was an exploitation based on purchase by the capitalist and sale by the worker of *Arbeitskraft*, labor in the physical sense of the term. *Exploitation today is less direct, but it goes deeper. It is no longer physical labor which is sold, but souls, meaning the entire mental outlook.* It is not a question of muscular force; it involves nervous energy. It is rarely tiring, but it is boring. It cannot be measured in terms of quantity, but it requires a qualitative re-orientation of labor activity. Physical obedience is no longer sufficient; what is wanted is psychological identification.

This is the paradox. The abundance and wealth of one part of mankind are of necessity paid for by all the rest. But this abundance is widespread and continues to expand. It gives rise to phenomena which over-zealous and over-optimistic sociologists have hastened to designate important phenomena of "anticipatory participation" by means of consumption, as a way of tranquilizing the consciences and suffocating the sense of guilt of satiate humanity. Is it not an important fact that today the lady and her maid buy and wear the same make of nylons? Can this not be read as the beginning of the end of social inequality? The obvious answer is that it cannot. But the analysis must cut deeper. Within the structure of that part of humanity which has progressed, new forms of exploitation must be examined, together with the manipulation which is effected through an inoculation with unreal needs and the creation of the customer. The typology of this new exploitation hinges not on the back-breaking sixteen hours of hard labor per day which we find so effectively described in the last chapters of Book I of *Das Kapital*, but on the new, really crucial variables of modern life, which are isolation, segregation, solitude, neglect, exclusion. *To be exploited in the modern world means to be on the fringes, to be cut off.* Our everyday experience and common sense might seem to contradict this conclusion. Mass media continue to spread. Decisions, at all levels of organized association, are more numerous, more clamorous, more widely known. But access to a center where these decisions are taken is more difficult. The center is remote: its arbitrary nature is consecrated by mystery. It is even hard to determine where exactly this center is located and who forms part. The message of power risks becoming the "message of the emperor." Kafka's solitary prophetic intuition has today become a sensation which is widely shared. Let us set aside, without pausing even to glance at time, the philosophical and sociological theories by which the various power elites defend themselves. Then a curious, and in many ways unexpected, fact must be pointed out. *Power today exploits and oppresses not by the use of direct action, which can be objectively and logically assessed on the basis of the objects in view and the results effectively obtained, but simply by ignoring, by failing to intervene, by refusing to take action, by taking refuge behind complex and perfectionist procedures through which formalism and paralysis come to each other's aid. The most serious sins of power today are sins of omission.* Today the genuine reactionary is not the man who has a gallows erected or applauds the censor, but the man who prevents action, who preaches resignation at all costs and urges men to put their trust in a spontaneous, automatic evolution.

OBLIVION OR EXCLUSION AS A PRESENT-DAY FORM OF EXPLOITATION

This is the reason for the decisive importance of social information. But it also explains the most serious obstacles in the path of social information. To understand and overcome these obstacles we have to distinguish and formulate clearly the triple perspective in which social information can carry out its function—three levels or differentiated planes of articulation with their respective contents.

In the first place we have social information about social assistance and social security services, which in many countries are established and permanent institutions. The role of this kind of social information is crucial, especially in the effective application to everyday life of the rules of social legislation. At this point of our analysis we are not concerned with the wider question of the ownership of property and the characteristics of the social structure. The question which concerns us here is connected with *the contents of social information in connection with the relation existing between citizens (as users of social assistance) and social security institutions providing such services.* How are these relations developed? Through what media do they operate? *By what channels does the citizen come into contact with the institution? What does he know of it? What does he expect from it?* It seems logical to suppose that his expectations will be colored by the extent of his information, and that his frustration or satisfaction will depend in strict proportion on the amount of information to which he has access. These questions arise in relation to the actual functioning of such institutions as exist in each country, quite apart from the whole question of this economic and political structure, the juridical system, the orientation, the institutional fabric of any given country. Let us concentrate our attention on the figure of the citizen standing before one of these institutions which exists to protect him from social injury or, in more urgent cases, to come to his aid. It should be remembered that this protection and assistance have already gone far beyond the concept of a purely charitable action. Today charity is regarded as inadequate, however valuable it may have been in the past. Such assistance is now universally felt to be the right of the citizen.

Social information is not always available when it is needed. It is not always expressed in such a way that the ordinary citizen to whom it is addressed can understand it. Specialist jargon—often not strictly necessary and stemming from bureaucratic officialese—conspires with a low general level of education to frustrate the most courageous social measures. *The people who need help most urgently are just the ones who get overlooked.* Their state of economic hardship creates psychological distance and social inferiority. The distinctions between the center and the outskirts are exaggerated, they become chronic. A field research carried out on behalf of UNESCO and UNRRA (United Nations Reconstruction and Recovery Administration) a few years ago at Pescocostanzo, a village in the poorer part of the Abruzzi, by Angela Zucconi and other social workers, brought to light the fact that there was no shortage of legally backed measures, and that financial provisions were available for prompt intervention. What was lacking was the request for intervention which should have come from the people in greatest need. The essential facts, the indispensable information, were lacking. This was the factor holding up the relation between the institution and the citizen. The lesson is easy to read: to simplify the relation, cut down bureaucratic procedure, see that social information is distributed more thoroughly, more quickly, and much more widely. Similar problems emerge from a recent study carried out among the poor in New York, in a group of the most hopelessly underprivileged in the eastern quarter of Harlem. Here the gap which splits off the citizen from social institutions is filled by unscrupulous profiteers, known as poverty pimps. In this way the East Harlem poor are doubly exploited, first by their state of poverty and neglect, and then by interested representatives who exploit their lack of information and the fact that it is practically impossible for them to have direct access to institutions.

In the second place we have *social information in connection with the application of development schemes and must consider its potential contribution to the carrying out of non-technocratic programs* as distinct from programs which operate unilaterally from above to below and which therefore give rise to a more or less rigidly bureaucratic process.

Here the situation is the opposite of the one considered previously. Social information in this context functions in a dynamic situation in which it is not merely a question of guaranteeing the practical actualization of measures which have already passed through formal legislation, but of accompanying and seconding a process of social change and of keeping present to both citizens and authorities the social objectives which justify it and the methods which will render it socially, and not merely technically, efficacious. *At this level social information is the fundamental requisite for the initial mobilization of the population.* We are still on the level of subordinate participation, in the sense that we are dealing with a participation which has been solicited from above, but at least the political and social authorities who take the important decisions can count on the advantage of learning the effects which their decisions have on the attitudes and behavior of the citizens. The process of planning loses some of its characteristic rigidity. It is no longer seen as an absolute, weighing down the destinies of all concerned with objectives which have been fixed once and for all, from which there is to be no turning back even if one realizes that the objectives have been mistaken or no longer meet the expectations of the majority of the citizens. The program loses all its metaphysical halo and becomes simply a way of graduating priorities. *That is, it becomes a way of establishing an order, prearranged but flexible, in the choices which society makes for itself by calculating with a certain degree of explicit reasonableness the relation between the desired ends and the available means.*

In the third place we have social information in regard to rational planning of social transformation. *Here the fundamental criterion is the interest of the greatest number of citizens, and the objective is that political power itself (i.e., the power to decide about men and their methods of coexistence, through the systematic participation of the people, institutionally guaranteed) should become a collective function instead of being the exclusive prerogative of a single person, group, or class.*

In this case the process of transformation affects the structural bases of society. It profoundly changes the dominance of certain social groups or classes. It influences the distribution of property and the motivation behind economic activity. And it postulates new orientations in culture and human values. At this point social information (esential if the plan is to prove successful) is required:

1. *to prevent popular initiative from dying away* as the result of the braking effect of bureaucratic complications;

2. *to guarantee the efficacy of the pressure from below*, not through slogans or emotional crisis, which would quickly die out, but by creating local autonomous institutions which ensure popular participation in the process of social transformation, especially in the aspects which affect day-to-day life;

3. *to ensure that political decisions and changes will coincide with the aspirations of the citizens and will be seen to do so* by controlling the times and rhythms of social transformation, protecting them against both authoritarian rashness and paternalistic tendencies.

It should be clear from what has been said above that I am suggesting a new model of social programming. In this new model the social moment and presence of social workers would not be simply additional and ornamental features, or the verbal tribute which financial imperatives, economic calculations, and technical resources are ready to pay to a vague, indefinite idea of socialization which is in no way binding on the practical level. From this time on we should be collecting the basic elements for the construction of this new model of "integral programming" in which the constructive nature of the technical and economic aspects is fundamentally guaranteed by the social aspects, that is to say, by the participation of the people.

SOCIAL INFORMATION AND DECISION-MAKING POWER

The limitations of social information are evident in a summary review of the situation. To begin with, it is doubtful whether social information alone has the power to change or influence the psycho-social attitudes of the masses or to modify positions which are soundly established on the existing state of affairs. *Social information demystifies, it lays bare, it brings about greater awareness, but of itself it cannot do anything to modify objective contradictions.* Left to itself it at best succeeds in exasperating them. Emargination is not a casual state, nor is it solely a question of good will. If we believed this we should run the risk of setting out to do something about the poor and the excluded and ending up by blaming them for everything. Anyone who has studied the living conditions in the shanties, in the *favelas*, in the *villa-miserias*, in the *barriadas* or *banlieue*, in the ghetto suburbs and in the villages which pay for the few miles separating them from the metropolis by a state of neglect and social distance measurable in light-years knows that emargination is a structural phenomenon, *and therefore that emargination is something which reproduces itself.* After two generations of ghetto-dwelling a human group is probably lost for good. It is essential to break the spiral at once, at its weakest point, at the point where the fundamental traits of the personality are formed and those value orientations are created which last for the whole life of the individual and condition him forever. It is necessary to strike at the weakest link in this reproductive chain of the phenomena of emargination: the point of primary socialization. Social information to this end must transform itself into organization. It must effectively change living conditions. It must change both the present situation and future prospects. But this is a difficult task which falls beyond its scope. Social information can (and must) point out the task, though it has no instruments, alone, with which to tackle the problems.

But there are also internal limitations—limitations, in the first place, linked to other sociological structures. Social information, mass communications, public opinion—these are three terms which send us to and fro without ever coming to terms with each other. *Public opinion is a social phenomenon which underlies private opinion but which is far from representing the arithmetic sum of private opinion.* What exactly is public opinion? Can we trust this anonymous and omnipresent monster (in the etymological sense of the word)? Is it true that it is omnipresent? An authoritative doubt has been expresssed in this respect. If a society were really characterized by public opinion—it has been observed—free discussion would be the dominant form of communication. Mass media, even if they existed, would serve merely to animate and to enlarge the dialogue. They would connect indirectly certain groups within which communication would continue to be direct. In a mass society, instead, the fundamental type of communication remains that of official media, and the public becomes simply the market for this media. The audience of a television program, for example, is defined as all the people exposed to it. In other words, the idea of an audience has lost, or at least is running the risk of losing, any suggestion of active significant participation, authentic and human—that is, spontaneous and incalculable. Where is social information to find its interlocutors? Or are we instead to consider social information as something impersonal and neutral, outside time and outside history, so that we must be satisfied with bureaucratic circulars or our documents, which achieve nothing and mean nothing to anybody?

In the second place there are still deeper internal limitations to be taken into consideration, in the sense that they have entered the very constitution of interpersonal information—*limitations connected with social mechanisms for the control and the exclusion of speech.* Social information can do nothing to protect itself from the action of such mechanisms, which are not to be confused with the manipulating of mass media because their roots lie much deeper. They seem in fact to spring from certain deep and primordial needs of man as a conversational animal, ritualistic and habit-forming, a maker of tools and customs (and thus of civilization). The only way to temper the paralyzing effects of such mechanisms is probably to become fully aware and conscious of their mode of operation. In every society—it has been observed—the production of speech is at one and the same time controlled, selected, organized, and distributed through a certain number of procedures intended to exorcise its powers and danger, to control its element of change, and to avoid its massive and overwhelming concreteness.[1]

To which instruments therefore should social information have recourse? How can it guarantee the achievement of its ends, and, in the first place, how is it to reach the citizens, its addressees? What screens must it throw down if it is to save the integrity of its message?

A systematic and adequate discussion of the instruments of social information is possible only insofar as we can distinguish the various levels at which such information takes shape. These levels extend from information as a knowledge of one's own rights and duties respecting institutions to the information that derives from significant participation. *It is the social institutions themselves which must take the first step.* Their information offices at the service of the citizen must be rendered more efficient and debureaucratized. It is clear that social information, not only in a reflected sense but also as innovation and as a stimulus, *is an integral part of the fundamental functions of the social service.* Social workers in the first place cannot help being responsible for social information. But what instruments and training have they? And what are the professional obstacles which prevent the full utilization of information techniques?

The problem is not merely a problem about the curriculum of training schools for social service, though this aspect of the question should not be neglected. The problem also concerns the relation between social workers and journalists, or even, in a wider vision, between social workers and mass media, that is to say newspapers, radio, and television. These three fundamental means of information—the written word, the spoken word, and the message transformed into image—merit detailed separate treatment as instruments of social information.

The daily and weekly papers hold great possibilities in this respect. But first of all the relation between social workers and journalists needs to be greatly improved. It is not a question of good will, which is unquestioned. The problem has two distinct aspects: the communicability of language, and the degree of privacy which is at times necessary if social action is to prove efficacious.

Setting the newspaper aside, the problem is still more serious when we come to radio and television. Here broadcasts which could be of interest for social information are either nonexistent or else have the character of specialist roundtable discussions among experts. This is still worse if we remember that, technically, with cable television (though this may not be imminent) we are certain to reach *a degree of cultural pluralism.* Cable television will make it possible to give that degree of expression to social groups and minority communities which in many countries, Italy among the first, is essential. Certainly substantial problems, such as the question of social information, cannot be reduced, as we said at the beginning, to problems of organization or engineering. But it is equally certain that, with cable television, *we can foresee a television which will result in practice and not merely in intention in the breaking down of existing barriers and socio-cultural inequalities. In this way it will be possible to represent the greatest number of real economic, social, and political interests.* The cable can, in fact, provide the space required by social, political, and trade union groups and communities which today are to be found on the fringes, shut outside the gates of both central and peripheral bureaucratic structures and no longer wishing to be represented by Rome or Washington, by Paris or London.

In this connection it is important to remember that a profound change in the process of education is being felt. The school is no longer the only source of knowledge. Television, radio, comics, factory classes, the daily press, even advertising are all important sources of information. For these reasons it is necessary today to keep for as long as possible, ideally for the whole of one's life, even as an adult, the assimilative, creative, and imaginative capacity of children.

Naturally, any consideration of the instruments of social information in the conditions of the modern world would be gravely defective and therefore misleading if it failed to remind us that the mass media are not moving in a political and social void. Especially in the capitalistic countries of the West, it has often been pointed out that the economic structure itself makes a certain degree of control over mass media indispensable on the part of large, vested interests. Industrial production today no longer depends on the laws of the market and on the theoretically free choice of individual customers. It is known that production programs for a given product are determined several years before the product is launched on the market and actually put up for sale. The setting up of a production program requires large-scale investment. It is therefore of the first importance that they can be assured of selling for a sufficient period and in sufficient quantities to pay off the basic investment. *Such consumer guarantees can only be obtained through intensive advertising campaigns, so as to convince and psychologically condition the customer, making a given product seem essential to him even when this is by no means the case.* The only instrument of these campaigns is the mass media. It is no exaggeration to affirm that if from one day to the next such mass media (radio, television, the press) were to cease their constant flow of advertising pressure, we should at very short notice find ourselves in a serious economic crisis in which the drop in sales of many products would immediately react on the productive system. This is not the place to go further into a discussion of this particular aspect of our theme, which would carry us a long way into an analysis of the complex phenomenon of consumption. It is important to remember, however, that a large part of modern economy is based, in the last analysis, on a systematic conditioning of men and women. This conditioning, if for no other reason than that it is concerned with the transmission of messages, cannot fail to concern those who are interested in the content, the limits, and the instruments of social information in the modern world. Given this situation, it is curious that few systematic efforts, if any, have been made to offer a critical understanding, at the theoretical level, of the process of mass communication. In this perspective, the recent contribution by Frank Böckelmann stands out, and its relevance becomes evident. A closer examination of this study might be useful.

MASS COMMUNICATION, INFORMATION, AND MANIPULATION

Frank Böckelmann's study is important in the first instance for a general reason which is at once one of method and one of essence.[2] We are inundated, besieged, and sometimes have the frustrating sensation of being inevitably overwhelmed, by a mass of studies and investigations referring to phenomena of the mass media and mass communications—from vaguely philosophical definitions to quantitative estimates concerning their social and individual consequences. Here at last is a contribution which does not form part of, and become absorbed by, the infinite number of such studies, like a crazy fragment. It tries to develop on the basis of an initial critical assessment of the field and the consequences which have been accumulated by other investigators, but in such a way as not to repeat their mistakes. At the same time it attempts to contribute to that degree of potential cumulation of the partial results which today seems so necessary for the social sciences. I do not know if one may in this instance talk of a real "theory" of mass communications. However, the settling of accounts with the great pioneers of research in this field and with their mania for quantification—from Paul F. Lazarsfeld to Feestinger and Klapper—is set out here in a rigorous and convincing fashion with no concession to the "engineering," modelling tendencies which are presented as a substitute for theory and which automaticaly result in a degradation of the truth, and its dilution into a series of fragmentary and disconnected patterns.

I see in Böckelmann's contribution more a series of practical-political suggestions than a complete "theory" in the classical sense of this much-abused term—in the sense of an "overview" which at once describes, explains, and interprets a specific constellation of phenomena and problems. However, for Böckelmann a theoretical design is certainly present and explicit. At the beginning, he says, "Certainly use of the microphone, lighting effects and other technical devices...lead to an increase in costs, a greater consumption of time and ever greater difficulties regarding organisation. *However this does not mean that radiophonic, film, and press techiques...can dominate the non-technological conditions which underlie the area of communication in general.*"[3]

It is therefore not legitimate to argue that Böckelmann is lacking in specific, problematic awareness and tends to give a reductive—though nevertheless very common—definition of mass commuications in terms of technical instrumentation and pure practical application. Indeed, his problematical awareness is so keen and demanding that it drives him to include before the really theoretical part of the book a detailed, historical discussion of the formation of a "public sphere" in the enlightenment sense, and of the dialectic between "public sphere" and "personal sphere," and hence of the "non-organised formation of opinion and will"—problematic areas which are first assaulted, and then, as now, deeply absorbed, by mass communications. In other words it comes as no surprise that Böckelmann should counterpose (even if in too scholastic a manner) mass communications and interpersonal or face-to-face communication, leaving to the last part of his book a rigorous critique of Lazarsfeld's famous theoretization of the two-step flow of communication and A. Moles' "cultural socio-dynamics." From the start of his investigation, Böckelmann cleary formulates the essence of the problem posed by mass communications. "Mass communications," he says "make possible a limitless expansion of the public political sphere. However, at the same time the public sphere and public opinion dissolve, and become mere illusions, produced and presented by professional commentators and publicity technicians."[4] In his day, C. Wright Mills was an unusually eloquent analyst of this aspect of the question, especially where he demonstrated the destruction of the public as such in the name of a standardization made necessary by technological imperatives and dominated by integrated interests which control both the technical structure and its social resonances as well as the juridical basis on which its formal power rests. However, it should perhaps be clarified in greater detail that, just as autonomous public opinion disappeared with the advent of the eighteenth-century type of integrated community and the "social control" which was natural to it, so similarly in today's conditions, the two terms "public" and "state" not only no longer coincide, but tend to diverge in an increasingly deeper and less reconcilable manner. This occurs as the tendency towards "statolatry" relentlessly negates those projects of social transformation of the political nuclei which are apparently most innovatory.

Böckelmann accurately notes the impoverishing effect of the "technical form of organisation" on the quality of social life. Referring rather to Jürgen Habermas and the Frankfurt School than to the profound insights of Walter Benjamin: "The restrictions which emanate from technological forms of organisation and circulation, and the levelling-down of vital rhythms in the field of free time, eliminate the 'strength of life histories'—the ability and the flux of perception, contrasting experiences which are continually assimilated, and a narrow horizon of hope and a persistent memory.''[5] However, without doubt what impresses him most is the systematic (or perhaps it would be better to say systemic) theory of Niklas Luhmann. In fact, he accepts and adopts, possibly even acritically, Luhmann's obsession regarding the "reduction of complexity"—a complexity which is derived from "the transcendence of the sphere of the family as the basis of meaning," insofar as "the meaning structures of the family community and of the individual can have no more value. . . as a social basis of the uniform interpretation of the world.''[6]

From this point of view, the organization of mass communications is made necessary by the interaction of intermediate systems with microsystems and the dominant macrosystem. It is no surprise that Böckelmann, at the end of his historico-political excursus, argues that "the concept of mass media refers to the complex of sophisticated communication techniques which allow simultaneous transmission by way of the press and films and of sound and visual telecommunications,''[7] and points out that "in contrast with face-to-face communication, in which there is a more or less continuous exchange between the sender and the receiver, the 'partners' of mass communications perform in a determined situation either only as communicators or only as receivers.''[8]

THE QUESTION OF SOCIAL COMPLEXITY

However, the basic question remains wholly untouched: In what sense is the modern world complex? What are the forms and the nature of the power relations which delimit mature capitalism or bureaucratic socialism? We are probably dealing with systems technically more complex than dynastic traditional societies, which are politically more simple. It is not an accident that we are dealing with systems in which the objective simplicity of political relations corresponds (*has* to correspond) to the manipulation—no longer artisan—of public opinion, and in which the mass media occupy a central position.

It seems to me that these limitations of Böckelmann's analysis are indisputable, but that they detract little—or not much—from the value of his *pars destruens* as regards contemporary investigation of the mass media. This is especially true in respect to North America: "A science of mass communications," he notes, "has to free itself from the obsessive question regarding the possibility of obtaining quantifiable results. Indeed, on closer examination it becomes clear that none of the possible replies to the questions regarding the effect of mass communications produces an increase in knowledge. What this science considers as a simple fact (individual attitude) it fetishizes at the same time, regarding it either as simply the most precise thing, as the most disconnected thing, or as the product of other disconnected attitudes independent of each other.... This research manipulates its object as if it had a value in itself."[9] It could not be put better. However, when the author moves on to the reconstruction of his theme and the positive part of his theoretical program (perhaps, too, because his critical questions—so intuitive and persuasive—raise our expectations to excess), a certain amount of disappointment is inevitable.

To state, as he does, that "the receivers only participate in mass communications when they consciously turn to mass communications in their free time," that "by necessity they 'receive' all their lives: the stereotypes of the whole of mass communications are omnipresent... and direct reception of the media of mass communication is also carried on in diverse processes and group conversations,"[10] is to say both too much and too little. In terms which seem to be borrowed from Jacques Lacan, Böckelmann expatiates on "communicating communication," insofar as this means that one "communicates to communicate communication": that is a turn of phrase which is not without theoretical suggestiveness, but which can also be seen as a demonstration of the superfluity of theoretical consideration in the real sense, just as Lacan talks about language as against *langue*, indeed *la langue*, which thus, as it communicates no further evidence, "communicates" the presence of the discourse, the moment or the "time" of the word.

Despite any expectation of greater equality or what some sociologists used to call "anticipatory participation," or vicarious participation by way of standardized consumption, social hierarchy is reproduced. Social equality makes no noticeable progress. Class "wounds" become partly secret, hidden behind consumerism, but they are not thereby less painful or less bloody. "Beneath the splendour of mass culture," says Böckelmann, "which levels all classes by making uniform the contents of leisure-time activities, there is an increasing difficulty in achieving communication of the masses who consume... since now the old multiplicity of specific class cultures and social differences has also disappeared, since they are no longer 'expressed' in a repressive relationship or one of solidarity, groups of consumers are immediately confronted with the hierarchy of the praxis of leisure time and labour, which is not resolved, and also with the privilege of access to mass communication. The hierarchy seems more evident and more unreasonable than ever."[11]

This is an analysis of unusual keenness which sees behind the persistence of social hierarchy the "communicative impoverishment" of industrial society, along with its necessary consequence: "a strict isolation whose correlate is cultural homogeneity." Paradoxically—up to a point—communication reinforces solipsistic isolation, and this, as Böckelmann points out, exists above all in the city satellites, where groups uniform from the point of view of social origin live together. In other words, mass communications effect the closing of nuclear families on themselves: "The non-organised communicative flow in individuals and groups is characterised by a ritualised obligatory, almost unmodifiable, behaviour, based on distance and competition."[12]

What is to be done? Böckelmann's study appears to arrive at a conclusion which contradicts common sense. Mass communication does not join together, but divides; it does not link up—it separates. It is based on a mutual exclusion: both the historical structures of mass communications and the individual parts of the whole of direct communication are expressions of the mutual isolation of both these aspects of communication." "The form in which mass communication takes shape is one of abstract standardisaton and it is maintained in an arbitrary fashion. The form in which interpersonal communication takes shape is a division without mediation. . . . The cause of communication is not social stratification, nor is the latter the cause of stratification. Both are reciprocally implied."[13] At this point the author suggests a series of "efforts at co-operation," which can be removed from abstract standardization, but also at the same time from aggressive parochial tendencies, "which in one way re-create the external form of pre-bourgeois spheres of circulation (the unlocked door, gossip among old people, local civic celebrations, popular festivals, etc.). Provincialism, parochialism, shattered fragments of interaction on which, however, 'there grows no protection of the urban democratic public sphere.' "[14]

MASS MEDIA DO NOT MEDIATE

How to decentralize without provincializing? How to democratize in the real sense without privatizing? The attempts at "co-gestion" (co-management) have been shown to be dangerously unprotected as regards bureaucratizing tendencies, and often "the joint formulation" of public messages not only furnishes certain journalists with a democratic alibi, but also "helps their self-confirmation."[15] Böckelmann glimpses a solution but does not make it explicit. Like Moses, he sees the Promised Land of the "democratic solution," but he dares not enter it. "The mutual development of the isolated spheres," he argues cautiously, "certainly can begin with the offer of greater possibilities of transmission and reception for those groups *which want to organise their interests and communicate with each other* . . . : apprentices, students, teenagers, *all those who plan their own freedom in common*: housewives, and other working women, women's organisations, groups of employees."[16]

Here the author is close to the ultimate problem, and almost arrives at it, even though he only pricks the skin: "Mass communications begins to free itself from institutions . . . when *it does not restrict itself to commenting on events*, but rather organises them as such and *does not deal with them as simple program material*" [author's emphasis].[17]

At last! The question of power has timidly arisen on the horizon of theoretical analysis. To plan one's own freedom in common requires the ability (the power) to *choose* and thus to *decide*. However, one can neither choose nor decide, save on the basis of what one knows.

At this point, certain theoretical inadequacies become evident. It is not sufficient to counterpose mass and interpersonal, or "face-to-face," communication. *Social* communication is socially relevant communication connected with a telos," which is more or less explicit. Collective communication, on the other hand, is generic mass communication, interpersonal only in a mediated sense, and not necessarily connected with a meaningful social end. This does not imply that it is without meaningfulness, but only that this meaning is not explicit, that it has to be "brought out." Thus, to be caught up in the network of a communication does not automatically mean to enter the framework of meaningful communication.

The question is multi-dimensional and very complex. Communication, information, deformation—these are interconnected terms and intercommunicating concepts, but their levels of interaction and reciprocal conditioning are differentiated. Who communicates, and what? Who is communicated with, and by whom? Why? In reality, mass information as "generic communication," amounts to deformation (de-information), potential and actual mystification, and manipulation. The meaning is buried in the—apparent—wealth of signs and messages. The most efficient censorship in modern conditions probably lies in multiplying the messages to bring out their "messages" (to use Marshall Mac-Luhan's formula), to assail the listener-spectator with a continuous flow of items, literally to bombard him without providing any means for him to recover. The items, by definition, exist on the same plane. *The mass media do not mediate.* No ordering of levels of priority—that is, no selective filter—can with ease be operated by the individual consumer.

Thus, public news is privatized, uprooted from the material basis of its significance ("the medium is the message"; on the other hand, for its receiver a "message" is a "massage"). It is in the apparent anonymity, the neutral objectivity, of the sender, in what I would call "orphan news," that there lies the risk of making the receiver politically powerless, a risk of spurious apoliticalness and hence of a passivity, however reluctant, refractory, or sceptical this may be. However, the transmitter of the message should not be viewed in conspiratorial terms. It is enough that he does his work well. An intention to manipulate does not have to be explicit, to be presented as a program. It is built in. The truth of this can be seen in the fact that the whole aggressive mythology which initially surrounded the arrival of certain technical means, such as videotape, which were held to be endowed with democratic virtues, essential for the construction of the self-awareness of the base, little by little—but inexorably—collapsed. The material base of the meaning of messages can never be obliterated or left in silence without in this way leading to an acritical fetishizing of practice.

The problem of the mass media is not, therefore, exhausted through the terms of Böckelmann's analysis—obsolescence of the word and primacy of the image. This is not only a more or less demogogic concession to a facile theorizing, even though it is true that the image can be more readily and lastingly perceived than the word or the abstract concept which lies behind it; the latter requires an additional effort of imagination to translate—decodify—what has been expressed at the level of verbal statement into an image related to concrete experience. Generally it is feared that the primacy of the image might diminish the efficiency of the work; it might drastically reduce its use and its capacity for criticism, and eventually void thought itself—ultimately drying out its basis of experience. One can certainly "watch as a group" (cinema and television), but one no longer talks. Even where it has not disappeared, conversation is in decline. Gabriel Tarde, in his *La conversation*

(1901) underlined the importance of an empirical study of conversations. "Who speaks, about what, and how much: all this in terms of the social characteristics of the parties and of changes in the historical environment."[18]

It is not by chance that Lazarsfeld refers to Tarde. He sees in him a precursor of his own theory of personal influence.[19] This theory has had, and continues to have, considerable influence on researchers. It has played the part of reassurance. There is an anxiety regarding the rationality of the modern individual, his capacity to keep his head and not be sucked in by the ceaseless flow of communications and messages. "The message is the massage," and "the medium is the content," MacLuhan warned, not altogether paradoxically. Lazarsfeld, with his theory of the two-step flow of communications, steps in to reassure the apocalyptics.

According to Lazarsfeld, it is wrong to think that there is on the one hand a means of mass communications which is solitary, mysterious, and omnipotent and on the other hand an amorphous, disarticulated, and tendentially passive "mass." He argues that in between the medium and the mass there is really a "small group"; it has a complex network of channels of communication, its structures of meaning and language, and the fluid, unforeseeable interpersonal relations which are nonetheless rich and dense and essentially critical, and which define it. Hence, in this case the theme of research on the mass media should no longer be seen in the media of mass communications in themselves, in those who control them, or in the equality of the messages they transmit: nor should mass society as such be studied. Rather, one should study the conditions in which the "small group" is formed and functions—"conversation." As Tarde discussed seventy years earlier, the "small group" consequently appears as last refuge and life-raft. However, are there "small groups"?

Glamorizing the "small group" bears the implication of an apologetic intention as regards mass industrial society. The image, the iconic message, as filtered by the small group which is formed (or was formed) between the media and the masses at the very moment in which it provided the greatest return for the smallest expenditure in reality deprives us of knowledge and real human participation: of a participation, that is, which is unpredictable and dramatic.

The incursion of the mass media into the world of information is both the effect of the process of general development of society and the cause of its articulation at the level of opinion. The progress of the technical conditions for the advancement of channels of information (radio, television, new press methods), the cancelling of distances between places, technological innovations which lead to a division of labor at the level of nations, different from the first phase—all these elements overcome the limits of information at the artisan level discussed in the preceding paragraph. However, at the same time the spread of a new method of information itself fixes a new world consciousness at the level of the individual, or societies, in a global manner—one which requires accurate and sophisticated information and one which is able to synthesize the various aspects of the reality it expounds. Marshall MacLuhan expressed this condition in the phrase "the global village": everyone is simultaneously "activated" through the very fact of becoming aware that something is happening in a certain place in the world.

In a general sense, the reality of the cultural industry springs from this. The recipient of the cultural product is defined, and this production itself enters a competitive process with all existing social structures. Immediate references and specific situations become fewer, and the whole framework of culture experiences the mediation of the new institutions. A high level of education, centers of professional instruction, and the definition of roles within each productive cycle are the complex responses to the new relation between producer and consumer of culture. As regards information, the realities to be borne in mind (and to be referred to) become progressively more complex. The objective widens from the primary transmitting group to the international and national interconnections of social classes. The information medium takes on autonomous importance, the use of which becomes itself a dialectical point. From information, one moves on to communication.

The media of communication become one of the central frameworks of the cultural industry. However, it is precisely in this phase that the asynchronic development between medium and operator becomes sharper. Since the news medium is directed at a large and heterogeneous number of receivers and readers, it has to modify its own organization. Once the areas of influence which can concern the reader (by way of the characteristic element of "global village" of which we were speaking) have been sounded out, they are subdivided according to two basic criteria: (1) the homogeneity of the areas of information to be covered: news of the day, internal politics, external politics, life style, sport, culture, etc.; (2) the relation of presumed interests between the mass of information and the specific social, economic, and cultural composition of the group of readers towards whom the news medium is directed.

The structure of the enterprises which operate in the area of information conforms to these criteria. News media as the expression of a single economic or political group become minimally productive at the level of influence on public opinion. There is thus a tendency to link up several components from identical interests involved in communication. It is not by chance that at this point the two major categories of the press take clearly divergent paths—that of information, and that of politics. This, however, is not enough. Because the political representativeness of the news medium must bring together different interest groups, even though these may be basically homogeneous, the political press is reduced to a simple organ of organized groups—that is, to party organs—and, as a further process of dissolution, only the parties which are connected with major ideological choices need an autonomous space to intervene in the area of communications. For the so-called "opinion" parties, the political option can be referred to the broad concept of representativeness, which is the basis of this major "organ of information." To confirm this development, one can consider international reality. In the Anglo-Saxon countries, where organized political representation (the parties) is formed as the coming-together of real socio-economic interests, at the maximum, information news media are developed. In the Latin countries, or in countries which have organized their state structure on the basis of the congruity of states and party—where, that is, party organization is derived from exact ideological options—the political press has an autonomous voice as regards the whole horizon of communications.

If we look at the ways in which the role of the journalist has developed following the movement of the medium into the terrain of the cultural industry, we have to proceed through three levels of deeper analysis:

1. the new division of labor in the professions;
2. specific functions in the organs of information;
3. specific functions within party organs.

The organization of the information enterprise, in its new dimension as cultural industry, rests on the double criterion of the homogeneous nature of the areas to be covered and of the assumed relation of interests between the mass of information and the composition of the group of readers, spectators, and consumers.

THE TECHNOCRATIC ILLUSION

In this way mass media have a function, over and above the structural level, which circumstances at times render unique: as for example in little villages which have not even been brushed by the process of industrialization, where the radio and newspapers are the only link, the only channel of communication, with the rest of the country. But in all cases, even in those which are less exceptional, it is this characteristic as a "link" which is the center of any inquiry into the action of mass media: wherever they are to be found, they serve as a connection between the limited and static local culture and urban culture, between a limited heritage handed down by tradition and a wider heritage. It seems to me that this potential capacity to unify and unite over a common denominator the contrasting and unequal cultural situations existing in a country (and I am thinking particularly of the situation in Italy) precedes both in time and in importance that other basic tendency which is towards homogeneity and levelling out.

For this reason it is particularly interesting to carry out research in a provincial center rather than in a great city. In a small community, however isolated it may be (and naturally the greater the isolation the truer this will be), cinema, television, press, and radio play a major role as channels of information and communication, while in an urban center they are simply one among many. The discovery of the new techniques of information should imply in the cultural field the spreading and rationalization of such culture comparable to the part played by the industrial revolution in the field of economics and labor, when both fields have been affected by the introduction of machinery, organization, and mass production; and the analogy is rounded out if we bear in mind the gap which exists in both fields between mechanical development, technology and the development of values, between the advantages brought about by technical development and the progress of critical self-knowledge.

Such expansion and rationalization are merely hypothetical; we have to take into account the actual use of the instruments of communication, the content of their messages, their irregular distribution (the fact that certain newspapers do not reach all the centers, the shortage of bookshops and libraries); and finally the accessibility of the general public, faced with a choice between information and entertainment, between high- and low-quality shows, between good and bad taste, between conscious assimilation and passive reception.

In conclusion, the meaning we can give to the word "culture" can be considerably restricted by defining it more precisely. If the concept of "culturalization" indicates the degree of penetration of the dominant culture (or the culture of national elites) among the lower or peripheric social groups, then an inquiry into the cultural life of a community linked to its mass media is the equivalent of any inquiry into the degree of culture to be found in the community—but at the same time it must take into account the content and the meaning of this culture.

If we go back to the analogy between rationalization in the field of labor and in the field of culture, then we see that with the former it is the structure which is modified, allowing for a conveniently clear-cut and straightforward plan of campaign; while on the other hand an inquiry into mass media operating in an area where interests and influence intersect, crisscross, and blend together, and which functions by means of a number of aims, suggestions, stimuli, then the problem of the method to be adopted becomes at once far more complex.

What is it that in effect we desire and hope to be able to discover when we take up a position in the midst of a community with the declared aim of inquiring into the instruments of mass media? The reply is apparently simple enough: We want to discover the peculiar influence exerted by those instruments on the inhabitants of the community, or, to use a term which is dear to the experts in this sector, to discover their "effects."

But this term is extremely elastic and is open to a number of interpretations. I would go so far as to say that, according to the meaning attributed to this word "effects" and according to the attitude towards the final aim, that is to say, towards the relation between the instrument and its audience, very different types of research can be set on foot, varying not only for what regards method and content but also, and more particularly, the usefulness and extent of the results obtained. It is necessary to have a clear view of this point if we are to solve even partially the problem of the choice of method.

Existing literature on the question of mass media is voluminous, and experimental research in the last decade has been intense; but insofar as it concerns an interpretation of the significance of the phenomenon, it has also been curiously sterile. To measure a specific influence of mass media on the behavior and psychology of the individual is no easy task, even though public opinion proclaims that such an influence exists and that it is extremely powerful; even research into phenomena which are commonly held to be serious (such as violence by children stimulated by the television or mass panic produced by communications causing alarm) has been forced to moderate considerably the hypotheses from which it started out.

Until the present day the inquiries carried out in England and in the United States have taken only two directions. The first is typical of market research and public opinion polls: the data produced by these inquiries show the areas within which the different instruments operate, the social factors which are to be found in concomitance with such variations, and the co-relations between the different groups of variants. The aim of such studies is to establish above all the range of the phenomenon and to identify the factors which contribute to its spread. Such studies should be restricted to institutes of statistics, organizations specializing in public opinion polls; in Italy this means the Doxa Institute and the RAI (Radio and Television) public opinion service, which have the necessary means to carry out such tests on a wide scale. Instead, what often happens is that all the energies of an entire research team, which has been set up at considerable expense, both in organizing and financing it, working in a carefully chosen region or zone, are wholly spent on qualitative measurements of this kind.

Examples of this are the study *The Communication of Ideas* which Cauter and Downham carried out in Derby (Great Britain) or, even more appropriately, Malcom MacLean's *Two Years with Film Audiences*, carried out at Scarperia in Tuscany. The chief discovery of this work, which had the benefit of the Michigan State Integral Computer for an elaboration of the data, boils down to the fact that attendance at the local cinema is in inverse ratio to the distance, that the age groups of the older inhabitants (in a township of 5,000 residents) is the least regular in attendance, while the younger inhabitants go to the cinema more frequently; that the ratio of book readers is much lower than that of the radio audiences; that perhaps the cinema and television exert a common attraction, and so on and so forth.

This kind of study, which is useful insofar as it provides the indispensable data for any research into any subject, hardly deserves the name of research. The "effects" to which it draws attention, and for which it provides the documentation, tell us nothing about the content of the relation between the people interviewed and the instruments they utilize—they are rather to be seen as inner products of the system. In the same way the information that a given factory employs a thousand workers and produces a hundred cars per day may define a certain commercial situation, but it throws no light on the relations between the workers and the factory.

It is important not to lose sight of the limitations of this type of inquiry. It exerts a strong attraction in that it is engaged with all that is clear, definable, measurable: in the eyes of a research worker imbued with a scientific spirit, the relations between the people interviewed and mass media at times take such indefinite and undefinable forms that they force him to take refuge in facts which, while they are obvious, are at least sure, and to lay aside all that would throw doubt on such certainties.

The other direction taken by research, which is followed by many workers in the United States who apply advanced methodological approaches, is characterized by a much subtler aim. Its objective is the pure "effect," the ideal stream which flows from the television screen or the printed page toward an audience, persuading it to perform certain actions or to modify, overturn, or confirm certain opinions. This pure state, known as "effectiveness," not only exists, according to research workers in the States, but can even be measured or, more properly, caught. It is a question of catching the specific potential of a social force by isolating it from the innumerable others which operate on the same plane, of analyzing its properties by the methods used by chemists. The whole operation is invariably carried out with strictly scientific processes: groups of individuals are deliberately "exposed" to a certain television program (or are taken from a background which ensures they are consistently so exposed) and are examined with specific tests and compared with similar individuals who have not been so exposed.

The results, when any are obtained, are very similar to a medical report on the effects of a cycle of injections. In fact, the great majority of the inquiries carried out in this way, as can be seen from J. Klapper's report, "The Effects of Mass Media," go to show that no one medium (or all four together) produces effects which depend unquestionably on its unaided action.[20]

Thus we end up being surrounded by the absurdity of large-scale and complex studies, which in order to measure slight differences, such as, for example, the difference between people who own a television set and those who do not, completely neglect the real and complex relationship existing between the television and its viewers.

This shift in the grounds of research away from the natural direction that an inquiry should take and towards one which proves so sterile and selective, so complicated in its checks, and so limited in its results is far from being purely casual. The motives go back to the disproportionate importance which American investigators give to two sectors among the many which make up mass communications: political propaganda and commercial advertising. They are without question all over the world the two sectors in which (to a greater or lesser extent, and by a variety of means) the techniques of persuasion are most openly applied. For this reason most of the attention is concentrated on them, while all the other products of mass culture are lumped together as ''entertainment''—and are anxiously examined for conclusive proofs of the efficacy of the media itself.

It has taken years of research to discover that even in these two sectors the action of the instruments cannot be considered either direct or sure, but has to be added to, or subtracted from, the action of a large number of mutually intersecting factors, such as, for example, the pre-existing attitudes of the subject (which may lead to a selective memorization of the message received), the prevailing opinion in his family, the opinion of his group leaders, and so on. I believe that this rapid survey of these two roads of research, and the wide margin of sterility which research of this kind is bound to allow for, enables us to fix some useful points and to avoid making certain mistakes.

THE IMPORTANCE OF SOCIAL CONTEXT

The first consideration which we must make is that our desire to estimate the potential of a given social force by isolating it under the microscope is probably an impossibility. Its direct result is in every case an abstract attitude which has nothing to do with the concrete conditions in which mass media operate, except insofar as these emerge in the course of an inquiry and are claimed as so many discoveries: for instance, the fact that the influence of a political message is conditioned by the opinions already held by the subject who receives it has been claimed a ''discovery.'' The validity of such an aim is, in any case, questionable. As C. Wright Mills has already observed, the attempt to distinguish between individuals exposed to different media to a greater or lesser extent certainly plays an important part for advertisers, but it is no sufficient basis on which to build a theory of the social significance of these media.

The second consideration, which is strictly connected with the former, is that it is a problem of influence, or at least that the weight carried by these new techniques of information can only be adequately formulated on a solid structural basis. It is necessary, that is to say, that the research should start out from a full knowledge of the social conditions and system of values current in the sample, the audience, or the community selected in order to be able to evaluate the part played in it by mass media and the reason why the influence of mass media is great or small in the community under examination. That is to say, we must bear in mind that cultural communications operate in a superstructural field, and that even the smallest phenomenon can be correctly understood only by taking into account the underlying structure. This means overturning the characteristic perspectives of the research as described above: the starting point should not be the media and the extent to which their messages are persuasive, but actual people who may assimilate or repel such messages; we should proceed not by extracting mass media from their social context, but by observing them as in fact they are, in relation to all the rest.

The research worker, in this way, is protected from certain risks. For example, he is no longer tempted to consider mass media as an independent variable, or to delude himself that he can use them to identify differences of behavior or shifts in the scale of values of the subjects interviewed, when it is extremely probable that they depend on more than one factor and possibly on real structural modifications. An example of this kind of aberration is the interpretation to be found in "Peasants and Television," by L. De Rita, in which the writer notes that the more assiduous viewers are less opposed to the idea of schooling for girls and puts forward the hypothesis, though with a certain caution, that this step forward is a result of the influence of television. But it is easy to realize that a number of other influences will all have been pulling in the same direction: the advice of relations who have emigrated into the towns, contact with the employees of the Reform Organization, (state agency for land reform in southern Italy) or, last but not least, new openings for employment which are the result of the establishment of a factory (in the case in question, the ANIC oil refineries).[21]

A further risk of this tendency to concentrate on "effects" is a mistaken attitude towards the sample, the attitude of a scientist who checks the efficacy of certain experiments on a more or less inert body. The American scholars who show a preference for this study of "effects" have never, unlike their English colleagues, questioned the appropriateness of the word "mass" and have rarely discussed the meaning to be given to the term, or the advisability of changing it.

Wilbur Schramm has pointed out that the study of mass media is concerned with the way in which the communication is effective, with the way in which it is understood and unequivocal, with the way in which people use mass media, with the way in which peoples communicate with each other, with the way in which society can utilize mass media for the advancement of its well-being, and, in general, with the way in which the fundamental processes of communication are carried out.[22]

It is easy to see from Schramm's outline that communication research, in its various sectors, represents a typically American approach to the study of certain important processes of interaction in mass society. The extension of the boundaries of communications research is such that today they embrace the most varied sectors of sociological, psychological, and anthropological investigation. Merton could state that the study of mass media is the American form of sociology of knowledge, in that American research into mass communications, like the work done by sociologists of knowledge in the European tradition, is concerned with the "reciprocal relation between the social structure and communications." In this way North American sociologists and political scientists believe that it is possible to explain complex socio-political phenomena by translating their mechanisms in terms of communications.

The advantages of this approach are that it enables them to interpret unequivocally and coherently, in the framework of a single conceptual model on the general level, a whole series of psycho-social phenomena which seem to be distinct and contradictory; but the risk is considerable and the price altogether too high. It is not only a question of the inevitable partiality of a model which in order to be general ends up by being generic, and which in an attempt to explain too much ends up by explaining nothing. Worse than this is the risk of losing sight of any critical dimension, of cutting down the critical analysis of the social conditioning operating on thought and culture until it is a mere neutral "evaluation" of the impact of different media on their audience, the critical consideration of the social structure to a "given social context" within which to ascertain the integrating functions of certain messages relayed by the mass media or by certain informal communication channels of the political system.

It is not hard to see how the study of mass media becomes sociology proper: nevertheless the limits of this approach, which, taking the instrument and the mass as its data (even through the mediation of a small group, in its turn selected) are likewise clear: it cannot ignore the major structural problems which underlie it. The limits of Lasswell's approach are comparable, even though he widens the sphere of analysis of mass media to the international level, as are those of Hovland, who, in Schramm's words, has built a new rhetoric in relation to mass media.

What remains in the shade is the whole problem connected with the wielders of power or control over the media, which implies power and control over the individual's electoral behavior, tastes, and inner values. What remains in the shade is an examination of the intentions of the wielders of power, the ways in which they apply it, and the extent to which there exists, or fails to exist, any real correspondence between such intentions and the effects of such messages transmitted through mass media.

The whole question of "manipulation" on the part of the proprietors and heads of private television networks in the United States is examined and criticized by Harry J. Skornia, who tackles a series of important social problems connected with mass society and mass culture in a country with a neo-capitalistic structure.[23]

The private structure of television organization in the United States, we are told, is a guarantee of democratic pluralism and leaves each man free, at least in theory, to utilize the powerful channels of communication which modern technology places at his disposal; furthermore, the upholders of the system are wont to add, competition forces such networks to take notice of public opinion, encouraging them to relay the messages which their audiences want to receive. They see this as a check on the chances of indoctrination and of the manipulation of consciences which a regime of public monopoly could give rise to. Finally, with a commercial-private system, the only cost to the viewer is the electricity needed to keep the set switched on. Each of these points is challenged in turn by Skornia. In the first place he denies that commercial television costs the user nothing. If we take into consideration the fact that many firms, especially in the field of cosmetics, spend over 50 percent of their total income on advertising, then every television user is, in effect, paying at least fifty dollars per year. There is no need of a long discussion to prove that the argument in favor of "democratic pluralism" is a mere screen which does little to hide the oligopoly behind. Can we accept the argument that the private television companies at least give their viewers what the viewers want? American radio and television networks have no doubts on this subject; for them this can be effected by means of audience research. The popularity rating has become a symbol, while the viewer rating, which calculates the size of the audience which listens in to a given program, is a sort of crystal ball on which the advertisers rely when commissioning programs.

Very few serious sociologists in the field of mass media are inclined to concede that popularity ratings can, in respect of what the viewers want, be considered to hold the power of discrimination that American television organizers claim for them. Skornia calls attention to the fact that the samples taken are so extremely limited and the data obtained are subject to distortions and manipulation. Furthermore, the spread of irritating advertisements which use the technique of drawing attention to the names of products in an aggressive fashion—names which nevertheless enter the subconscious of the consumer—seems to furnish a further proof of the lack of attention paid to giving the viewers what they want.

The whole question of popularity ratings needs to be developed in theoretical and methodological terms. This is the more necessary because the techniques of sampling popularity ratings has been exported to many countries without taking into account the fact that this technique in the United States serves certain definite purposes. It is in the interest of the American companies to give their advertisers long lists showing high popularity ratings in order to encourage further advertising commitments or else to raise the price of television advertising time. This both accounts for the deformations of data which Skornia challenges and also explains the logic underlying popularity ratings and viewer ratings. Obviously this is a typically private logic, which is scarcely applicable to a public monopoly. The limitations of the usual techniques for obtaining popularity ratings are well known, especially as regards the problem of sampling. Even the methods used by the Italian radio and television cannot be exempted from these criticisms. But the basic problem consists in the substitution of the logic of private enterprise for the logic of a public service, the substitution of a policy of popularity ratings for an educational policy. This can be done only if we possess precise data on the effects of mass media on the audience (and not simply information regarding the extent to which the audience does or does not enjoy a particular type of program) in order to determine the most effective way of conveying messages of a certain type not in the name of a mythical High Culture but with the intention of acting on the very forms of mass culture rather than of accepting them as data to which the programs should be expected to adapt themselves.

Mass media of communication. Communication, then. But, who communicates? And what? And to what effect? Is it man who uses language or is it the language which uses man? Who is speaking? Are we speaking through language or is language speaking through us? That is, are we *spoken* by our language? Are we then just living "codes," cultural stenograms, as it were?

There is little doubt that communication is the most powerful instrument of social control, at least in two ways, either through blocking or censorship of the information flow, and therefore through mystification, or through "fagocitation," that is, an excess of indiscriminate, acritical supply of data and information items without any priority in such a way that the individual to whom the communication flow is directed cannot help being overwhelmed and feeling vaguely mastered by things he cannot control. Evaluation is practically prevented and any personal judgment is likely to be paralyzed. One must add the tendency towards a purely formal consideration of "messages" which dispenses with objective content in favor of the *form* in which content is expressed. As pure form, there is no doubt that sign, word, message have a great importance. But by forgetting about content one loses the historical and political perspective which is essential to pass responsible (personal) judgment on specific issues.

NOTES

1. In this connection, see Michel Foucault, *L'ordre du discours*, Paris, 1980.

2. Cfr. F. Böckelmann, *Theorie der Massenkommunikation—das System Hergestellter "Offentlichkeit, Wirkungsforschung und Gesellschaftliche Kommunikationsverhältnisse"*. Frankfurt a.M., 1975.

3. Ibid., p. 28 (emphasis added).

4. Ibid., p. 7.

5. Ibid., p. 15.

6. Ibid., p. 22.

7. Ibid., p. 28.

8. Ibid., p. 30.

9. Ibid., pp. 152–53.

10. Ibid., p. 163.

11. Ibid., pp. 196–97.

12. Ibid., p. 199.

13. Ibid., p. 202.

14. Ibid., p. 212.

15. Ibid., p. 230.

16. Ibid., p. 241 (emphasis added).

17. Ibid., p. 241–42.

18. Cfr. P. F. Lazarsfeld, *Metodologia e ricerca sociologica*, V. Capecchi, (Ital. trans. of most of his methodological writings), Bologna, 1974, p. 771.

19. Cfr. Elihu Katz and Paul F. Lazarsfeld, *Personal Influence*, Glencoe, Ill., 1955.

20. J. Klapper, "The Effects of Mass Media," New York, Columbia University Press, 1949; see also J. Klapper, *What Do We Know about the Effects of Mass Communication: The Brink of Hope*, New York, Columbia University Press, 1958.

21. Cfr. L. De Rita, *Cotadini e televisione*, Bologna, Mulino, 1965.

22. Cfr. W. Schramm, *The Science of Human Communication*, New York, 1963.

23. Cfr. Harry J. Skornia, *Television and Society*, New York, 1955.

A Bibliographical Essay

1. As regards the process of industrialization in historical perspective, the reader already has in the text the basic references. Clearly, we are dealing with suggestions and references which are very far from exhaustive. The literature on the subject is in fact very substantial, though of uneven value. I do not so much refer to the textbook material, in which we may include C. Barbagallo, *Le origini della grande industria*, Florence, 1929, or to standard works like T. S. Ashton's *Economic History of England: The Eighteenth Century*, New York, 1958, London, 1964, nor again to impressive works like John U. Nef's *The Rise of the British Coal Industry*, 2 vols., London, 1932, and *Industry and Government in France and England, 1540–1640*, Philadelphia, 1940, Ithaca, N.Y., 1964; I am thinking rather of the Dobb–Sweezy debate on the transition from feudalism to the modern world (see *Science and Society*, 14, 2, Spring 1950, pp. 134–67), and books like the highly stimulating collection of essays by A. Gerschenkron, *Economic Backwardness in Economic Perspective*, Cambridge, Mass., 1962, which prick and deflate a whole series of myths around industrialization ingenuously conceived as a unilinear and basically homogeneous process, quite closed to local cultures and deaf, ultimately, to the problem of historical variation. Then, it is scarcely necessary to mention the great names: Weber, in addition to whose famous essay on the *Protestant Ethic*, one should recall the *Allgemeine Wirtschaftgeschichte*, which are the lectures for his last academic course held in Munich in the winter 1919–20 session; W. Sombart, whose qualities as interpreter and researcher, though not always at a critical level, shine through more in the weighty *Der moderne Kapitalismus*, Munich, 1902, than in the slender monograph *Der Bourgeois*, Munich, 1913, Eng. trans., *The Quintessence of Capitalism*, New York, 1967; Arnold Toynbee, whose papers and lectures on the *Industrial Revolution*, London, 1884; Boston, 1956, greatly contributed to popularizing this term undoubtedly of a "barricade" origin; R. H. Tawney, whose *Religion and the Rise of Capitalism*, London and

New York, 1926, Gloucester, Mass., 1962, gathers together his Holland Memorial Lectures of 1922 and is intended to be a comment and response to Weber's works and also those of Troeltsch, Choisy, Sombart, Brentano, and Levy.

2. Still more classical and, so to speak, consecrated names should be recalled as regards the process of industrialization seen as global social process. What distinguished, from the start, Marx's work, probably decisively assisted by Engels in its descriptive-empirical aspects—Engels, who had direct experience of the industrial factory environment—was precisely their global nature, the attempt to see how the technical datum in its objective finality influenced the social relationship in which working activity was taking shape, and how this in turn crystallized into complex institutions (that is, into more or less rigidly crystallized collective behavior) which ultimately sought their justification through the codification of elaborate ideological and doctrinal constructs. Where Engels gave in to mechanistic attitudes of an ingenuous positivism, letting himself be swamped by empirical data, Marx constantly stressed the need for the dialectical link between the analytical datum and the totality of the human situation under consideration. However, at least in the first volume of *Capital* and the remarkable thirteenth chapter, which we may see as the birth of industrial sociology, rarely does the systematic or dialectical-abstract requirement prevail over the minute, very careful description of technological characteristics and the daily processes not so much of the machines seen in isolation, but of what with a most fortunate insight he terms a "system of machines," a basis and support of what was later to be known as the "factory system." An example of this global, typically sociological reasoning is: the incorporation of the tool in the machine specializes the machine and degrades the worker; the worker can then be replaced by female labor, which is more "docile" and costs less; thus a technical innovation creates among the workers who become prey to alcoholism, the new slave merchants, and breaks up the traditional family nucleus—all in the name of the ideology of the free market as a new factor for integration and of "lay assistance."

However, the concept of industrialization as new type of global society belongs more to the "founders" of sociology than to Marx—to Saint-Simon and Comte. In other works, but especially my *La piccola citta'*, Milan, 1957, *Macchina e uomo nella societa' industriale*, Turin, 1963, and *La sociologia— storia, concetti e metodi*, Turin, 1965, (4th edition), I have brought out how much of modern theories on industrial society as new type of society—at least tendentially meta-ideological as is analyzed mainly in Raymond Aron's work— should be attributed to Saint-Simon and Comte, whose basic works should be read; of the former, *Du système industriel*, Paris, 1820–22, and of the latter, *Cours de philosophie positive*, 6 vols., Paris, 1830–42, especially the last three volumes, shortly to appear in an Italian translation edited by myself from UTET, Turin.

3. Among the more recent works, I shall restrict myself to noting a number with no attempt at evaluating them, and indeed with the warning that we are concerned with a stimulus for the reader to develop on his own account the themes which interest him. However, to help him find his way through the forest of a literature which grows perceptibly and in which the confusion between objective discovery, ideological preference, and simple vulgarizing propaganda is quite frequent, here I shall refer to the four dominant critical schemas.

a. *the genetic or historical approach*, in which one may collect together disparate contributions, mostly monographs, but held together by the purpose of providing accounts of development of specific institutional wholes. These regard industry as a phenomenon by itself, or corporate managers, or the working-class movement in the double sense of union organization and political party; in the majority of cases we are dealing with accounts which I have elsewhere termed "dynastic" precisely because the phenomenon under investigation is seen as a reality closed in on itself, almost a datum moving in a void instead of a variable, however variously important, in a universe of factors—structures, forces, social groups—which altogether make up the living essence of the social process;

b. *the approach characterized by "theories of economic development,"* which has secured a quite special stress from the recent entrance into history as autonomous agents, the people, and in general the ex-colonial countries, who today with understandable patience set to open up the path of industrial development, often giving rise to the disturbing paradox of the simultaneous defeat and victory of the European West, defeated from the point of view of political supremacy and jealously courted from that of technology. For the most, we are dealing with studies on the non-economic aspects of economic development, which demonstrates the unease of economists when faced with behavior not reducible to the socio-psychological hypothesis—in truth, fairly simplistic—of man as necessarily drawn to maximize his own individual profit, which underlies the theoretical apparatus of marginalist economics. However, one has the impression that recognizing the importance of structures and value sets as regards self-generating economic development on a local scale, stops short at its verbal elaboration and at most is translated into the attempt to add from without, almost as a harmless (if elusive and ultimately frustrating) additive, conclusions of a vaguely sociological, anthropologico-cultural and psychological kind, to the normal economic considerations;

c. *the interpretative approach*, marked by research and studies in which there prevails the criterion of synoptic globality, intended to bring out the interaction between phenomena and the simultaneous, coordinated evolving process of institutional wholes; herein one might easily include Weber and his many discussants from Sombart and Wunsch to the latest, Kurt Samuelsson, *Religion and Economic Action*, Eng. trans., New York, 1961, along with studies like

like those of Clark Kerr, John T. Dunlop, Frederick Harbison, and Charles A. Myers, *Industrialism and Industrial Man*, Cambridge, Mass., 1960, and John U. Nef, *La naissance de la civilisation industrielle et le monde contemporaine*, Paris, 1954;

d. lastly, *the ideological approach*, or the prescriptive approach, in the doctrinal sense, in which more or less consciously the scientific analysis and factual testing are replaced by schemas and models presented as desirable, and in which the very concept of industrial society or civilization is charged with negative or positive connotations according to the preferences of the authors, independently of the empirical tests employed for the plausibility of the arguments used.

4. Among the many contributions to the discussion, in addition to those cited in the text, I shall confine myself to mentioning the following from among the most important:

Ackoff, R. L., *Redesigning the Future*, New York, 1974.

Aronowitz, S., *False Promises*, New York, 1974.

Bell, D., *The Coming of Post-industrial Society: A Venture in Social Forecasting*, New York, 1973.

Bennis, W., *Changing Organizations*, New York, 1966.

Bennis, W., and Slater, P., *The Temporary Society*, New York, 1968.

Berger, J., and Offe, C., "*Die Entwicklungsdynamik des Dienstleistungssektors*," *Leviathan*, 80, 1, 1980.

Berkley, G. E., *The Administrative Revolution: Notes on the Passing of Organization Man*, Englewood Cliffs, N.J., 1971.

Berle, A. A., *The Twentieth Century Capitalist Revolution*, New York, 1954. *Bibliography on Industrialization in Underdeveloped Countries*, UN, New York, 1956.

Blake, R.R., and Mouton, J.S., *The Managerial Grid*, New York, 1964.

Braverman, H., *Labor and Monopoly Capital*, New York, 1974.

Bruce, M., *The Coming of the Welfare State*, London, 1961.

Burns, T., and Stalker, G.M., *The Management of Innovation*, London, 1961.

Chandler, A.D., *Strategy and Structure*, Cambridge, Mass., 1962.

———, *The Visible Hand: The Managerial Revolution in American Business*, Cambridge, Mass., 1977.

Clapham, J. H., *Economic development of France and Germany, 1716–1814*, Cambridge, 1923, 1936.

Clark, C., *The Conditions of Economic Progress*, New York, 1940; London and New York, 1957.

Clawson, D., *Bureaucracy and the Labor Process*, New York, 1980.

Clemens, R., *La mentalité d'entrepreneur aux premières phases du développement*, in *Fifth World Congress of Sociology*, vol. 2.

De Maria, G., *Il progresso tecnico e l'economia moderna*, in "Progresso technologico e la societa' italiana," Guiffre', Milan, 1961.

Drucker, P., *The New Society*, New York, 1951, 1962.

———, *The Practice of Management*, New York, 1973.

Duchene, F., ed., *The Endless Crisis: America in the Seventies*, New York, 1970.

Evan, W.E., *Organization Theory*, New York, 1976.

Ferrarotti, F., *An Alternative Sociology*, New York, 1979.

———, *L'evoluzione interna del capitalismo dal proprietario al manager*, in "Rassegna italiana di sociologia," 2, 2, April–June 1961, pp. 171–85.

———, *Max Weber and the Destiny of Reason*, Armonk, N.Y., 1982.

———, *Sindacato, Industria, Societa*, Turin, UTET, 1968.

Fourastie, Y., *Les répercussions économiques de l'automation et la problème de l'emploi*, CNR, Rome, 1956.

Freidson, E., "Professionalization and the Organization of Middle-class Labor in Post-industrial Society." In *Professionalization and Social Change*, edited by P. Halmos, Sociological Review Monograph, no. 20, 1973.

———, "Professions and the Occupational Principle." In *The Professions and Their Prospects*, edited by Eliot Freidson, Beverly Hills, Calif., 1973.

Fuchs, V., *The Service Economy*, New York, 1969.

Fusfeld, D.R., "The Rise of the Corporate State in America," *Journal of Economic Issues*, 6 (March): 1-22, 1972.

Galbraith, J.K., *The New Industrial State*, New York, 1967.

Gartner, A., and Riessman, F., *The Service Society and the Consumer Vanguard*, New York, 1974.

Gershuny, J., *After Industrial Society: The Emerging Self-Service Economy*, Atlantic Highlands, N.J., 1978.

Habermas, J., and Luhmann, N., *Theorie der Gesellschaft oder Sozialtechnologie?*, Frankfurt, 1971.

Hall, R.H., *Organization: Structure and Process*, Englewood Cliffs, N.J., 1982.

Hammond, J. L., and Hammond, B., *The Rise of Modern History*, London, 1926; New York, 1937.

Heydebrand, W., and Noell, J., "Task Structure and Innovation in Professional Organizations." In *Comparative Organizations*, edited by W. Heydebrand, Englewood Cliffs, N.J., 1973.

Hirschmann, A. O., *The Strategy of Economic Development*, New Haven, 1958.

Hoselitz, B. F., *Lo sviluppo economico sotto la prospettiva sociologica, Atti del congresso internazionale di studio sul problema delle aree arretrate*, Giuffre', Milan, 1955.

———, *Sociological Aspects of Economic Growth*, Glencoe, Ill., 1960.

———, *Non-economic Barriers to Economic Development*, "Economic Development and Cultural Change," March 1952.

————, and Moore, W. E., eds., *Industrialization and Society*, UNESCO, The Hague, 1963.

Hughes, E.C., *Men and Their Work*, New York, 1958.

Jun, J.S., and Storm, W.D., *Tomorrow's Organizations*, Glenview, Ill., 1973.

Katon, G., *Psychological Analysis of Economic Behavior*, New York, 1961.

Kraemer, P.E., *The Societal State Meppel*, Boom en Zoon, 1966.

Kraft, P., *Programmers and Managers: The Routinization of Computer Programming in the United States*, New York, 1977.

Kumar, K., *Prophecy and Progress: The Sociology of Industrial and Post-industrial Society*, London, 1978.

Lewis, W. A., *The Theory of Economic Growth*, London, 1955.

Lindblom, C.E., *Politics and Markets*, New York, 1977.

Luhmann, N., *Legitimation durch Verfahren*, Neuwied, 1976.

Mattick, P., *Marx and Keynes: The Limits of the Mixed Economy*, Boston, 1969.

Mead, M., *Cultural Patterns and Technical Change*, Paris, 1953; New York, 1955.

Mills, C.W., *White Collar*, New York, 1951.

Moore, W. E., *Industrialization and Labor: Social Aspects of Economic Development*, Ithaca, N.Y., 1951, 1965.

Naisbitt, J., *Megatrends*, New York, 1982.

Noble, D., *America by Design: Science, Technology, and the Rise of Corporate Capitalism*, London, 1977.

O'Connor, J., *The Fiscal Crisis of the State*, New York, 1973.

Ogburn, W. F., *How Technology Causes Social Change*, in "Technology and Social Change," New York, 1957.

Parsons, T., *The System of Modern Societies*, Englewood Cliffs, N.J., 1971.

Pennings, J.M., *Interlocking Directorates*, San Francisco, 1980.

Pietsch, M., *La révolution industrielle*, Payot, Paris, 1961.

Rogers, E. M., *Diffusion of Innovations*, Glencoe, Ill., 1962.

Schmitter, P.C., "Still the Century of Corporatism?" In *The New Corporatism*, edited by F.B. Pike and T. Stritch, Notre Dame, Ind., 1974.

Scott, R.W., *Organizations: Rational, Natural, and Open Systems*, Englewood Cliffs, N.J., 1981.

Shonfield, A., *Modern Capitalism*, London, 1965.

Sklar, H., ed., *Trilateral Commission and Elite Planning for World Management*, Boston, 1980.

Smelser, N. J., *The Sociology of Economic Life*, Englewood Cliffs, N.J., 1963, 1976.

Steiner, G.A., and Ryan, William G., *Industrial Project Management*, New York, 1968.

Toffler, A., *Future Shock*, New York, 1970.

Weick, K.E., *The Social Psychology of Organizing*, Reading, Mass., 1979.

Wilensky, H.L., "The Professionalization of Everyone?" *American Journal of Sociology*, September: 136-158, 1964.

Wolfe, A., *The Limits of Legitimacy: Political Contradictions of Contemporary Capitalism*, New York, 1977.

Whyte, W.H., *The Organization Man*, New York, 1956.

Zaltman, G.; Duncan R.; and Holbek, J., *Innovations and Organizations*, New York, 1973.

Zweig, F., *Productivity and Trade Unions*, Oxford, 1951.

Index

About the Author
FRANCO FERRAROTTI is Professor of Sociology at the University of Rome. His previous English-language works include *An Alternative Sociology* and *Max Weber and the Destiny of Reason*, and he has written many books in other languages. His articles have appeared in *Social Research*.